SRA Connecting Math Concepts

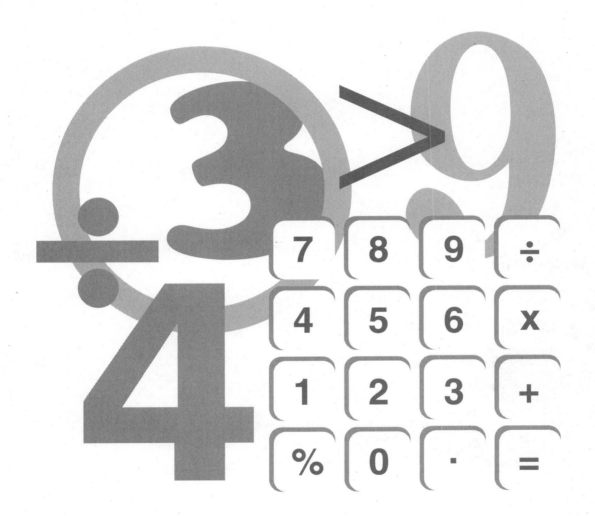

Columbus, Ohio

The McGraw·Hill Companies

www.sra4kids.com

 **SRA
McGraw-Hill**

The *McGraw·Hill* Companies

Contents

Introduction

Crisis in Mathematics

The poor performance of U.S. students in mathematics has been widely documented. In the 1973 National Assessment of Educational Progress, only 25% of fourth graders and 62% of eighth graders could solve five story problems (one for each operation and one requiring two operations).[1] Five years later, performance on the National Assessment had dropped even farther. At that time, only one-third of seventh graders could add fractions such as $\frac{1}{3}$ and $\frac{1}{2}$.[2]

Average performance in mathematics improved slightly on the 1986 National Assessment, but the gains occurred on lower-level computational skills.[3] In 1989, two directors of the National Assessment estimated that only 50% of current high school juniors and seniors had mastered the content of a typical eighth-grade mathematics textbook.[4]

Their estimate was confirmed by later assessments which indicated that less than 20% of current eighth graders had attained the proficiency in mathematics expected for that grade.[5]

Educational researcher Andrew Porter has identified four weaknesses in mathematics instruction that could account for poor student performance in areas such as problem solving:

1. An inordinate amount of time spent teaching computational skills at the expense of concept understanding.
2. At least 70% of topics given less than 30 minutes of instructional time (topics "taught for exposure").
3. Large differences in the amount of time engaged in mathematics.
4. Prevalence of a "low-intensity" curriculum[6].

The fourth weakness was also cited in a report on the Second International Mathematics Study. This report attributes major blame for student failure to the predominance of the "spiral curriculum" used in most mathematics programs, in which topics are taught, dropped, and reintroduced later (sometimes months or years later).[7]

Reforming Mathematics

The mathematics curriculum is currently defined in most schools by the mathematics textbook used in the classroom. Research makes it clear that improving performance is only possible with systematic reform of mathematics textbooks.

The *Connecting Math Concepts* program embodies the following reforms:

1. Organizing lessons around a number of topics rather than a single topic.
2. Making connections between important concepts.
3. Designing lessons to maximize instructional time, so that all students have an opportunity to learn and apply concepts.
4. Introducing concepts at a reasonable rate.
5. Providing guided and independent practice.
6. Field testing and revising instructional materials before publication.

Organization of Connecting Math Concepts

The organization of *Connecting Math Concepts* (CMC) is unique and powerful. Unlike traditional basal programs, in which each lesson is devoted to a single topic, CMC is designed around curriculum **strands.** Each CMC lesson is divided into a number of five- to ten-minute segments addressing topics from different strands.

There are three principal reasons for organizing the curriculum in this way.

• First, students are **more easily engaged** with a variety of topics. For example, 30 minutes on subtraction with regrouping becomes tedious. In contrast, a lesson consisting of 10 minutes on regrouping, followed by 5 minutes on estimation, 5 on facts, and 10 on word problems is more likely to keep students engaged. Increased student attentiveness increases learning. Having students work thirty to forty exercises on regrouping, estimation, facts, and word problems is reasonable; having them work thirty to forty exercises all on regrouping is not.

• Second, lessons composed of several segments make **cumulative introduction** feasible. In cumulative introduction, concepts are introduced gradually and systematically and integrated with related concepts. Cumulative introduction, as an alternative to the traditional spiral introduction, has two important advantages: essential components can be introduced and mastered early, and adequate practice can be provided on both new and previously introduced concepts.

• Third, arranging the content of a mathematics program in strands allows for a more **systematic application** of the concept introduced. For example, instead of a single major unit on problem solving, CMC coordinates instruction in place value, number families, and computation in a way that allows students to apply these concepts to problem-solving activities that gradually become more difficult throughout the entire program.

Overview of Connecting Math Concepts

WHOM IT'S FOR

CMC is a complete basal mathematics program. It has been designed so that all students will learn to compute, solve problems, and think mathematically.

Levels A through F are appropriate for regular-education students in first through sixth grade. The program is particularly effective with students who are at risk in mathematics. The Bridge program is also suitable for older students performing at a fifth- or sixth-grade level.

RATIONALE

CMC is based on the rationale that understanding mathematics requires making connections—
- among related concepts within mathematics
- across daily instructional activities involving mathematics
- between mathematics and the world around us

CMC does more than expose students to connections; it ensures that they understand these connections, and it establishes relationships between concepts and their applications.

RESEARCH BASED

Connecting Math Concepts is a case study in equally balanced mathematics instruction. CMC provides a balanced emphasis on symbolic mathematics (computation), manipulative activities, and problem solving, as well as a balance between understanding and the type and amount of practice necessary to secure that understanding.

The research base for such balance is well established, as is the research base for many of the specifics of CMC, such as selection and sequence of examples, variation in instruction, focus on key concepts, discrimination practice, and so on.

In contrast, there is little research base for many mathematics programs used or proposed today.

LEARNER VERIFIED

The authors believe that if teachers or students have trouble with instructional materials, the materials are at fault.

CMC was thoroughly field tested in a variety of classrooms with a variety of learners. The authors carefully reviewed teacher critiques and student performance on every lesson and used this feedback in making extensive revisions to correct problems and insure instructional effectiveness. This work was completed *before* the program was published.

The authors also noted approaches that were especially successful. For example, teachers frequently commented on how much they liked the specific teaching of problem solving and the fact that it was included in many lessons.

The field testing demonstrated that success leads to confidence for both students and teachers. Students found that the success they experienced enabled them to communicate their understandings and to value mathematics in their lives.

INSTRUCTION

CMC is like no other basal mathematics program on the market.

First, for each lesson there is a scripted, step-by-step presentation that is both effective and highly interactive. The presentation allows the teacher to use the program equally well with groups or the whole class.

Second, instruction in CMC is organized by **tracks.** A track is the ongoing development of a particular topic. Within each lesson, students work on four to six different tracks.

New information is introduced in small steps from lesson to lesson, so that instruction proceeds at a reasonable rate and students are not overwhelmed. Continuous review is provided, so that students learn, remember, and integrate the concepts they are taught.

When students have received enough practice to understand and master the content developed in a track, that track is incorporated with other tracks. That is how connections are made. The instructional tracks for Levels A through F are indicated on each scope-and-sequence chart included in this book.

Application and extension activities are provided in every lesson. These include problem solving, games, activities with manipulatives, and cooperative-learning opportunities to expand concepts taught in the lesson.

NUMBER AND LENGTH OF LESSONS

Levels A, B, C, and D each contain 120 lessons. Level E contains 125 lessons. The Bridge contains 70 lessons. Level F contains 100 lessons. The teacher-directed instruction for each lesson takes approximately 30 to 55 minutes. Independent student work is also provided for each lesson.

Usually the program is taught five days per week.

EVALUATION

Each level (except Level F) contains a placement test to determine whether students have the prerequisite skills necessary for success in the program. In addition, each level contains tests given at ten-lesson intervals, designed to detect any difficulties students are having. Remediation suggestions are included at each checkpoint.

Cumulative Tests and remediation suggestions are provided approximately every thirty lessons.

Test Preparation activities are also provided. The lessons will help students become familiar with standardized test formats and will help them tackle some of the challenges of standardized tests.

MATERIALS FOR TEACHER AND STUDENTS

Teacher materials for Levels A, B, C, D, and E consist of two *Presentation Books*, a *Teacher's Guide,* and an *Answer Key* for each level. The Bridge and Level F each have a *Presentation Book*, a *Teacher's Guide,* and an *Answer Key.*

Student materials consist of two workbooks for each of Levels A and B, a workbook and textbook for each of Levels C, D, and E, and a textbook for the Bridge and Level F.

From time to time, students need a ruler, dice, counters, pennies, and scissors. A calculator is used in Levels C through F.

IN BRIEF

Connecting Math Concepts is a balanced, research-supported mathematics program that teaches students to use mathematics in their everyday lives with understanding and success.

On the following pages, you will find more information about each level of the program, along with sample lessons.

REFERENCES

1. T.D. Carpenter, T.G. Coburn, R.E. Reyes, and J.N. Wilson. "Notes from the National Assessment: Problem Solving." *Mathematics Teacher,* 32 (1976): 389–393.
2. T.D. Carpenter, M.K. Corbitt, H.S. Kepner, Jr., M.M. Lindquist, and R.E. Reyes. *Results from the Second Mathematics Assessment of the National Assessment of Educational Progress.* Reston, VA: National Council of Teachers of Mathematics, 1981.
3. J.A. Dossey, I.V.S. Millis, M.M. Lindquist, and D.L. Chambers. *The Mathematics Report Card: Are We Measuring Up?* Princeton, NJ: Educational Testing Service, 1988.
4. G.R. Anrig and A.E. Lapointe. "What We Know about What Students Don't Know." *Educational Leadership,* 47 (1989): 4–9.
5. For example, K. De Witt. "Eighth Graders' Math Survey Shows No State Is 'Cutting it.' " *New York Times,* June 7, 1991:1.
6. A. Porter. "A Curriculum out of Balance: The Case of Elementary School Mathematics." *Education Researcher,* June–July 1989: 9–15.
7. C.C. McKnight, F.J.Crosswhite, J.A. Dossey, E. Kifer, J.O. Swafford, K.J. Travers, T.J. Cooney. *The Underachieving Curriculum: Assessing U.S. School Mathematics from an International Perspective.* Champaign, IL: Stipes Publishing Company, 1987.

Scope and Sequence for

Connecting Math Concepts, Level A

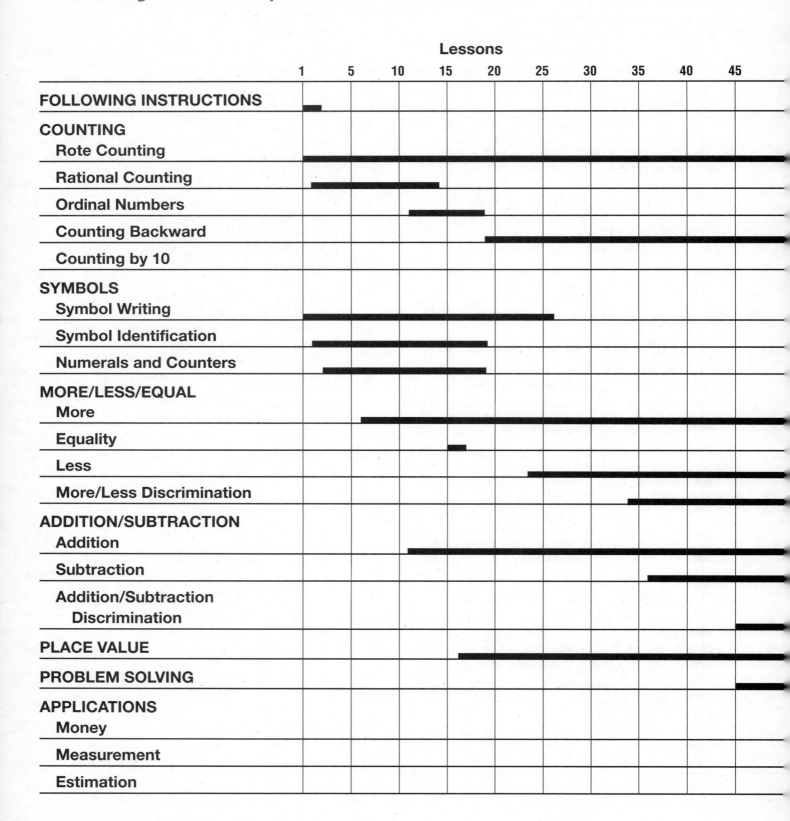

Lessons

	1	5	10	15	20	25	30	35	40	45
FOLLOWING INSTRUCTIONS	▬									
COUNTING										
Rote Counting	▬▬▬▬▬▬▬▬▬▬▬▬▬▬▬▬▬▬▬▬									
Rational Counting		▬▬▬▬▬▬▬								
Ordinal Numbers			▬▬▬▬							
Counting Backward					▬▬▬▬▬▬▬▬▬▬▬▬					
Counting by 10										
SYMBOLS										
Symbol Writing	▬▬▬▬▬▬▬▬▬▬▬▬▬									
Symbol Identification		▬▬▬▬▬▬▬								
Numerals and Counters		▬▬▬▬▬▬▬								
MORE/LESS/EQUAL										
More		▬▬▬▬▬▬▬▬▬▬▬▬▬▬▬▬▬▬								
Equality				▬						
Less						▬▬▬▬▬▬▬▬▬▬▬▬				
More/Less Discrimination								▬▬▬▬▬▬		
ADDITION/SUBTRACTION										
Addition			▬▬▬▬▬▬▬▬▬▬▬▬▬▬▬▬▬							
Subtraction									▬▬▬	
Addition/Subtraction Discrimination										▬
PLACE VALUE				▬▬▬▬▬▬▬▬▬▬▬▬▬▬▬▬						
PROBLEM SOLVING										▬
APPLICATIONS										
Money										
Measurement										
Estimation										

Connecting Math Concepts, Level A builds on the aspect of mathematics that is most familiar to children—counting. Counting experiences are developed in a variety of contexts, expanded to the concepts of more and less, and then to addition and subtraction. This foundation in number sense is extended to the representation of numbers and place value. Finally, this number sense is systematically applied to problem solving, estimation, money, and measurement. The Scope and Sequence Chart shows where each track or major topic begins and where it ends.

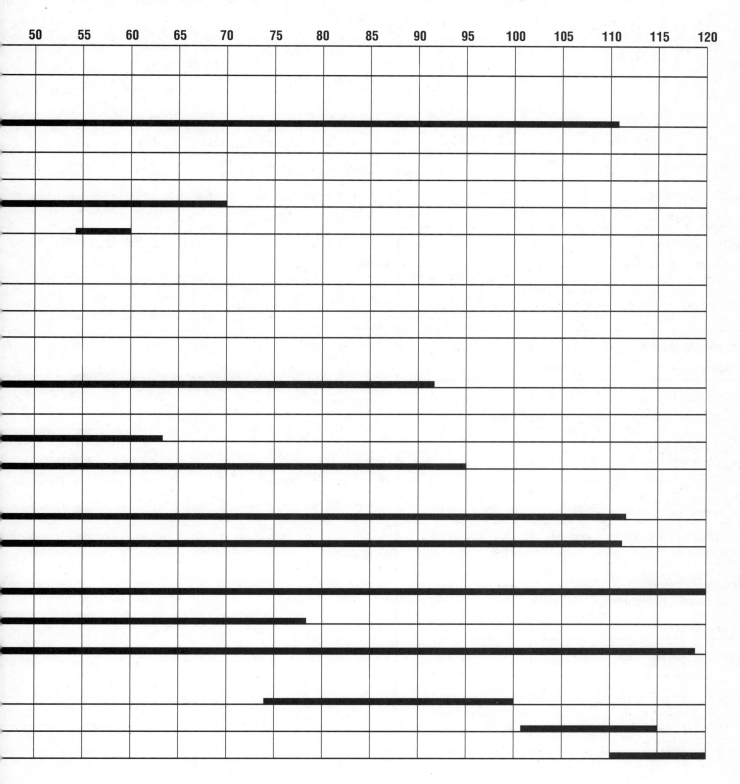

Level A Contents

Skills	Taught in these Lessons	Date Lessons Completed
FOLLOWING INSTRUCTIONS		
Crosses out specified pictures	1, 2	
COUNTING **Rote Counting**		
Says the next number	1–8	
Counts to a specified number	4–7	
Counts from a number to a number	12–111	
Rational Counting		
Counts events	2–14	
Ordinal Numbers		
Follows insturctions with ordinal numbers	11–16	
Answers questions involving ordinal numbers	17–19	
Counting Backward		
Counts backward to a specified number	18–70	
Counting by 10		
Completes a tens number line	54–60	
SYMBOLS **Symbol Writing**		
Copies symbols	1–19	
Writes number series	11–20	
Writes symbols and groups of symbols from dictation	21–26	
Symbol Identification		
Crosses out backward digits	2–15	
Says the name	2–19	
Numerals and Counters		
Draws lines for numerals	3–9	
Writes numerals for counters	4–10	
Matches numerals and counters	10–19	

Skills	Taught in these Lessons	Date Lessons Completed
MORE/LESS/EQUAL **More**		
Says (marks) numbers that are more	6–30	
Writes numbers that are more	17–29	
Marks groups that are more than a given number	18–20	
Says (writes) numbers that are 2 more	19–23	
Says (writes) numbers that are 3 more	70–76	
Circles numbers on a number line that are more than a specified number	88, 89	
Circles the larger number	88–92	
Equality		
Makes both sides of equations have the same number	15, 16	
Less		
Says (writes) the number just before a specified number	23–26	
Indicates groups that are less than a specified number	27–31	
Says (writes) numbers that are 1 less	34, 35	
Says numbers that are 2 less	91–95	
More/Less Discrimination		
Discriminates values that are more, less or equal	34, 35	
Makes the greater-than or less-than sign between numbers	91–95	

Level A Contents

Skills	Taught in these Lessons	Date Lessons Completed
ADDITION/SUBTRACTION **Addition**		
Says (marks) answers to + 1 questions	11–14	
Writes answers to + 1 questions	15–29	
Says (writes) answers to +2 questions	24–31	
Writes problems from dictation or from a number line	25–44	
Writes answers to orally presented + 1 problems	29–42	
Writes answers to + 1 and + 2 problems	32–36	
Writes answers to zero + problems	37–47	
Writes (says) answers to orally presented problems with a 2-digit value and an addend of 0, 1 or 2	40–90	
Writes answers to "turned around" + 1 and +2 addition problems	42–51	
Writes answers to orally presented problems that start with 0 +, 1 + or 2 +	50–67	
Writes and solves addition problems with tens numbers	57–63	
Writes (says) answers to problems that add 10 and 20	64–80	
Writes answers to orally presented problems that begin with a tens number	67–112	
Writes answers to problems that + 3	77–80	
Uses fact derivation to solve + 3 problems	81–85	
Writes answers to problems with 3 addeneds	85–88	
Writes answers to + 2 and + 3 problems	86–88	
Represents "doubles" facts on the number line	89, 90	
Says "doubles" facts	91–97	

Skills	Taught in these Lessons	Date Lessons Completed
Writes answers to orally presented problems with 2 tens numbers	95–100	
Writes answers to "turned around" + 3 facts	96–102	
Responds to "add" rather than "plus"	101, 102	
Writes answers to column addition problems	101–105	
Subtraction		
Writes answers to − 1 problems	36–40	
Writes answers to problems that − 1 or − 0	52, 53	
Writes answers to − 2 problems	64–66	
Writes answers to problems that − 0, − 1, or − 2	67–71	
Writes answers to problems that begin with 2-digit numbers and − 1 or − 2	72–104	
Writes answers to problems that − 10 or − 20	73–78	
Writes subtraction problems with an answer of zero	100–102	
Writes subtraction problems with an answer of 1	103–108	
Writes answers to column subtraction problems	106–108	
Works subtraction problems with an answer of 0 or 1	109–111	
Addition/Subtraction Discrimination		
Writes addition and subtraction facts from number lines	45–63	
Writes addition and subtraction facts based on number-family relationships	64–86	
Writes answers to problems with tens numbers	85–87	
Responds to mental arithmetic questions	49–120	

Level A Contents

Skills	Taught in these Lessons	Date Lessons Completed
Responds to the words "add" and "subtract"	104, 105	
Writes answers to column-addition and column-subtraction problems	109, 110	
Reads "box" as "how many"	118–120	
PLACE VALUE		
Writes teen numbers from dictation	16–24	
Writes teen numbers	30–33	
Writes 2-digit numbers (beyond 20) from dictation	31–56	
Writes tens and twenties numbers from representations	41–74	
Counts to identify digits	51, 52	
Works with facts or numbers in columns	52–96	
Writes Ts for tens, then writes the 2-digit numeral	70–78	
Represents 2-digit numerals with Ts and lines	70–78	
PROBLEM SOLVING		
Finds missing addend or subtrahend for number problems	45–47	
Writes problems and answers for stories about a bug-on-a-number-line	47–53	
Finds missing middle term (number and sign) in number problems	48–60	
Solves bug-on-a-number-line problems with a missing addend or subtrahend	53–58	
Solves bug-on-a-number-line problems with the unknown as the middle or last term	59–72	
Writes facts for more/less story problems on the number line	73–77	

Skills	Taught in these Lessons	Date Lessons Completed
Indicates whether an action story calls for addition or subtraction	76–83	
Solves action problems	78–83	
Solves comparison problems	84–90	
Solves problems involving "joining"	91, 92	
Solves various problems of previously taught types	92–120	
Solves problems with the phrase "all but"	94–100	
Solves 3-addend problems	97–102	
Figures out whether to add or subtract	104–107	
Solves problems that start with a number and add 2 numbers or subtract 2 numbers	105–108	
Solves problems that require 5, ,, or . sign	109–111	
Solves 2 problems, then writes the sign that compares the answers	112–115	
Solves problems with multiple solutions	116–119	
APPLICATION **Money**		
Writes the cents for a row of dimes and pennies	74–76	
Writes the cents for 2 groups of dimes	80, 81	
Writes the cents for dimes and pennies mixed in a row	82, 83	
Identifies coins and their values	91	
Writes the cents for a nickel, a dime or a quarter followed by pennies	92–94	
Adds pennies to a row of coins to obtain a price-tag value	95–97	
Adds or crosses out pennies in a row of coins to obtain a price-tag value	98–100	

Level A Contents

Skills	Taught in these Lessons	Date Lessons Completed
MEASUREMENT		
Shows 1 and 2 inches with fingers	101, 102	
Measures horizontally and vertically oriented lines to the nearest whole inch	103–107	
Measures rectangles	108–115	

Skills	Taught in these Lessons	Date Lessons Completed
ESTIMATION		
Estimates to identify particular rectangles	110–113	
Estimates relative height, then measures height using non-standard units	111–116	
Estimates to complete rectangles that approximate descriptions	114–120	
Estimates height in multiples of 10 feet	117–120	

For Level A Placement Test, see page 176.

Level A, Lesson 63 (Presentation Book)

Objectives

- **Count backward from 15 to 5.** (Exercise 1)
- Use a number line and answer the question, "What number is 2 less than . . ." (Exercise 2)
- **Write addition and subtraction statements based on a number line representation.** (Exercise 3)
- Write numerals for **T's** and lines. (Exercise 4)
- Write questions and answers for word problems with the missing term in the middle or at the end. (Exercise 5)
- Write and solve addition problems with tens numbers. (Exercise 6)

EXERCISE 1 COUNTING BACKWARD

a. Everybody, say **10** and count backward to zero. Get ready. (Signal.) *10, 9, 8, 7, 6, 5, 4, 3, 2, 1, zero.*
b. My turn to say **15** and count backward to 10. Here I go: 15, 14, 13, 12, 11, 10.
- Your turn: Say **15** and count backward to 10. Get ready. (Signal.) *15, 14, 13, 12, 11, 10.*
c. Again. Say **15** and count backward to 10. Get ready. (Signal.) *15, 14, 13, 12, 11, 10.* (Repeat step c until firm.)
d. My turn to say **15** and count backward to 5. Here I go: 15, 14, 13, 12, 11, 10, 9, 8, 7, 6, 5.
- Your turn: Say **15** and count backward to 5. Get ready. (Signal.) *15, 14, 13, 12, 11, 10, 9, 8, 7, 6, 5.* (Repeat step e until firm.)
e. Again. Say **15** and count backward to 5. Get ready. (Signal.) *15, 14, 13, 12, 11, 10, 9, 8, 7, 6, 5.*

EXERCISE 2 SAYING 2 LESS
Cover-Up Game

a. (Write on the board:)

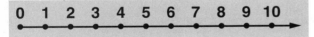

- You're going to tell me the number that is 2 less than the number next to the arrow card.
b. (Cover the numerals before **5,** using the arrow card:)

- What's the number next to the card? (Signal.) *5.*
- Think big. What number is 2 less than 5? (Signal.) *3.*
- (Uncover **4** and **3** as you say:) 1 less, 2 less.
- Everybody, were you right?

c. (Cover the numerals before **10.**)
- New game. What's the number next to the card? (Signal.) *10.*
- Think big. What number is 2 less than 10? (Signal.) *8.*
- (Uncover **9** and **8** as you say:) 1 less, 2 less.
- Were you right?
d. (Cover the numerals before **7.**)
- New game. What's the number next to the card? (Signal.) *7.*
- Think big. What number is 2 less than 7? (Signal.) *5.*
- (Uncover **6** and **5** as you say:) 1 less, 2 less.
- Were you right?
e. (Cover the numerals before **8.**)
- New game. What's the number next to the card? (Signal.) *8.*
- Think big. What number is 2 less than 8? (Signal.) *6.*
- (Uncover **7** and **6** as you say:) 1 less, 2 less.
- Were you right?
f. (Cover the numerals before **3.**)
- Last game. What's the number next to the card? (Signal.) *3.*
- Think big. What number is 2 less than 3? (Signal.) *1.*
- (Uncover **2** and **1** as you say:) 1 less, 2 less.
- Were you right?
g. (Do **not** erase the number line.)

EXERCISE 3 NUMBER RELATIONSHIPS

a. (Draw a bug and arrow on the number line:)

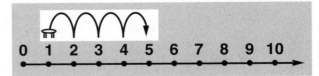

- The arrow shows a bug problem. You can see where the bug started and how many places the bug plussed. Listen: What number did the bug start at? (Signal.) *1.*

- Did the bug plus or minus? (Signal.) *Plus.*
- Raise your hand when you know how many places the bug plussed.
- Everybody, how many places did the bug plus? (Signal.) *4.*
- What number did the bug end up at? (Signal.) *5.*

Workbook Practice

a. Open your workbook to lesson 63 and find part 1. √
- You're going to write the fact for the problem. You start your fact where the bug started. What number did the bug start at? (Signal.) *1.*
- Write **1** at the beginning of the line for item A. √
b. Now you have to tell whether the bug plussed or minused. What did the bug do? (Signal.) *Plussed.*
- How many places did the bug plus? (Signal.) *4.*
- So write **plus 4** for the next part of the number problem. Raise your hand when you're finished. √
- Now write the part that tells where the bug ends up. Remember to write **equals** for **ends up.** Raise your hand when you're finished. √
- (Write on the board:)

> **A. 1 + 4 = 5**

- Check your work. Here's what you should have for fact A: 1 plus 4 equals 5. Raise your hand if you got it right.
c. (Change the number line to show:)

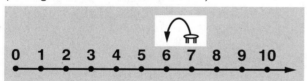

- Here's problem B. What number did the bug start at? (Signal.) *7.*
- Did the bug plus or minus? (Signal.) *Minus.*
- How many places did the bug minus? (Signal.) *1.*
- What number did the bug end up at? (Signal.) *6.*
- Touch the line for item B.
  Your turn: Write the whole fact for problem B. Remember, tell where the bug started, how many places the bug minused, and the number the bug ended up at. Remember, this is a fact you know. Don't write anything silly. Raise your hand when you're finished.
  (Observe children and give feedback.)
- (Write on the board:)

> **A. 1 + 4 = 5**
> **B. 7 − 1 = 6**

- Check your work. Here's what you should have for fact B: 7 minus 1 equals 6. Raise your hand if you got it right.
d. (Change the number line to show:)

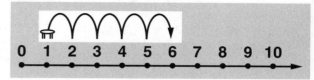

- Here's problem C. What number did the bug start at? (Signal.) *1.*
- Did the bug plus or minus? (Signal.) *Plus.*
- How many places did the bug plus? (Signal.) *5.*
- What number did the bug end up at? (Signal.) *6.*
- Touch the line for item C. Your turn: Write the whole fact for problem C. Remember, tell where the bug started, how many places the bug plussed, and the number the bug ended up at. Raise your hand when you're finished.
  (Observe children and give feedback.)
- (Write on the board:)

> **C. 1 + 5 = 6**

- Check your work. Here's what you should have for fact C: 1 plus 5 equals 6. Raise your hand if you got it right.
e. (Change the number line to show:)

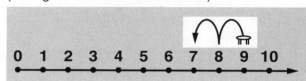

- Here's problem D. What number did the bug start at? (Signal.) *9.*
- Did the bug plus or minus? (Signal.) *Minus.*
- How many places did the bug minus? (Signal.) *2.*
- What number did the bug end up at? (Signal.) *7.*
- Touch the line for item D.
  Your turn: Write the whole fact. Remember, the bug is minusing 2 places. Raise your hand when you're finished.
  (Observe children and give feedback.)
- (Write on the board:)

> **C. 1 + 5 = 6**
> **D. 9 − 2 = 7**

- Check your work. Here's what you should have for fact D: 9 minus 2 equals 7. Raise your hand if you got it right.

EXERCISE 4 PLACE VALUE
2-Digit Numerals

a. Find part 2.
   This is tough. Count the **T's** for item A and raise your hand when you know how many there are.
- Everybody, how many **T's?** (Signal.) *4.*
- So what number do you start with? (Signal.) *40.*
b. Count the **T's** for item B and raise your hand when you know how many there are.
- Everybody, how many **T's?** (Signal.) *5.*
- So what number do you start with? (Signal.) *50.*
c. Count the **T's** for item C and raise your hand when you know how many there are.
- Everybody, how many **T's?** (Signal.) *4.*
- So what number do you start with? (Signal.) *40.*
d. Your turn: Count carefully to yourself and write the numerals for part 2. Raise your hand when you're finished.
   (Observe children and give feedback.)
e. Check your work.
- Item A has 4 **T's.** So you said **40** and then counted the lines. Everybody, what numeral did you write for item A? (Signal.) *43.*
- Item B has 5 **T's.** So you said **50** and then counted the lines. Everybody, what numeral did you write for item B? (Signal.) *52.*
- Item C has 4 **T's.** So you said **40** and then counted the lines. Everybody, what numeral did you write for item C? (Signal.) *45.*
- Item D has 3 **T's.** So you said **30** and then counted the lines. Everybody, what numeral did you write for item D? (Signal.) *34.*
f. Raise your hand if you wrote the correct numerals in all the boxes.
- Good for you.

EXERCISE 5 PROBLEM SOLVING
Word Problems

a. Find part 3.
   I'm going to tell you bug problems. Some of these problems tell how many places the bug plusses or minuses. Some don't. I'll read each problem two times. Then you'll write the whole problem.
b. Problem A: A bug starts at **10** on the number line. Then the bug plusses some places. The bug ends up at **11.**
- Listen again: A bug starts at **10.** Then the bug plusses some. The bug ends up at **11.** Write the problem and the answer for A. Raise your hand when you're finished.
   (Observe children and give feedback.)
- (Write on the board:)

$$\text{A. } 10 + \boxed{} = 11$$

- Check your work. Here's the problem you should have for A. Everybody, what's the answer? (Signal.) *1.*
- (Write **1.**)
- Yes, if the bug starts at **10** and ends up at **11,** the bug plusses 1 place. Raise your hand if you got everything right.
c. Problem B: A bug starts at **10** on the number line. Then the bug minuses 1 place. The bug ends up at what number?
- Listen again: A bug starts at **10.** Then the bug minuses 1. The bug ends up at what number? Write the problem and the answer for B. Raise your hand when you're finished. √
- (Write on the board:)

$$\text{A. } 10 + \boxed{1} = 11$$
$$\text{B. } 10 - 1 = \boxed{}$$

- Check your work. Here's the problem you should have for B. Everybody, what's the answer? (Signal.) *9.*
- (Write **9.**)
- Yes, if the bug starts at **10** and minuses 1, the bug ends up at **9.** Raise your hand if you got everything right.
d. Problem C: A bug starts at **7** on the number line. Then the bug plusses some places. The bug ends up at **9.**
- Listen again: A bug starts at **7.** Then the bug plusses some. The bug ends up at **9.** Write the problem and the answer for C. Raise your hand when you're finished. √
- (Write on the board:)

$$\text{A. } 10 + \boxed{1} = 11$$
$$\text{B. } 10 - 1 = \boxed{9}$$
$$\text{C. } 7 + \boxed{} = 9$$

- Check your work. Here's the problem you should have for C. Everybody, what's the answer? (Signal.) *2.*
- (Write **2.**)
- Yes, if the bug starts at **7** and ends up at **9,** the bug plusses 2 places. Raise your hand if you got everything right.
e. Problem D: A bug starts at **6** on the number line. Then the bug plusses 2 places. The bug ends up at what number?
- Listen again: A bug starts at **6.** Then the bug plusses 2. The bug ends up at what number? Write the problem and the answer for D. Raise your hand when you're finished. √

- (Write on the board:)

B.	10 − 1	=	$\boxed{9}$
C.	7 + $\boxed{2}$	=	9
D.	6 + 2	=	$\boxed{}$

- Check your work. Here's the problem you should have for D. Everybody, what's the answer? (Signal.) *8.*
- (Write **8.**)
- Yes, if the bug starts at **6** and plusses 2, the bug ends up at **8.** Raise your hand if you got everything right.
f. Raise your hand if you got all the answers right.

EXERCISE 6 ADDING TENS

a. Find part 4.
First you're going to read all the problems in part 4. Then you're going to write the answers.
b. Touch problem A.
Everybody, read it. (Signal.)
10 plus 10 equals what number?
- Touch problem B.
Everybody, read it. (Signal.)
40 plus 20 equals what number?
- Touch problem C.
Everybody, read it. (Signal.)
50 plus 10 equals what number?
- Touch problem D.
Everybody, read it. (Signal.)
20 plus 70 equals what number?
c. Your turn to write answers to the problems. Remember to look at the first digit of each numeral. The first digits tell you the first digit of the answer. Write the answers to the problems. Raise your hand when you're finished. **(Observe children and give feedback.)**
d. Check your work. Read each problem and the answer.
- Problem A. Read it. (Signal.)
10 plus 10 equals 20.
- Problem B. Read it. (Signal.)
40 plus 20 equals 60.
- Problem C. Read it. (Signal.)
50 plus 10 equals 60.
- Problem D. Read it. (Signal.)
20 plus 70 equals 90.
e. Raise your hand if you got all of them right.

EXERCISE 7 INDEPENDENT WORK

a. You'll finish the rest of the workbook parts on your own.
- Find part 5.
You'll write the numerals in a column.
Remember how to line them up.
b. (Assign **Connecting Math Concepts** *Independent Worksheet* 23 as classwork or homework. Before beginning the next lesson, check the students' independent work.)

Manipulative Activity—Addition and Subtraction

Materials: 10 beans and a can for each pair of children.

Activity: Children can work in pairs and take turns. The first child drops beans, one at a time, into the can. The second child counts and says the number. The first child then drops one or two more beans into or removes one bean from the can. The second child says the addition or subtraction fact that describes the first child's actions. The first child dumps out all the beans in the can and counts them to verify the sum or difference.

Level A, Lesson 63 (Workbook)

For each item in **part 1,** students write an addition or subtraction statement based on a number-line diagram.

For example, for item A, students write: $1 + 4 = 5$ for

the diagram: 0 1 2 3 4 5 6 7

In later lessons (73–77) students translate verbal descriptions into addition/subtraction problems. For example: A bug starts at 5 on the number line. Then the bug goes to the number that is 1 less. The bug ends up at what number?

In earlier lessons (6–35) students translated "more" and "less" with the number line. Getting "more" implies moving to the right. Getting "less" implies moving to the left.

The items in **part 2** require students to write 2-digit numerals. The T's stand for tens and the lines stand for ones. A necessary prerequisite for this task is skip-counting by tens, taught in lessons 54–60. In later lessons (66–69), students confirm the "T" representation by crossing out groups of ten lines, writing a T for each group, and then writing a 2-digit numeral.

Lesson 63

Part 1

A. _____

B. _____

C. _____

D. _____

Part 2

A.

T T T | | |
 T

B.

T T T | |
 T T

C.

T T T | | | | |
 T

D.

T T T | | | |

Part 3

A. _____

B. _____

C. _____

D. _____

Part 4

A. $10 + 10 = \boxed{}$ C. $50 + 10 = \boxed{}$

B. $40 + 20 = \boxed{}$ D. $20 + 70 = \boxed{}$

5

For **part 3,** students solve a mixture of addition and subtraction problems based on spoken descriptions of a bug on a number line. For example, for item B, students hear: A bug starts at 10 on the number line. Then the bug minuses 1 place. The bug ends up at what number? Students write: $10 - 1 = \square$, and solve the problem.

For item C, students hear: A bug starts at 7 on the number line. Then the bug plusses some places. The bug ends up at 9. Students write: $7 + \square = 9$.

This is the fifth consecutive lesson where students solve spoken problems with the unknown as the middle or last term. Prior to spoken descriptions, students have worked number problems for missing addend/subtrahend and for regular addition/subtraction problems.

Addition of tens numbers was introduced in lesson 57. This is the seventh consecutive lesson in which this problem type has occurred. Students use what they know about simple facts to solve the problems in **part 4.** For example, problem B represents 4 tens plus 2 tens. $4 + 2 = 6$. Therefore, 4 tens + 2 tens = 6 tens. Students write the numeral for 6 tens as the answer: 60. Problems with 1 or 2 as one of the addends were practiced in lessons 32–36 and lessons 42–51.

Subtraction problems with tens numbers appear in lessons 73–78. In later lessons (95–100), students will write answers to orally presented problems, such as: 40 plus 30 equals what number?

Parts 5 through 7 are the independent work for lesson 63. These parts review problem types that were practiced in a structured form in earlier lessons.

In **part 5,** students copy the numerals with the proper column alignment. Students worked with column alignment in lessons 52–61. This work consolidates earlier place-value work with tens and ones. In later lessons (74–76, 80–83), students also represent dimes and pennies as 2-digit values.

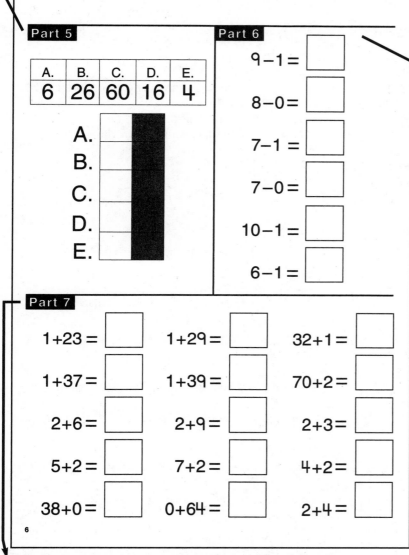

Part 6 reviews minus 1 and minus zero facts. Minus 1 problems were introduced and taught in lessons 36–40. A mix of minus 1 and minus zero facts appeared in lessons 52 and 53. Review sets appear in all but two lessons between 53 and 63. A set of problems of this type also appears in test 6.

Part 7 provides a review of a wide range of addition facts introduced prior to lesson 63. This range includes: a) simple facts that add 2 (e.g., 5 + 2), initially taught in lessons 24–31; b) 2-digit values that add 0, 1 or 2 (e.g., 38 + 0, 70 + 2), taught in lessons 51–62; c) "turned around" add 1 or 2 problems (e.g., 1 + 37), taught in lessons 42–51; and d) problems that begin with "zero plus" (e.g., 0 + 64), taught in lessons 37–41. This mixed review integrates previous types and promotes student retention of what has been taught.

Level A

Sample Track: Place Value

Level A teaches the following concepts about place value in 2-digit numerals:
- Numerals have digits.
- The first digit represents tens.
- The second digit represents ones.
- When 2-digit numerals are written in a column, the digits should be aligned.
- 2-digit numerals can be modeled using "counters" (tens counters for the first digit and individual counters for the second digit, or ones.)
- For models made with tens counters and individual counters, it is possible to write 2-digit numerals using symbols for the corresponding values.

Because place value assumes column alignment, many place-value activities require children to write numerals from dictation. The first dictation exercise is in Lesson 14. The introduction presents the terminology "first digit" and "second digit." It shows conventions for aligning digits, and it makes the connection between the teen numerals and the familiar 1-digit numerals.

In Lesson 30 children are introduced to the notion that the digits in 2-digit numerals have different values. Children are shown that the first digit is a ten and can be represented with a **T.** Then they write appropriate numerals for models that show a single **T** and a group of lines. The following is from Lesson 30:

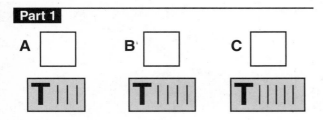

EXERCISE 2 PLACE VALUE

a. (Write on the board:)

Ten

- (Point to **Ten.**)
  This word is **ten.** Everybody, what's the first letter in **ten?** (Signal.) *T.*
- Watch this.
  (Erase **en.**)
- We'll use the letter **T** to stand for **ten.**
  What does the **T** stand for? (Signal.) *Ten.*

b. (Write on the board:)

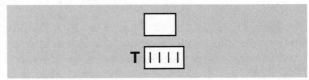

- Here's **10** and some lines. When I touch the **T,** I'll say **10.** Then I'll count the lines. Watch. (Touch the **T** and then each line as you say:) 10, 11, 12, 13, 14.
- Your turn: Remember to say **10** for the **T.**
c. (Point to **T.**)
  Get ready.
  (Touch the **T** and then each line as children say:) *10, 11, 12, 13, 14.*
  (Repeat step c until firm.)
d. There are **14** in this group. So I write **14** in the box.
  (Write **14:**)

e. (Write on the board:)

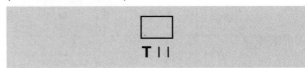

- New problem. What are you going to say for the **T?** (Signal.) *Ten.*
- Get ready.
  (Touch the **T** and then each line as children say:) *10, 11, 12.*
- There are **12** in this group. So I write **12** in the box.
  (Write **12:**)

f. (Write on the board:)

- New problem. What are you going to say for the **T?** (Signal.) *Ten.*
- Get ready.
  (Touch the **T** and then each line as children say:) *10, 11, 12, 13, 14, 15, 16.*
- How many are in this group? (Signal.) *16.*
- So what do I write in the box? (Signal.) *16.*

- (Write **16:**)

WORKBOOK PRACTICE

a. Open your workbook to Lesson 30 and find part 1. √
b. Touch group A.
   What are you going to say for the **T** in the group? (Signal.) *Ten.*
- Start with **10** and count group A. Raise your hand when you know how many are in group A.
- Everybody, how many in group A? (Signal.) *13.*
- Yes, **13.** Write **13** in the box for group A. √
- (Write on the board:)

A. 13

- Here's what you should have for group A. Raise your hand if you got it right.
c. Touch group B.
   Start with **10** and count group B. Raise your hand when you know how many are in group B.
- Everybody, how many in group B? (Signal.) *14.*
- Yes, **14.** Write **14** in the box for group B. √
- (Write on the board:)

B. 14

- Here's what you should have for group B. Raise your hand if you got it right.
d. Touch group C.
   Start with the number for **T** and count group C. Raise your hand when you know how many are in group C.
- Everybody, how many in group C? (Signal.) *15.*
- Yes, **15.** Write **15** in the box for group C. √
- (Write on the board:)

C. 15

- Here's what you should have for group C. Raise your hand if you got it right.

During structured work, children generally do not have any trouble with Ts and lines; however, good performance in this activity does not suggest that children have learned the fundamental assumptions of place value. They have practiced only the first step.

Starting in Lesson 52, children write numerals in columns. The ones column is shaded. Children discriminate between 1-digit and 2-digit numerals and indicate whether each numeral begins in the first column or in the second column. Many children benefit from explicit instruction in the ideas that 1-digit numerals do not begin in the first column:

Part 1

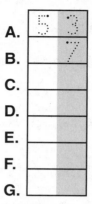

EXERCISE 3 PLACE VALUE
Dictation

a. (Draw columns on the board:)

- I'm going to write numerals. You'll tell me whether to write a 1-digit numeral or a 2-digit numeral. Let's practice.
b. Listen: **17.** How many digits? (Signal.) *2.*
- Listen: **4.** How many digits? (Signal.) *1.*
- Listen: **34.** How many digits? (Signal.) *2.*
- Listen: **9.** How many digits? (Signal.) *1.*
- Listen: **29.** How many digits? (Signal.) *2.*
- Listen: **30.** How many digits? (Signal.) *2.*
- Listen: **10.** How many digits? (Signal.) *2.*
   (Repeat step b until firm.)
c. (Point to the columns on the board.)
   I'm going to write the numerals in these columns. Writing numerals in columns is very tricky because you don't always start in the **first** column. Here's the rule: You start in the first column if it's a 2-digit numeral. You don't start in the first column if it's a 1-digit numeral. Remember, you don't start in the first column unless the numeral has **two digits.**
d. (Touch the tens column.)
   Here's the first column. You're going to tell me if I start writing in this column. Listen: **14.** Would I start **14** in the first column? (Signal.) *Yes.*
- My turn: Why would I start **14** in the first column? Because it's a 2-digit numeral. Your turn: Why would I start **14** in the first column? (Signal.) *Because it's a 2-digit numeral.*

e. Listen: **29**. Everybody, would I start **29** in the first column? (Signal.) *Yes.*
- Why? (Signal.) *Because it's a 2-digit numeral.*
- Listen: **4**. Everybody, would I start **4** in the first column? (Signal.) *No.*
- Right. **4** is not a 2-digit numeral.
- Listen: **1**. Everybody, would I start **1** in the first column? (Signal.) *No.*
- Why not? (Signal.) *Because it's not a 2-digit numeral.*
(Repeat step e until firm.)
- This time I'm going to write the numerals. Listen: **36**. Do I start **36** in the first column? (Signal.) *Yes.*
f. (Write **36:**)

g. Listen: **5**. Do I start **5** in the first column? (Signal.) *No.*
- (Write **5:**)

h. Listen: **2**. Do I start **2** in the first column? (Signal.) *No.*
- (Write **2:**)

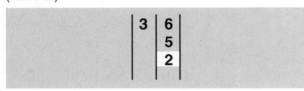

i. Listen: **12**. Do I start **12** in the first column? (Signal.) *Yes.*
- (Write **12:**)

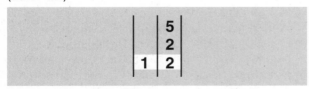

j. Listen: **22**. Do I start **22** in the first column? (Signal.) *Yes.*
- (Write **22:**)

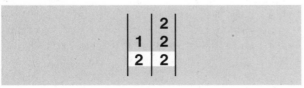

k. Listen: **17**. Do I start **17** in the first column? (Signal.) *Yes.*
- (Write **17:**)

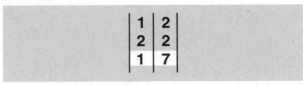

l. Listen: **3**. Do I start **3** in the first column? (Signal.) *No.*
- (Write **3:**)

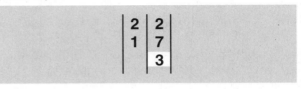

WORKBOOK PRACTICE

a. Open your workbook to Lesson 52 and find part 1. √
- Now it's your turn. The first column in part 1 is not shaded. The second column is shaded.
b. Numeral A is **53**.
It's already written with dotted lines. Do you start **53** in the first column? (Signal.) *Yes.*
- Why? (Signal.) *Because it's a 2-digit numeral.*
- Your turn: Trace **53**. Raise your hand when you're finished. √
c. Touch numeral B.
That numeral is **7**. It doesn't have two digits, so it doesn't start in the first column. Your turn: Trace **7**. Raise your hand when you're finished. √
d. Touch the space for numeral C.
Listen: Numeral C is **17**. What numeral? (Signal.) *17.*
- Do you start **17** in the first column? (Signal.) *Yes.*
- Write **17**. Raise your hand when you're finished. (Observe children and give feedback.)
- (Write on the board:)

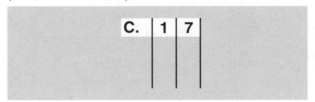

- Here's what you should have for numeral C.
e. Touch the space for numeral D.
Listen: Numeral D is **9**. What numeral? (Signal.) *9.*
- Do you start **9** in the first column? (Signal.) *No.*
- Write **9**. Raise your hand when you're finished. √

- (Write **9:**)

```
C.  | 1 | 7 |
D.  |   | 9 |
```

- Here's what you should have for numeral D.
f. Touch the space for numeral E.
  Listen: Numeral E is **50**. What numeral? (Signal.) *50.*
- Do you start **50** in the first column? (Signal.) *Yes.*
- Write **50**. Raise your hand when you're finished. √
- (Write **50:**)

```
C.  | 1 | 7 |
D.  |   | 9 |
E.  | 5 | 0 |
```

- Here's what you should have for numeral E.
g. Touch the space for numeral F.
  Listen: Numeral F is **51**. What numeral? (Signal.) *51.*
- Do you start **51** in the first column? (Signal.) *Yes.*
- Write **51**. Raise your hand when you're finished. √
- (Write **51:**)

```
D.  |   | 9 |
E.  | 5 | 0 |
F.  | 5 | 1 |
```

- Here's what you should have for numeral F.
h. Touch the space for numeral G.
  Listen: Numeral G is **1**. What numeral? (Signal.) *1.*
- Do you start **1** in the first column? (Signal.) *No.*
- Write **1**. Raise your hand when you're finished. √
- (Write **1:**)

```
E.  | 5 | 0 |
F.  | 5 | 1 |
G.  |   | 1 |
```

- Here's what you should have for numeral G.
i. Raise your hand if you wrote all the numerals correctly.

An ongoing activity that first appears in Lesson 58 presents numerals in a row. Children write them in columns. Here's the introduction from Lesson 58.

A.	B.	C.	D.	E.	F.	G.
23	8	80	18	81	1	21

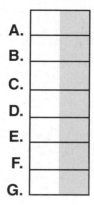

EXERCISE 3 PLACE VALUE
Alignment

a. Find part 2.
   There's a row of numerals. You're going to write them in columns.
b. Touch numeral A.
   Everybody, what numeral? (Signal.) *23.*
- Touch numeral B.
   What numeral? (Signal.) *8.*
- Touch numeral C.
   What numeral? (Signal.) *80.*
- Touch numeral D.
   What numeral? (Signal.) *18.*
- Touch numeral E.
   What numeral? (Signal.) *81.*
- Touch numeral F.
   What numeral? (Signal.) *1.*
- Touch numeral G.
   What numeral? (Signal.) *21.*
c. Touch the space in the columns for numeral A.
   That's where you'll write numeral A. Everybody, what's numeral A? (Signal.) *23.*
- Touch the space in the columns for numeral B.
   What numeral goes in that space? (Signal.) *8.*
- Touch the space in the columns for numeral C.
   What numeral goes in that space? (Signal.) *80.*
d. Your turn: Write the numerals in the columns. Write numeral A in space A; write numeral B in space B; and so forth. Remember the rule about 2-digit numerals. Don't get fooled. Raise your hand when you're finished.
(Observe children and give feedback.)

e. (Write on the board:)

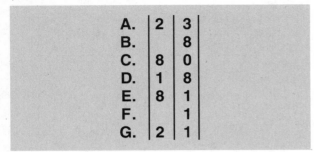

A.	2	3
B.		8
C.	8	0
D.	1	8
E.	8	1
F.		1
G.	2	1

- Check your work. Here's what you should have for the numerals. Check your numerals carefully. Make sure all of the 2-digit numerals start in the first column and none of the 1-digit numerals start in the first column.

f. Raise your hand if you wrote all the numerals correctly.

The set of examples presented to the children gives them practice in writing potentially confusing numerals in a context that all but eliminates errors. In this exercise, children do not have to concern themselves as much with how to compose the numeral but can concentrate on how to write it and in which column to start.

Last, children write **T**s and lines for 2-digit numerals. The first activity is in Lesson 70. The teacher describes the numerals using the expanded form. "34 is 30 plus 4." Children learn to make the **T**s under the first digit of the number and the lines under the second digit. This activity ensures that students understand the concepts of place value:

Part 3

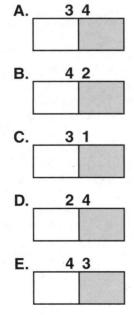

A. 3 4

B. 4 2

C. 3 1

D. 2 4

E. 4 3

EXERCISE 4 PLACE VALUE
2-Digit Numerals

a. You've learned to make numerals from **T**'s and lines. Now you're going to make **T**'s and lines for 2-digit numerals.

b. Listen: 10. How many **T**'s do you make for 10? (Signal.) *1.*

- Listen: 50. How many **T**'s do you make for 50? (Signal.) *5.*
- Listen: 70. How many **T**'s do you make for 70? (Signal.) *7.*
- Listen: 30. How many **T**'s do you make for 30? (Signal.) *3.*

c. Listen: 32. That's 30 plus 2. How many **T**'s do you make for 30? (Signal.) *3.*

- How many **lines** do you make for 2? (Signal.) *2.*
- Listen: 53. That's 50 plus 3. How many **T**'s do you make for 50? (Signal.) *5.*
- How many **lines** do you make for 3. (Signal.) *3.*
- Listen: 86. That's 80 plus 6. How many **T**'s do you make for 80? (Signal.) *8.*
- How many **lines** do you make for 6? (Signal.) *6.* (Repeat step c until firm.)

WORKBOOK PRACTICE

a. Find part 2.
You're going to write **T**'s and lines for numerals.

b. Touch numeral A.
Everybody, read the numeral. (Signal). *34.*

- That's 30 plus 4. How many **T**'s do you make for 30? (Signal.) *3.*
- How many **lines** do you make for 4? (Signal.) *4.*
- Your turn. Make the **T**'s and lines for 34. Make the **T**'s under the digit for 30. Make the lines under the 4. Raise your hand when you're finished. (Observe children and give feedback.)
- (Write on the board:)

A. 3 | 4
    T T T | I I I I

- Check your work. Here's what you should have for numeral A. 34 has 3 **T**'s plus 4 leftover lines. Raise your hand if you got it right.

c. Touch numeral B.
Everybody, read the numeral. (Signal.) *42.*

- That's 40 plus 2. How many **T**'s do you make for 40? (Signal.) *4.*
- How many **lines** do you make for 2? (Signal.) *2.*
- Your turn: Make the **T**'s and lines for 42. Make the **T**'s under the digit for 40. Make the lines under the 2. Raise your hand when you're finished. (Observe children and give feedback.)

- (Write on the board:)

$$\text{B.} \quad \frac{4 \,|\, 2}{\text{T T T T} \,|\, \text{I I}}$$

- Check your work. Here's what you should have for numeral B. 42 has 4 **T's** plus 2 leftover lines. Raise your hand if you got it right.
d. Touch numeral C.
   Everybody, read the numeral. (Signal.) *31.*
- That's 30 plus 1. How many **T's** do you make for 30? (Signal.) *3.*
- How many **lines** do you make for 1? (Signal.) *1.*
- Your turn: Make the **T's** and lines for 31. Raise your hand when you're finished.
   (Observe children and give feedback.)
- (Write on the board:)

$$\text{C.} \quad \frac{3 \,|\, 1}{\text{T T T} \,|\, \text{I}}$$

- Check your work. Here's what you should have for numeral C. 31 is 3 **T's** plus 1 leftover line. Raise your hand if you got it right.
e. Touch numeral D.
   Everybody, read the numeral. (Signal.) *24.*
- That's 20 plus 4. How many **T's** do you make for 20? (Signal.) *2.*

- How many **lines** do you make for 4? (Signal.) *4.*
- Your turn: Make the **T's** and lines for 24. Raise your hand when you're finished.
   (Observe children and give feedback.)
- (Write on the board:)

$$\text{D.} \quad \frac{2 \,|\, 4}{\text{T T} \,|\, \text{I I I I}}$$

- Check your work. Here's what you should have for numeral D. 24 is 2 **T's** plus 4 leftover lines. Raise your hand if you got it right.
f. Touch numeral E.
   Everybody, read the numeral. (Signal.) *43.*
- That's 40 plus 3. How many **T's** do you make for 40? (Signal.) *4.*
- How many **lines** do you make for 3? (Signal.) *3.*
- Your turn: Make the **T's** and lines for 43. Raise your hand when you're finished.
   (Observe children and give feedback.)
- (Write on the board:)

$$\text{E.} \quad \frac{4 \,|\, 3}{\text{T T T T} \,|\, \text{I I I}}$$

- Check your work. Here's what you should have for numeral E. 43 is 4 **T's** plus 3 leftover lines. Raise your hand if you got it right.

Scope and Sequence for

Connecting Math Concepts, Level B

Connecting Math Concepts, Level B provides many illustrations of how mathematical concepts are linked to each other and to the outside world. For example, money is used to illustrate renaming, regrouping, multiplication, problem solving, and

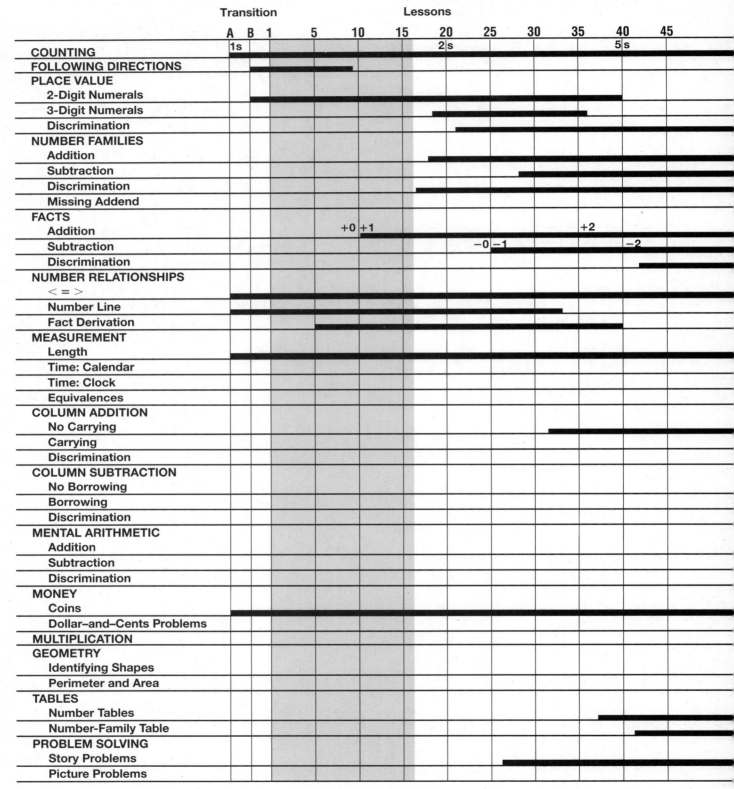

	Transition		Lessons							
	A B 1	5 10	15	20	25	30	35	40	45	
COUNTING	1s			2s				5s		
FOLLOWING DIRECTIONS										
PLACE VALUE										
2-Digit Numerals										
3-Digit Numerals										
Discrimination										
NUMBER FAMILIES										
Addition										
Subtraction										
Discrimination										
Missing Addend										
FACTS										
Addition		+0 +1					+2			
Subtraction					−0 −1			−2		
Discrimination										
NUMBER RELATIONSHIPS										
< = >										
Number Line										
Fact Derivation										
MEASUREMENT										
Length										
Time: Calendar										
Time: Clock										
Equivalences										
COLUMN ADDITION										
No Carrying										
Carrying										
Discrimination										
COLUMN SUBTRACTION										
No Borrowing										
Borrowing										
Discrimination										
MENTAL ARITHMETIC										
Addition										
Subtraction										
Discrimination										
MONEY										
Coins										
Dollar–and–Cents Problems										
MULTIPLICATION										
GEOMETRY										
Identifying Shapes										
Perimeter and Area										
TABLES										
Number Tables										
Number-Family Table										
PROBLEM SOLVING										
Story Problems										
Picture Problems										

many other concepts. CMC includes both symbolic and physical representations of place value, regrouping, renaming, and so forth. As discussed previously, the linking of these concepts from one lesson to the next makes the program unique. Regrouping, for example, is not limited to one "chapter," but is distributed across many successive lessons in the subtraction track. In this way, all students from the slowest to the fastest have ample time to become competent and successful at each of the strategies presented. The Scope and Sequence Chart shows where each track or major topic begins and where it ends.

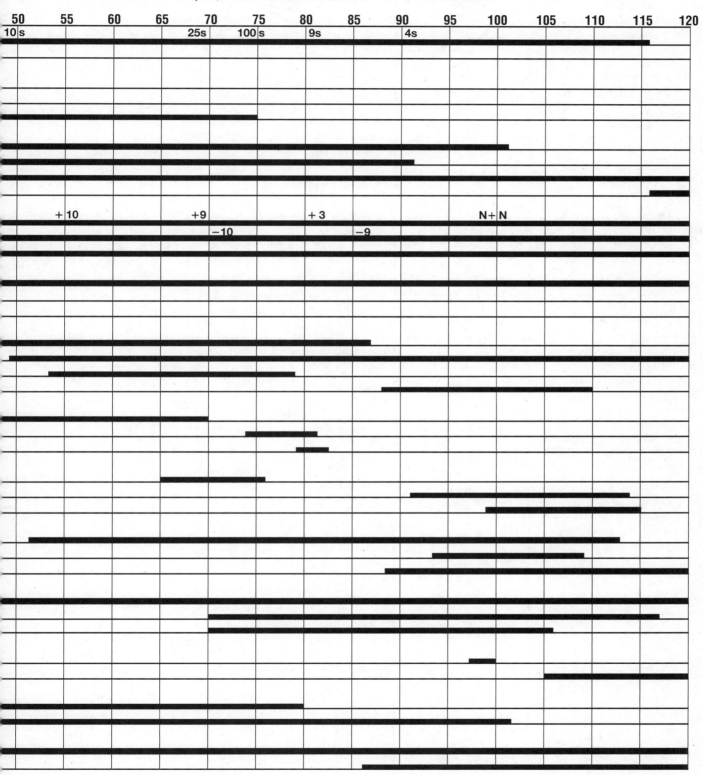

Level B Contents

Skills	Taught in these Lessons	Date Lessons Completed
COUNTING		
Counts forward from different numbers	A-40	
Identifies objects by ordinal numbers	58	
Counts backwards from 10	71–80	
Counts by 2	19–116	
Indicates which number comes next in the series for counting by 2	32–35	
Counts by 5	39–116	
Counts by 10	49–111	
Counts by 25	67–72	
Counts by 100	74–78	
Counts by 9	81–116	
Counts by 4	92–116	
FOLLOWING DIRECTIONS		
Plays a team game that requires following directions	B-9	
Crosses out specific items quickly in a following-directions race	2, 3	
PLACE VALUE **2-Digit Numerals**		
Reads/writes 2-digit numerals	1–36	
Identifies or writes 2-digit numerals from counters or from descriptions	24–35	
Writes 2-digit numerals in expanded notation	37–40	
3-Digit Numerals		
Reads/writes 3-digit numerals	18–33	
Writes 3-digit numerals from counters	31–33	
Writes 3-digit numerals from descriptions	35, 36	
Discrimination		
Identifies digits in numerals according to their ordinal position	21, 22	
Determines the number of digits in numerals	22, 23	

Skills	Taught in these Lessons	Date Lessons Completed
Writes 1-, 2-, or 3-digit numerals from dictation, counters or descriptions	27–38	
Indicates the number of hundreds, tens and leftovers (ones) for numerals	TL3-44	
Indicates how many digits are in a numeral and identifies the digit in the tens column	74, 75	
NUMBER FAMILIES **Addition**		
Writes 2 addition facts for a number family	18–23	
Indicates the missing big number in number families	23–99	
Writes the big number and the addition fact for families that have small numbers that are the same	100, 101	
Subtraction		
Writes the missing small number in number families	27–91	
Indicates the subtraction facts for number families	33–91	
Writes both small numbers for number families that have 1 as a small number, using the number-family table	34, 35	
Writes subtraction problems for number families that have a missing small number	37–40	
Discrimination		
Identifies the 2 small numbers and the big number in a number family	17, 18	
Puts numbers in a number family	21–TL5	
Indicates the missing small number or the missing big number in number families	29–67	
Writes 2 addition facts and 2 subtraction facts for a number family	38–41	
Writes column problems for number families that have 2-digit or 3-digit numerals	107–120	

Level B Contents

Skills	Taught in these Lessons	Date Lessons Completed
Missing Addend		
Writes the missing addend in problems based on familiar number families	116–120	
FACTS		
Addition: Zeros and Ones		
Says the number that comes after (or is 1 more than) a specified number	TL1, 23	
Works +1, 1+ or +0 problems	11–26	
Adds single-digit numbers in a column and writes the 1-digit sum	27, 28	
Addition: Twos		
Works +2 or 2+ problems	36–55	
Writes answers to +2 problems and finds the appropriate number family in the number family table	39, 40	
Indicates the number that is 2 more than the odd numbers 1, 3, 5, 7 and 9	49–51	
Addition: Tens		
Writes the place-value addition for teen numerals	55, 56	
Works +10 or 10+ problems	59–TL6	
Addition: Nines		
Indicates the answers to problems that add 10 and that add 9	69, 70	
Indicates answers to problems that add 9	69–78	
Addition: Threes		
Works problems that add 2 and that add 3	81	
Indicates answers to +3 or 3+ problems	86–88	
Addition: "Doubles"		
Indicates answers to "doubles" problems	98–105	
Subtraction: Zeros and Ones		
Writes numbers that are 1 smaller than specified numbers	25–27	
Works −1 or =1 problems	TL4, 41	
Works −0 problems	45	

Skills	Taught in these Lessons	Date Lessons Completed
Subtraction: Twos		
Writes the number that is 2 less than specified numbers	42–44	
Works −2 or =2 problems	46–61	
Subtraction: Tens		
Works 210 or 510 problems	72, 73	
Subtraction: Nines		
Works 29 or 59 problems	87–104	
Discrimination		
Works mixed sets of addition/ subtraction problems	42–67	
Plays a team game with addition/ subtraction problems	50–118	
Plays a fact game with addition/ subtraction problems	TL6–TL12	
NUMBER RELATIONSHIPS		
< = >		
Indicates which of 2 numbers is more	A-6	
Writes 3 numerals in order, from least to greatest	7–119	
Answers questions about the greater-than and less-than signs	9, 10	
Completes the sign between: 2 numerals	B-12	
2 groups of lines	19	
2 groups of coins	20, TL2	
pairs of numbers that are added or subtracted	116–120	
Number Line		
Uses a number line (or ruler) to solve simple addition/subtraction problems	A-33	
Circles the numbers on a number line that are greater than a specified number	4–6	

Level B Contents

Skills	Taught in these Lessons	Date Lessons Completed
Fact Derivation		
Indicates answers to pairs or sets of related addition problems	5–TL4	
Fills in missing addends and writes answers for a set of related addition problems	13–15	
MEASUREMENT **Length**		
Measures lines	A-23	
Makes lines a specified number of inches longer	A-23	
Uses measurement to make lines that correspond to addition/subtraction facts	B-48	
Constructs number families from addition/subtraction measurement problems	25–33	
Shows the length of 1 foot and 1 inch	85–87	
Time: Calendar		
Answers questions by referring to a calendar	49–120	
Uses a calendar to determine the date that is —days or —weeks after a given date	53–57	
Identifies numbers on a calendar as ordinals	58, 59	
Time: Clock		
Identifies the hour hand and the minute hand	54–57	
Writes the numbers that come before and after selected numerals on clock faces	56–59	
Identifies the hour on clock faces	59–62	
Indicates the number of minutes on clock faces	61–63	
Writes the time for clock faces	64–79	
Equivalences		
Completes the sign between foot/inch or pound/ounce designations	88–110	

Skills	Taught in these Lessons	Date Lessons Completed
COLUMN ADDITION **No Carrying**		
Works problems that add 2 or 3 numerals	32–TL7	
Carrying		
Works problems that require carrying to the tens/hundreds column	74–81	
Discrimination		
Works problems, some of which require carrying to the tens column or the hundreds column	79–82	
COLUMN SUBTRACTION **No Borrowing**		
Works problems that involve 2- or 3-digit subtrahends and 1-, 2- or 3-digit minuends	65–76	
Borrowing		
Rewrites 2-digit numerals for borrowing	92–95	
Indicates whether a subtraction problem starts with the big number	95–98	
Works problems that involve 2- or 3-digit numerals	96–114	
Discrimination		
Works 2- or 3-digit problems, some of which require borrowing	99–115	
MENTAL ARITHMETIC **Addition**		
Indicates answers to problems that add 1 to larger numbers	52, 53	
Indicates answers to problems that add 10	63–106	
Indicates answers to problems that add tens/hundreds numbers	80–113	
Subtraction		
Indicates answers to problems that subtract 10 or tens numbers	94–109	

Level B Contents

Skills	Taught in these Lessons	Date Lessons Completed
Discrimination		
Indicates answers to problems that add or subtract 10 or tens numbers	88–117	
Indicates answers to problems that add or subtract hundreds numbers	88–118	
Indicates answers to word problems that require addition or subtraction	116–120	
MONEY **Coins**		
Identifies coins and states their values	A-14	
Determines the value of groups of mixed coins	B-106	
Determines the value of groups of like coins	59–73	
Writes multiplication problems for rows of coins	TL8–86	
Counts coins to reach specified amounts	107–112	
Uses a specified number of coins to reach a specified amount	113, 114	
Solves coin problems using a table	115–120	

Skills	Taught in these Lessons	Date Lessons Completed
Dollar-and-Cents Problems		
Reads or writes dollar-and-cents values	70–79	
Works column-addition/subtraction problems that involve money	77–85	
Works money problems that require carrying	83–85	
Adds pennies, dimes and dollars in the same way as ones, tens and hundreds	87–96	
Solves money problems by referring to a table	109–117	
MULTIPLICATION		
Translates multiplication problems into count-by operations	70–72	
Figures out answers to multiplication problems	71–114	
Writes answers to multiplication problems and reads multiplication facts	103–106	

Level B Contents

Skills	Taught in these Lessons	Date Lessons Completed
GEOMETRY **Identifying Shapes**		
Identifies triangles, circles, rectangles	97–100	
Perimeter and Area		
Figures out the perimeter of rectangles, triangles	105–120	
Figures out the area of rectangles	110–112	
Figures out the area and perimeter of rectangles or squares	113–120	
TABLES **Number Tables**		
Identifies the smallest and largest numbers in the rows/columns of a table	38–41	
Identifies row and column designations for cells in a table	42, 43	
Answers questions by referring to a table	44–TL8	
Determines totals and interprets data in a table to answer questions	62–65	

Skills	Taught in these Lessons	Date Lessons Completed
Number-Family Table		
Identifies the number families for addition/subtraction problems	41–48	
Finds specified number families in the number-family table	68–102	
PROBLEM SOLVING **Story Problems**		
Writes number problems (symbols) for story problems	26–32	
Writes 1- or 2-digit number problems and answers for story problems	42–103	
Solves problems by referring to a calendar	103–106	
Solves number-family story problems that involve 2- or 3-digit numerals	112–119	
Picture Problems		
Writes answers to price-tag problems that require addition or subtraction	86–120	

Standard Sequence: Lessons 1, 2, 3, through 120.
Accelerated Sequence: Transition lessons A, B, then 16–120.
Test lessons (TL1–TL12) follow every tenth lesson.
For Level B Placement Test, see page 179.

Level B, Lesson 108 (Presentation Book)

Materials

A primary ruler for each child, a penny for each pair of children and an object that weighs about 1 pound, for example a 6" × 9" softcover book of 250 pages.

Objectives

• Practice mental arithmetic by adding and subtracting 10. (Exercise 1)

• **Complete an equality or inequality sign for pound/ounce designations.** (Exercise 2)
Note: Children learn that there are 16 ounces in 1 pound.

• Write column problems for number families that have 2-digit numerals. (Exercise 3)

• **Figure out the perimeter of a rectangle.** (Exercise 4)

• Count coins to reach specified amounts. (Exercise 5)

• Write answers to subtraction problems, some of which require borrowing. (Exercise 6)

• Play the fact game that requires saying subtraction problems and answers for families with missing small numbers. (Exercise 7)
Note: The fact game may take too much time to complete within the regular lesson. If so, schedule the game for some other period before lesson 109 is scheduled.

EXERCISE 1 MENTAL ARITHMETIC
Adding and Subtracting 10

a. Get ready to add 10 and subtract 10 from different numbers.
b. Listen: 50 plus 10. What's the answer? (Signal.) *60.*
• Listen: 60 minus 10. What's the answer? (Signal.) *50.*
• Listen: 50 minus 10. What's the answer? (Signal.) *40.*
• Listen: 40 minus 10. What's the answer? (Signal.) *30.*
• Listen: 40 plus 10. What's the answer? (Signal.) *50.*
(Repeat step b until firm.)

EXERCISE 2 MEASUREMENT
Ounces and Pounds

Note: You will need an object that weighs 1 pound.

a. You're going to learn about units of weight. A pound is a unit of weight. The more pounds you weigh, the heavier you are.
• Raise your hand if you know how many pounds you weigh.
(Call on individual children. Ask each child:) How much do you weigh? ____ *pounds.*

b. (Present an object that weighs 1 pound.) This ____ weighs about 1 pound. If I piled 10 of these ____, I'd have 10 pounds. How many pounds would I have with a pile of 100 ____? (Signal.) *100 pounds.*

c. Listen: An ounce is much lighter than a pound. Here's the rule about an ounce: It takes 16 ounces to make 1 pound. Once more: It takes 16 ounces to make 1 pound. How many ounces are in 1 pound? (Signal.) *16.*

d. Your ruler weighs a little over an ounce. Pick up your ruler and feel how much it weighs.
• You would need about 16 of those rulers to have 1 pound of rulers.

Workbook Practice

a. Open your workbook to lesson 108 and find part 1.
• You're going to complete the sign for each item. Everybody, how many ounces are in 1 pound? (Signal.) *16.*
• Yes, 16 ounces. Remember that.
b. Item A has **17 ounces** on 1 side and **1 pound** on the other side. Everybody, which is heavier, 17 ounces or 1 pound? (Signal.) *17 ounces.*
• Yes, 17 ounces is more than 16 ounces. And a pound is 16 ounces. Circle **17 ounces.** That's the side that's heavier.
c. Item B has **15 ounces** on 1 side and **1 pound** on the other side. Everybody, which is heavier? (Signal.) *1 pound.*

- Yes, 1 pound is 16 ounces, and that's more than 15 ounces. Circle **1 pound**. √

d. Item C has 16 ounces on 1 side and 1 pound on the other side.
   (Call on a student:) Which is heavier?
   (Ideas: *Neither; they are the same.*)
- Right, they're the same. So don't circle anything.

e. Your turn: Circle the side that is heavier in item D. Then complete the signs for all the items. Raise your hand when you're finished.
   (Observe children and give feedback.)

f. (Write on the board:)

   > a. 17 ounces ⪺ 1 pound
   > b. 15 ounces ⪡ 1 pound
   > c. 16 ounces = 1 pound
   > d. 1 pound ⪡ 19 ounces

- Check your work. Here's the sign you should have for each problem.

g. Raise your hand if you got all the problems right.

EXERCISE 3 NUMBER FAMILIES
Writing Column Problems

a. Find part 2.
   These are number families with 2-digit numerals. Remember, if you go forward along the arrow, you add. If you go backwards along the arrow, you subtract.

b. Touch family A.
   Do you go forward along the arrow or backwards along the arrow for this problem? (Signal.)
   Forward.
- Say the problem. (Signal.)
   26 plus 56 equals how many.
- Touch family B.
   Do you go forward along the arrow or backwards along the arrow for this problem? (Signal.)
   Backwards.
- Say the problem. (Signal.)
   79 minus 59 equals how many.
- Touch family C.
   Do you go forward along the arrow or backwards along the arrow for this problem? (Signal.)
   Backwards.
- Say the problem. (Signal.)
   80 minus 51 equals how many.
- Touch family D.
   Do you go forward along the arrow or backwards along the arrow for this problem? (Signal.)
   Forward.
- Say the problem. (Signal.)
   75 plus 73 equals how many.
   (Repeat step b until firm.)

c. Your turn: Write the column problem for family A. Remember the sign and the equal line. Raise your hand when you're finished. √
- (Write on the board:)

   > a. 26
   > + 56

- Check your work. Here's what you should have for problem A. Raise your hand if you got it right.

d. Your turn: Write the column problems for the rest of the families in part 3. Raise your hand when you're finished.
   (Observe children and give feedback.)

e. (Write on the board:)

   > b. 79   c. 80   d. 75
   > − 59   − 51   + 73

- Check your work. Here's what you should have for the problems.

f. Make sure all your column problems are right. Then write the answer to each problem. Raise your hand when you're finished.
   (Observe children and give feedback.)

g. Check your work. Read each problem and the answer.
- Problem A. (Signal.) *26 plus 56 equals 82.*
- Problem B. (Signal.) *79 minus 59 equals 20.*
- Problem C. (Signal.) *80 minus 51 equals 29.*
- Problem D. (Signal.) *75 plus 73 equals 148.*

h. Raise your hand if you got all the problems right.

EXERCISE 4 GEOMETRY
Perimeter of a Rectangle

> *Note:* **Each child will need a primary ruler.**

a. Find part 3.
   You learned a rule about rectangles. The sides that are across from each other are the same length. Two of the sides on the rectangle have circled letters. What sides are those? (Signal.)
   B and C.

b. Touch side B.
   Which side is the same length as side B? (Signal.) *Side D.*
- Touch side C.
   Which side is the same length as side C? (Signal.) *Side A.*
   (Repeat step b until firm.)

c. Your turn: Measure the sides with circled letters. Then write the lengths of **all 4** sides. Remember, don't measure sides A and D. You'll know how long they are when you measure sides B and C.

Raise your hand when you're finished.
(Observe children and give feedback.)

d. Check your work. Tell me the length of each side.
- Side A. (Signal.) *2 inches.*
- Side B. (Signal.) *1 inch.*
- Side C. (Signal.) *2 inches.*
- Side D. (Signal.) *1 inch.*

e. Raise your hand if you got all the sides right.

f. Below the rectangle is a line that shows the total distance around the rectangle. That's the distance something would have to go if it went around all 4 sides of the rectangle. The first part of the line is side A, the next part is side B, the next part is side C, and the last part is side D.

g. Your turn: Measure the whole line and write the number at the end of the line. Raise your hand when you're finished.
(Observe children and give feedback.)
- Check your work. Everybody, how long is the distance around the whole rectangle? (Signal.) *6 inches.*

h. You can get the same answer by adding up the length of each side. You've written those numbers in the box. Write a plus sign. Then add up all the numbers. You should get the same answer you got when you measured the line that shows the distance around the rectangle. Raise your hand when you're finished. (Observe children and give feedback.)
- Check your work. Everybody, what does 2 plus 1 plus 2 plus 1 equal? (Signal.) *6.*

i. You figured out the distance around the whole rectangle. Remember how to do it. You just add up the lengths of all the sides.

EXERCISE 5 COUNTING MONEY
Specific Amounts

a. Find part 4.
Each problem has 2 rows of coins. The number of cents at the end of each problem shows the number of cents that should be shown, but there are too many coins.

b. Touch the number for problem A.
Everybody, how many cents should be in problem A? (Signal.) *45.*
- So you start with the top row. Count the cents. Cross out any coins that take you past 45 cents. Raise your hand when you've fixed up the top row. √
- Everybody, how many quarters did you cross out? (Signal.) *2.*
- Raise your hand when you know how many cents are left in the quarter row.

- Everybody, how many cents? (Signal.) *25.*
- You're at 25. Count for the dimes to 45. Cross out any dimes that take you past 45. Raise your hand when you're finished. √
- Listen: How many dimes did you cross out? (Signal.) *2.*
- Count the cents for the coins that are not crossed out. Start with the quarters. Get ready. (Signal.) *25, 35, 45.*
- So you fixed up problem A to have 45 cents.

c. Touch the number for problem B.
Everybody, how many cents should be in problem B? (Signal.) *40.*
- So you start with the top row. Count the cents. Cross out any coins that take you past 40 cents. Raise your hand when you've fixed up the top row. √
- Everybody, how many quarters did you cross out? (Signal.) *2.*
- Raise your hand when you know how many cents are left in the quarter row.
- Everybody, how many cents? (Signal.) *25.*
- You're at 25. Count for the nickels to 40. Cross out any nickels that take you past 40. Raise your hand when you're finished. √
- Listen: How many nickels did you cross out? (Signal.) *1.*
- Count the cents for the coins that are not crossed out. Start with the quarters. Get ready. (Signal.) *25, 30, 35, 40.*
- So you fixed up problem B to have 40 cents.

d. Touch the number for problem C.
Everybody, how many cents should be in problem C? (Signal.) *34.*
- So you start with the top row. Count the cents. Cross out any coins that take you past 34 cents. Raise your hand when you've fixed up the top row. √
- Everybody, how many dimes did you cross out? (Signal.) *1.*
- Raise your hand when you know how many cents are left in the dime row.
- Everybody, how many cents? (Signal.) *30.*
- You're at 30. Count for the pennies to 34. Cross out any pennies that take you past 34. Raise your hand when you're finished. √
- Listen: How many pennies did you cross out? (Signal.) *1.*
- Count the cents for the coins that are not crossed out. Start with the dimes. Get ready. (Signal.) *10, 20, 30, 31, 32, 33, 34.*
- So you fixed up problem C to have 34 cents.

EXERCISE 6 SUBTRACTION
Borrowing Discrimination

a. Find part 5.
   You have to borrow to work some of these subtraction problems. Remember, you read the problem in the ones column. If the problem in the ones column does not start with the big number, rewrite the top number. Then you work the problem. But if the problem in the ones column starts with the big number, you just work the problem.
b. Work problem A. Raise your hand when you're finished. (Observe children and give feedback.)
• (Write on the board:)

$$\text{a.} \quad \begin{array}{r} \overset{8}{\cancel{9}}\,16 \\ -\,7\quad7 \\ \hline 1\quad9 \end{array}$$

• Check your work. Here's what you should have for problem A.
c. Your turn: Work the rest of the problems in part 5. Raise your hand when you're finished.
   (Observe children and give feedback.)
d. (Write on the board:)

$$\begin{array}{ccc} \text{b.} \ \begin{array}{r} 9\ 6 \\ -2\ 5 \\ \hline 7\ 1 \end{array} & \text{c.} \ \begin{array}{r} \overset{4}{\cancel{5}}\,14 \\ -3\ 9 \\ \hline 1\ 5 \end{array} & \text{d.} \ \begin{array}{r} \overset{2}{\cancel{3}}\,18 \\ -2\ 9 \\ \hline 9 \end{array} \end{array}$$

$$\begin{array}{cc} \text{e.} \ \begin{array}{r} \overset{5}{\cancel{6}}\,16 \\ -3\ 9 \\ \hline 2\ 7 \end{array} & \text{f.} \ \begin{array}{r} 9\ 4 \\ -2\ 4 \\ \hline 7\ 0 \end{array} \end{array}$$

• Check your work. Here's what you should have for each problem.
e. Raise your hand if you got all of them right.

EXERCISE 7 FACT GAME
Subtraction

Note: For this game, each pair of children will need a penny.

a. (Draw on the board:)

	Superstars	Stars	Totals
A			
B			

• We're going to play the fact game. Everybody, sit with your partner.

b. A team, raise your hand. √
• B team, raise your hand. √
• Everybody, find the game sheet on page 110 of your workbook. B team, put your penny in the start box.
• A team, circle the number **3** in scorebox 3. You'll make your tally marks in the part of that scorebox that is not shaded.
• B team, you'll move your penny and say the subtraction fact that starts with the big number. Everybody, ready? Here we go.
c. (Roll the die and tell the class the number.)
• B team, go. A team, raise your hand when you're ready for the answer.
• Here's the fact: _____. A team, make a tally mark if the answer is wrong.
   (Repeat step c until you've completed the table.)
d. That's the end of the first game.
   B team, find scorebox 3. Then circle the number **3** in the scorebox.
• A team, count the tally marks you made. Then tell your partner the number. B team, write that number in **the shaded part** of **your** scorebox 3. B team, raise your hand when you're finished.
   (Observe children and give feedback.)
• B team, raise your hand if you made no mistakes. Those are superstars!
   (Count children with hands raised and write the number in row B under **Superstars.**)
• B team, raise your hand if you made only 1 mistake.
   Those are stars.
   (Count children with hands raised and write the number in row B under **Stars.**)
e. Now it's the A team's turn. A team, put your penny in the start box. B team, you'll make tally marks in the part of box 3 that's not shaded. Remember, A team, move the penny and say the subtraction fact. B team, make a tally mark in box 3 if the answer is wrong. Everybody, ready?
   Here we go.
f. (Roll the die and tell the class the number.)
• A team, go. B team, raise your hand when you're ready for the answer.
• Here's the fact: _____. B team, make a tally mark if the answer is wrong.
   (Repeat step f until you've completed the table.)
g. B team, count the tally marks you made. Then tell your partner the number. A team, write that number in **the shaded part** of **your** scorebox 3. Raise your hand when you're finished.
   (Observe children and give feedback.)
• A team, raise your hand if you made no mistakes. Those are superstars!
   (Count children with hands raised and write the number in row A under **Superstars.**)

- A team, raise your hand if you made only 1 mistake.
  Those are stars.
  (Count children with hands raised and write the number in row B under **Stars.**)
h. I'll write the totals of superstars and stars for each team.
  (Write the totals in the **Totals** boxes.)
- Which team has the larger total of superstars and stars? (Signal.)
- But anybody who is a star or a superstar is really learning a lot of math.

EXERCISE 8 INDEPENDENT WORK

a. Finish the rest of the worksheet on your own.
b. (Assign **Connecting Math Concepts** *Independent Worksheet* 80 and *Math Facts Worksheet* 88 as classwork or homework. Before beginning the next lesson, check the students' independent work.)

Estimation Activity

- Materials: Cards, each with a question, such as:

  Would a man weigh 150 pounds or 150 ounces?
  Would a candy bar weigh 6 pounds or 6 ounces?
  Would a cup weigh 12 pounds or 12 ounces?
  Would a dog weigh 9 pounds or 9 ounces?

- Activity: A child (or teacher) draws a card and reads the question. The child answers the question.

Level B, Lesson 108 (Workbook)

For **part 1**, students complete each statement with the sign >, <, or =. In lessons 11 and 12, students used the signs to complete statements with numerals. In lessons 19 and 20, they also used the signs with groups of lines and with groups of coins. Prior to lesson 108 they also completed signs shown between two lengths. In the final application (introduced in lesson 116) students complete the sign between pairs of numbers that are added or subtracted (e.g., 7 + 7 _____ 5 + 10).

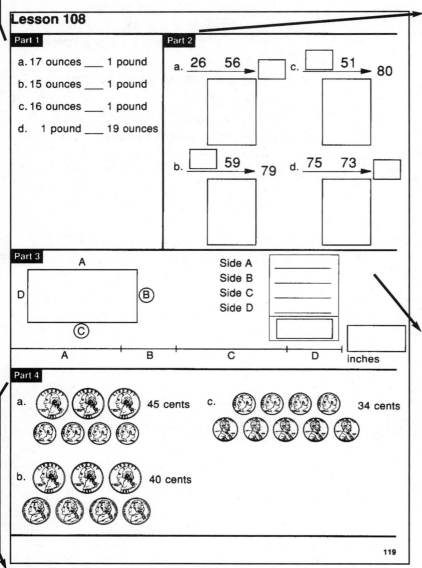

For **part 2**, students translate the number families into addition/subtraction statements. For item a, the "big number" (total) is missing, so students write the problem:

$$\begin{array}{r} 26 \\ + 56 \\ \hline \square \end{array}$$

For item b, a "small number" is missing, so students work the problem:

$$\begin{array}{r} 79 \\ - 59 \\ \hline \square \end{array}$$

Number families are introduced in the context of addition/subtraction facts (see the fact game, page 40). Students have worked with number families in various forms since lesson 18. Lesson 108 is the second consecutive day of the problem type shown in **part 2**. After five consecutive lessons, students will construct similar number families from written descriptions.

Part 3 introduces the concept of perimeter. Students measure two sides of the rectangle, deduce the length of the other two sides, and work the addition problem. Students confirm their answer by measuring the perimeter shown below the rectangle. Perimeter exercises continue through the end of the program.

Area is introduced in lesson 110. By the end of the program, students figure out the area and perimeter of rectangles and squares and the perimeter of triangles.

The task in **part 4** is the culmination of many prerequisites taught in Level B. In order to correctly represent the number of cents for each item, students must: a) know the value of coins (lessons 13, 14); b) skip-count by 5, 10 and 25 (in over 30 previous lessons); c) count on from a multiple of 5 (lessons 62, 63); and d) count to reach a specified amount (introduced in lesson 107). Problems of the type in part 4 appear for six consecutive lessons. In later lessons (113, 114), students count out different combinations of coins to reach a specified amount.

Part 5 requires students to discriminate subtraction problems that call for regrouping and problems that do not. Column problems were introduced in lessons 65–67. Discrimination tasks and component tasks for renaming appeared in lessons 92–98. Renaming problems were introduced in lessons 96–98. Mixed sets such as **part 5** have appeared since lesson 99.

Parts 6 through 10 are worked independently. These parts review problem types that were practiced in a structured form in earlier lessons.

Part 6 reviews related facts that have 9 or 10 as one of the "small" numbers. The sequence of introduction for these facts was: a) minus 10 or end up with 10 (lessons 72, 73); b) minus 9 (lessons 87–90, 93–94); c) minus 9 or end up with 9 (lessons 102–104).

Part 7 reviews related addition facts that start with 3 or plus 3. These facts were introduced in lesson 81 and practiced in lessons 86 through 88.

The items in **part 8** review addition with problems carrying to the tens column. Some result in a 3-digit answer. Column addition was introduced in lesson 32 and appeared in over a dozen lessons before carrying to the tens column was introduced in lesson 74.

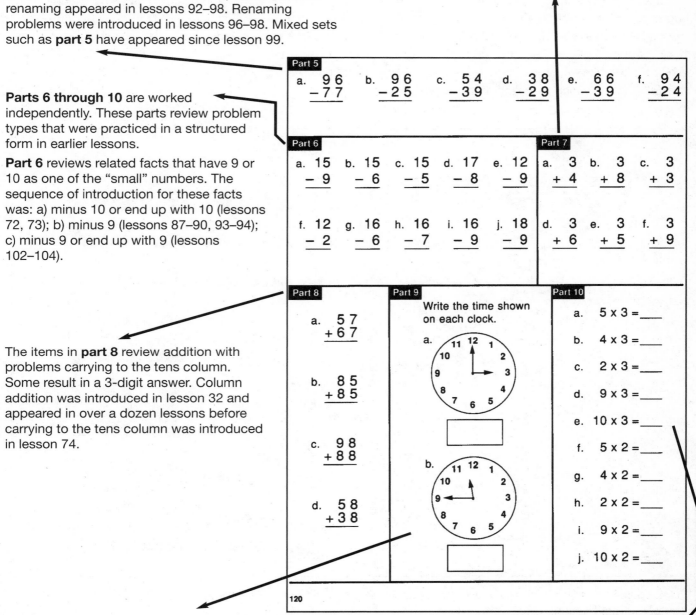

Students write "digital" times (3:00, 11:45) for the clocks in **part 9**. Prerequisites for telling time to the 5 minutes (count by 5, identify hour/minute hands and the number of minutes for numbers on the clock face) were taught in lessons 39–63, after which time-telling occurred for five more consecutive lessons.

Part 10 reviews two sets of related multiplication facts (times 3 and times 2).

Students translate each problem in order to solve it. For example, for item a students read: "Count by 5 three times." This type of problem is introduced in lesson 71 and appeared in 19 lessons prior to lesson 108.

Addition/subtraction facts are introduced through the concept of a number family. For any addition/subtraction situation, there are two "small" numbers and a "big" number (the sum). In this number family: $\xrightarrow[\quad]{3 \quad 4} 7$, 3 and 4 are the small numbers; 7 is the big number. The family generates four facts: 3 + 4 = 7; 4 + 3 = 7; 7 − 4 = 3; 7 − 3 = 4. Number families lighten the load for fact memorization by presenting all 200 addition/subtraction facts through 55 families.

In Level B, students work with related sets of facts. The fact game below includes facts that have 1, 2, 9, or 10 as a small number.

When a die is thrown, students move a penny the specified number of places and say the subtraction fact implied by the family on which they land. For example, the fact for $\xrightarrow[\quad]{2} 9$ is: 9 − 2 = 7.

The game gives an opportunity for rapid random practice of previously introduced facts.

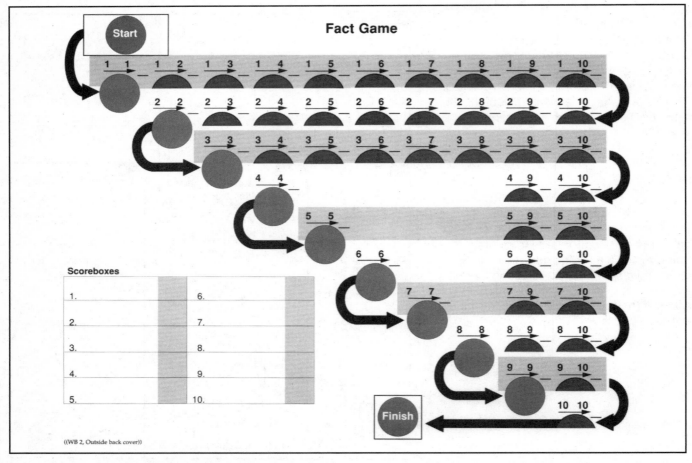

In later levels, number families are applied extensively to a variety of problem-solving situations involving whole numbers, fractions, and ratios/proportions.

Level B

Sample Track: Number Families

In *Connecting Math Concepts* the **number family** is the principal vehicle for teaching basic addition and subtraction facts, as well as the relationships between addition and subtraction.

A number family consists of three numbers written on an arrow; for example, $\underset{\longrightarrow}{6 \quad 9}$ 15. In this number family, 6 and 9 are the "small numbers" and 15 is the "big number."

A number family can be transformed into addition and subtraction statements. For the number family $\underset{\longrightarrow}{6 \quad 9}$ 15, each of the two related addition facts starts with a small number and adds the other small number to produce the big number: $6 + 9 = 15$ and $9 + 6 = 15$. The two subtraction facts start with the big number and subtract one of the small numbers: $15 - 6 = 9$ and $15 - 9 = 6$. Because one number family leads to four facts, a student who memorizes only 55 number families can figure out all 200 basic addition and subtraction facts.

Number families promote integration of the concepts of addition and subtraction. Students learn that when a small number is missing in a number family, as in $\underset{\longrightarrow}{\square \quad 9}$ 17, they should start with the big number and subtract the other small number to determine the missing number: $17 - 9 = \square$. If the big number is missing, as in $\underset{\longrightarrow}{8 \quad 9}$ $\square$, they should add the two small numbers to determine the big number: $8 + 9 = \square$.

Number families first appear in Lesson 17:

EXERCISE 2 NUMBER FAMILIES
Introduction

a. (Draw on the board:)

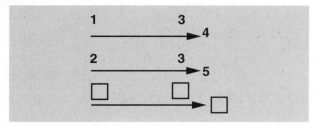

- These are number families. Each family shows the 3 numbers that always go together in addition facts and subtraction facts.

b. (Point to the top number family.)
This number family is just like the last measurement problem you worked. It has 3 numbers—the number you start with, the number you plus, and the number you end up with. It shows 1 plus 3 equals 4.

c. Here is a rule about number families. Listen: The big number is always at the end of the arrow.

d. (Point to the **4** in the first family.)
Here's the big number in this family. What's the big number in this family? (Signal.) *4.*

- (Point to the **5** in the second family.)
Here's the big number in this family. What's the big number in this family? (Signal.) *5.*

- Remember, the big number is always at the **end** of the arrow. The small numbers are **above** the arrow.

e. (Point to the first family.)
The small numbers in this family are 1 and 3.

- (Point to the second family.)
What are the small numbers in this family? (Signal.) *2 and 3.*

f. (Point to the bottom family.)
Let's see how smart you are. You can't see the numbers in this number family. But you know that one of the boxes is the big number and the other 2 boxes are the small numbers.

g. Tell me if I touch the **big number** or a **small number.**

- (Touch the third box.)
What did I touch? (Signal.) *Big number.*

- (Touch the second box.)
What did I touch? (Signal.) *Small number.*

- (Touch the first box.)
What did I touch? (Signal.) *Small number.*

- (Touch the third box.)
What did I touch? (Signal.) *Big number.*

- (Touch the first box.)
What did I touch? (Signal.) *Small number.* (Repeat step g until firm.)

h. Let's review the number families one more time. (Point to the first family.)
Listen: What's the big number in this family? (Signal.) *4.*

- What are the 2 small numbers? (Signal.) *1 and 3.*

- (Point to the second family.)
Listen: What's the big number in this family? (Signal.) *5.*

- What are the 2 small numbers? (Signal.) *2 and 3.*

i. (Point to the first family.)
Each number family shows you how to make addition facts and subtraction facts. Here's how you make addition facts: You add the two **small** numbers to get the big number.

- What are the 2 small numbers in this number family? (Signal.) *1 and 3.*
- Here's an addition fact. (Touch the numbers as you say:)
  1 plus 3 equals 4.

j. Your turn: I'll touch the numbers. You say that addition fact. Get ready.
  (Touch 1, 3, and 4 as children say:)
  1 plus 3 equals 4.

k. Here's another addition fact. (Touch the numbers as you say:)
  3 plus 1 equals 4.

l. Your turn: I'll touch. Say the addition fact that starts with 3. Get ready.
  (Touch 3, 1, and 4 as children say:)
  3 plus 1 equals 4.

m. (Point to the second family.)
  Remember, we add the two small numbers to get the big number. Say the two small numbers for this family. (Signal.) *2 and 3.*
- Here's an addition fact. (Touch the numbers as you say:)
  2 plus 3 equals 5.
- Here's the other addition fact. (Touch the numbers as you say:)
  3 plus 2 equals 5.

n. Listen: Say the addition fact that starts with 2. Get ready.
  (Touch the numbers as children say:)
  2 plus 3 equals 5.
- Now start with the other small number and say the addition fact.
  (Touch the numbers as children say:)
  3 plus 2 equals 5.
  (Repeat step n until firm.)

o. (Point to the first family.)
  What are the small numbers in this number family? (Signal.) *1 and 3.*
- Say the addition fact that starts with 1.
  (Touch the numbers as children say:)
  1 plus 3 equals 4.
- Now start with the other small number and say the addition fact.
  (Touch the numbers as children say:)
  3 plus 1 equals 4.
  (Repeat step o until firm.)

p. Remember how number families work because you'll be doing a lot with them in this program.

Children play team games involving missing numbers in number families. They also practice writing facts from number families. In Lesson 38 children begin writing two addition facts and two subtraction facts for specified number families.

The relationship between number families and measurement is introduced in Lesson 25. The following activity is done after children have worked with number families involving 1s:

Part 6

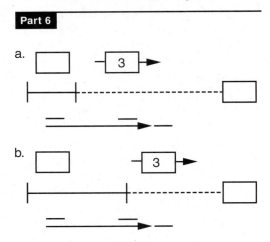

EXERCISE 7 MEASUREMENT AND NUMBER FAMILIES

a. Find part 6
  Touch line A.
- The line has an arrow box with a number in it. Measure the solid part of the line. Write that number above the solid part. Make the line longer. Then measure the whole line and write that number at the end of the line. Raise your hand when you're finished.
  (Observe children and give feedback.)

b. Check your work.
  How long is the solid part? (Signal.) *1 inch.*
- How much longer did you make the line? (Signal.) *3 inches.*
- How long is the whole line? (Signal.) *4 inches.*

c. The line works just like a number family. The two small numbers are above the line. The small numbers are 1 and 3. The big number is at the end of the line. Everybody, what's the big number? (Signal.) *4.*
- Touch the number-family arrow for line A. It's right below the lines.
- Your turn: Put the numbers from the line in the number family. Raise your hand when you're finished.
- (Write on the board:)

- Check your work. Here's what you should have for line A. Raise your hand if you got it right. (Praise children who raise their hand.)

d. Everybody, what are the small numbers for line A? (Signal.) *1 and 3.*
   What's the big number? (Signal.) *4.*
   (Repeat step d until firm.)
e. Touch line B.
   Measure the solid part of the line. Write that number above the solid part. Make the line longer. Then measure the whole line and write that number at the end of the line. Raise your hand when you're finished.
   (Observe children and give feedback.)
f. Check your work. Listen: What are the 2 small numbers for line B? (Signal.) *2 and 3.*
   • What's the big number for line B? (Signal.) *5.*
   (Repeat step f until firm.)
g. Put those numbers in the number family for line B. Raise your hand when you're finished.
   • (Write on the board:)

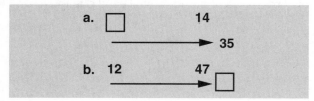

   • Check your work. Here's what you should have for line B. Raise your hand if you got it right.
   (Praise children who raise their hand.)
   • Remember, the lines work just like number families.

Starting in Level C, students use number families to help them analyze word problems and compute solutions—a strategy that teaches them not to make quick judgments because they see a "key word" such as *more.* The foundation for this work is laid in Level B. For example, children write column problems for families with 2-digit numbers beginning in Lesson 107:

EXERCISE 3 NUMBER FAMILIES
Writing Column Problems

a. (Write on the board:)

   • These are number families with 2-digit numerals. You're going to write a column problem for each family.
b. (Point to family A.)
   Is a small number or a big number missing in this family? (Signal.) *A small number.*

• So the problem you write goes backwards along the arrow. Everybody, say the subtraction problem for this family. (Signal.) *35 minus 14 equals how many.*
• (Point to family B.)
   Is a small number or the big number missing in this family? (Signal.) *The big number.*
• So the problem you write goes forward along the arrow. Everybody, say the addition problem for this family. (Signal.) *12 plus 47 equals how many.*
   (Repeat step b until firm.)
c. I'm going to write the problems in columns. (Point to family A.)
   Say the problem for this family and I'll write it. Get ready. (Signal.)
   (As children say the problem write:)

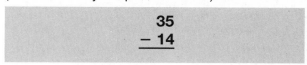

• You must remember to write the sign and the equal line.
d. (Point to family B.)
   Say the problem for this family and I'll write it. Get ready. (Signal.)
   (As children say the problem write:)

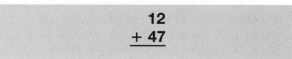

• You don't need to write the box for these column problems, but you need a sign and an equals line.

Part 2

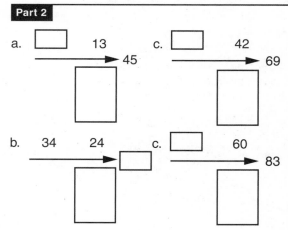

WORKBOOK PRACTICE

a. Your turn: Find part 2.
   Remember, if you go forward along the arrow, you add. If you go backwards along the arrow, you subtract.

b. Touch family A.
   Do you go forward along the arrow or backwards along the arrow for this problem? (Signal.)
   Backwards.
   • Say the problem. (Signal.)
   45 minus 13 equals how many.
c. Touch family B.
   Do you go forward along the arrow or backwards along the arrow for this problem? (Signal.)
   Forward.
   • Say the problem. (Signal.)
   34 plus 24 equals how many.
d. Touch family C.
   Do you go forward along the arrow or backwards along the arrow for this problem? (Signal.)
   Backwards.
   • Say the problem. (Signal.)
   69 minus 42 equals how many.
e. Touch family D.
   Do you go forward along the arrow or backwards along the arrow for this problem? (Signal.)
   Backwards.
   • Say the problem. (Signal.)
   83 minus 60 equals how many.
f. Your turn: Write the column problem for family A. Remember the sign and the equals line. Raise your hand when you're finished.
   (Observe children and give feedback.)
   • (Write on the board:)

$$\text{a.} \quad \begin{array}{r} 45 \\ -\ 13 \\ \hline \end{array}$$

   • Check your work. Here's what you should have for problem A. Raise your hand if you got it right.
g. Write the column problem for family B. Remember the sign. Raise your hand when you're finished.
   (Observe children and give feedback.)
   • (Write on the board:)

$$\text{b.} \quad \begin{array}{r} 34 \\ +\ 24 \\ \hline \end{array}$$

   • Check your work. Here's what you should have for problem B. Raise your hand if you got it right.

h. Write the column problem for family C. Raise your hand when you're finished.
   (Observe children and give feedback.)
   • (Write on the board:)

$$\text{c.} \quad \begin{array}{r} 69 \\ -\ 42 \\ \hline \end{array}$$

   • Check your work. Here's what you should have for problem C. Raise your hand if you got it right.
i. Write the column problem for family D. Raise your hand when you're finished.
   (Observe children and give feedback.)
   • (Write on the board:)

$$\text{d.} \quad \begin{array}{r} 83 \\ -\ 60 \\ \hline \end{array}$$

   • Check your work. Here's what you should have for problem D. Raise your hand if you got it right.
j. Make sure all your column problems are right. Then write answers to all the problems. Remember, you have to add for some and subtract for others. Be careful and don't write silly answers. Raise your hand when you're finished.
   (Observe children and give feedback.)
k. Check your work. Read each problem and the answer.
   • Problem a. (Signal.) *45 minus 13 equals 32.*
   • Problem b. (Signal.) *34 plus 24 equals 58.*
   • Problem c. (Signal.) *69 minus 42 equals 27.*
   • Problem d. (Signal.) *83 minus 60 equals 23.*
l. Raise your hand if you got all the problems right.

NUMBER-FAMILY TABLES

The first variation of the number-family table is introduced in Lesson 41, after children learn about row and column designations. The initial table has only two rows of number families and is found on the inside front cover of *Workbook 1*.

The introduction relates addition facts to the number family table and provides an important rule about the organization of number families: If an addition problem has a 1 in it, the family for that problem is in row 1; if the problem has a 2, the family is in row 2, and so on:

Number Families
Rows 1 and 2

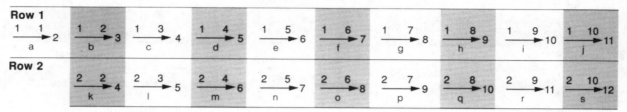

EXERCISE 5 NUMBER FAMILIES

a. Find rows 1 and 2 on the inside front cover of your workbook.

- I'm going to say addition problems. You'll find the number family for each problem I say. Listen big: If the problem has a **1** in it, it's in row 1. If a problem has a **2** in it, it's in row 2.

b. Listen: 6 plus 1. Say that problem. (Signal.) *6 plus 1.*

- Find the family in row 1 that has small numbers 6 and 1. Be careful, because 6 may not be the first small number. Raise your hand when you've found it.
(Observe children and give feedback.)

- Everybody, look at the letter below the number family that has small numbers of 6 and 1. What's the letter below that family? (Signal.) *F.*

c. New problem: 6 plus 2. That's in row 2. Find the family that has small numbers of 6 and 2. Raise your hand when you've found it.
(Observe children and give feedback.)

- Everybody, what's the letter below that family? (Signal.) *O.*

d. New problem: 8 plus 2. Find the family that has small numbers of 8 and 2. Raise your hand when you've found it.
(Observe children and give feedback.)

- Everybody, what's the letter below that family? (Signal.) *Q.*

e. New problem: 10 plus 1. Find the family that has small numbers of 10 and 1. Raise your hand when you've found it.
(Observe children and give feedback.)

- Everybody, what's the letter below that family? (Signal.) *J.*

f. New problem: 3 plus 1. Find the family that has small numbers of 3 and 1. Raise your hand when you've found it.
(Observe children and give feedback.)

- Everybody, what's the letter below that family? (Signal.) *C.*

g. Turn back to Lesson 41 and find part 6. For each problem, you'll write the letter of the number family.

- Problem A: 8 plus 2 equals how many? Write the letter of the family that has small numbers of 8 and 2. Raise your hand when you're finished.
(Observe children and give feedback.)

- Check your work. Everybody, what letter did you write? (Signal.) *Q.*

h. Your turn: Write letters for the rest of the problems in part 6. Raise your hand when you're finished.
(Observe children and give feedback.)

i. Check your work.

- Problem B: 7 plus 2 equals how many? Everybody, what letter? (Signal). *P.*

- Problem C: 8 plus 1 equals how many? Everybody, what letter? (Signal). *H.*

- Problem D: 3 plus 2 equals how many? Everybody, what letter? (Signal). *I.*

- Problem E: 4 plus 1 equals how many? Everybody, what letter?(Signal). *D.*

j. Later you'll write answers to the problems in part 6. After you write the answers, you can check them by looking at the number family for the problem. The answer is the big number in the family.

Children play fact games based on number-family tables beginning in Test Lesson 6, before Lesson 61. The first fact game involves a table that shows both small numbers.

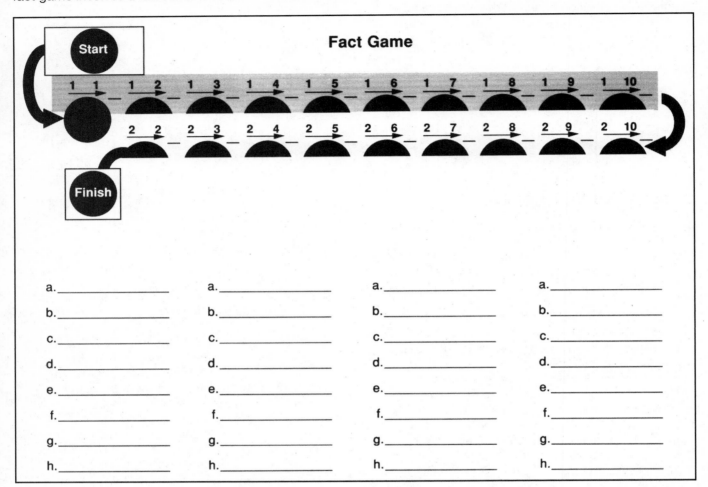

a._____   a._____   a._____   a._____

b._____   b._____   b._____   b._____

c._____   c._____   c._____   c._____

d._____   d._____   d._____   d._____

e._____   e._____   e._____   e._____

f._____   f._____   f._____   f._____

g._____   g._____   g._____   g._____

h._____   h._____   h._____   h._____

EXERCISE 2 FACT GAME

a. (You will need a die for this game. Each child will need a penny.)

• We're going to play a new kind of game. (Call on a child.) ((Child's name)) will be my helper.

b. Everybody, find the fact game on page 4. Put a penny in the start box. The box says **start** and has a round space for your penny. √

• For this game, you'll move your penny. You'll follow the arrow from the start box and move your penny to the right place below the number families.

c. Everybody, move your penny from the start box and move it 2 places along row 1. Raise your hand when your penny is in place. √

• Your penny should be right below the family that has the small numbers of 1 and 2. Raise your hand if your penny is in the right place. If it isn't, move it to the family with the small numbers of 1 and 2.

d. Listen: Move your penny 4 more places. Raise your hand when you're finished. √

• Everybody, what are the small numbers for the family your penny is under? (Signal.) *1 and 6.*

• Raise your hand if you got it right.
(Praise children who raise their hand.)

e. Listen: Move your penny 4 more places. Raise your hand when you're finished. √

• Everybody, what are the small numbers for the family your penny is under? (Signal.) *1 and 10.*

f. Listen: Move your penny 3 more places. Follow the arrow down to row 2 and count 3 places along the arrows. Raise your hand when you're finished. (Observe children and give feedback.)

• Everybody, what are the small numbers for the family your penny is under? (Signal.) *2 and 8.*

• Raise your hand if you got it right.
(Praise children who raise their hand.)

g. Put your penny in the start box.

• This time, we'll play the game. My helper will roll the die and tell you the number of dots on top. That's the number of places you'll move.

h. (Tell the helper to roll the die and say the number of dots.)

• Everybody, move your penny ____ places. Raise your hand when you're finished.

• Everybody, what are the small numbers for the family your penny is under? (Signal.)

• Your turn: Write the first addition fact for that family. Write it on line A. Do it fast. You have 5 seconds.

• (Write fact A on a piece of paper.)

i. (Tell the helper to roll the die and say the number of dots.)

• Everybody, move your penny ____ places. Raise your hand when you're finished.

• Now write the first addition fact for that family. Write it on line B. Do it fast. You have 5 seconds.

• (Write fact B on a piece of paper.)

j. (Repeat step i until you complete the second row.) We've finished one game. Put your penny back in the start box.

k. Let's check your work for the first game. Mark each fact that you got wrong.

• Fact A. Read it. (Signal.)

• Fact B. Read it. (Signal.)

• Fact C. Read it. (Signal.)

• (Continue through the facts.)

l. Raise your hand if you got them all right.
(Praise children who raise their hand.)

m. Let's play one more game. Write the facts for this game in the second column.

• (Direct the helper to roll the die. Tell the children to move that number of places. Direct them to write the first addition fact for that family. Tell the letter of that fact. Repeat the procedure until you complete the second row. Direct the children to read the fact for each letter, starting with the first letter of the second game.)

• Raise your hand if you got all the facts right. Good thinking!

n. (Collect the workbooks.)

Children use the game board again in Lesson 61, where they write facts in the next column. The remaining columns can be used for any additional fact-game practice the teacher wishes. In later lessons, children play variations of the game.

Scope and Sequence for

Connecting Math Concepts, Level C

Connecting Math Concepts, Level C places a strong emphasis on higher-order thinking. Students learn a variety of mapping techniques for relating problem solving to real-life situations. With word problems, measurement, money, time, and various

Lessons

Skill	Lessons (approx. range)
ADDITION AND SUBTRACTION NUMBER FAMILIES	1–47
ADDITION FACTS	1–29
SUBTRACTION FACTS	7–48
MULTIPLICATION FACTS	6–48
DIVISION FACTS	
MENTAL ARITHMETIC	46–48
MORE/LESS	20–32
NUMBER RELATIONSHIPS	38–47
PLACE VALUE	1–47
COLUMN ADDITION	1–42
COLUMN SUBTRACTION	7–42
COLUMN MULTIPLICATION	
DIVISION WITH REMAINDERS	
ESTIMATION	22–48
CALCULATOR SKILLS	
EQUATION CONCEPTS	
PROBLEM SOLVING	18–48
ANALYZING DATA: TABLES	14–48
FRACTIONS	
COORDINATE SYSTEM	39–42
GRAPHS	
AREA	9–30
VOLUME	
TIME	14–48
STATISTICS: RANGE	
MONEY	9–48

projects, students graphically represent information before they attempt to calculate an answer. The detailed instructions lead both teachers and students to develop positive feelings about problem solving.

In addition, instruction covers place value, geometry, estimation, and calculator use. Concepts and computational skills are also taught for regrouping, multiplication, division, and fractions. The Scope and Sequence Chart shows where each track or major topic begins and where it ends.

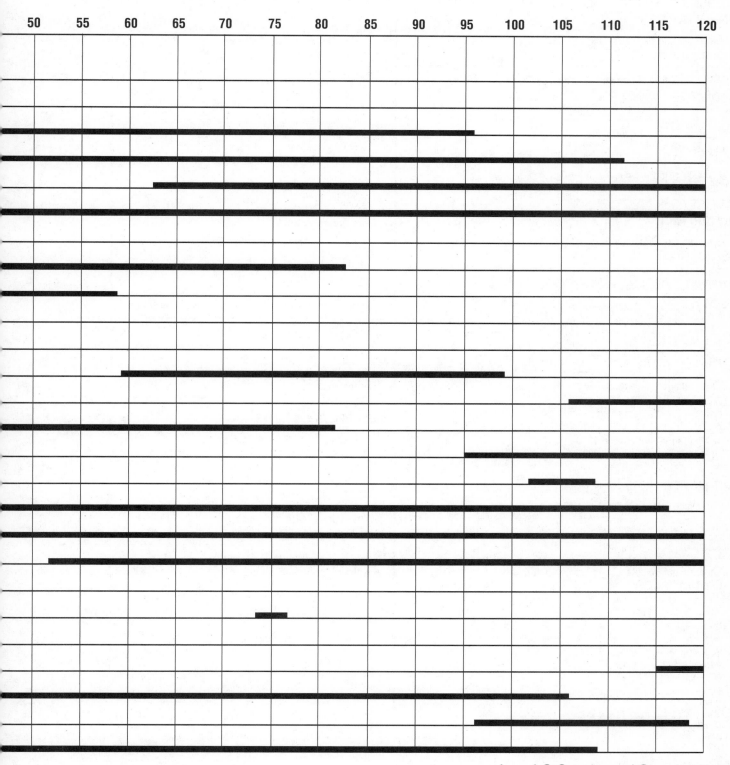

Level C Contents

Skills	Taught in these Lessons	Date Lessons Completed
ADDITION AND SUBTRACTION NUMBER FAMILIES		
Completes number families and writes the related facts	1–12	
Solves column-addition and column-subtraction problems using number families with a missing small number	5–46	
Writes two addition facts for each number family	10–12	
Writes column problems for number families with 1-, 2- and 3-digit numerals	47, 48	
ADDITION FACTS		
Reviews facts with addends of 1, 2, 3, 9, and 10	1–21	
Writes answers to "doubles" problems	8–10	
Works on addition facts based on number families with a small number of 6	9–27	
Works on addition facts based on number families with a small number of 4	14–24	
Works on addition facts based on number families with a small number of 5	19–23	
Works with the two addition statements for the number family with small numbers of 7 and 8	29	
SUBTRACTION FACTS		
Works facts that subtract 9 or 10	6–21	
Works facts that have an answer of 9 or 10	9–15	
Works facts that subtract 4 (through 8 − 4)	22–39	
Works facts that subtract 5 (through 10 − 5)	28–37	
Works remaining facts that subtract 4 or have 4 as the answer	41–51	
Works facts that subtract 6 (through 12 − 6)	52–59	

Skills	Taught in these Lessons	Date Lessons Completed
Works facts with an answer of 5 or 6	61, 62	
Practices in a pair with subtraction facts	27–96	
Writes subtraction facts for "doubles" problems	71–76	
Works facts that subtract 3	73–75	
Works facts that subtract 3 or have 3 as the answer	76, 77	
Works remaining facts that subtract 5	79–81	
Writes answers to subtraction problems, some of which subtract 5 or have an answer of 5	82, 83	
Writes the related subtraction fact for a known fact (for example: for 12 − 5 = 7, student writes the answer for 12 − 7 = □)	82	
Works remaining facts that subtract 6	85–87	
Works facts that subtract 6 or have 6 as the answer	64–89	
Works facts that subtract 7 or have 7 as the answer	91–96	
MULTIPLICATION FACTS		
Counts by 10 to 100 and by 5 to 50	4, 7	
Translates multiplication problems into count-by operations (for example: for 5 × 3, student "counts by 5, 3 times")	4	
Writes answers to multiplication problems using number lines	5	
Writes answers to multiplication problems without referring to a number line	6–8	
Counts by 2 to 20	8	
Writes answers to multiplication problems with a factor of 1	9–14	
Counts by 9 to 90	5–62	

Level C Contents

Skills	Taught in these Lessons	Date Lessons Completed
Writes two multiplication facts for number families	32–43	
Works on multiplication facts with a factor of 1 or 10	34–50	
Works on multiplication facts with a factor of 2	41–50	
Counts by 4 to 40	42–48	
Works on multiplication facts with a factor of 4	49–76	
Works on multiplication facts with a factor of 5	55–98	
Practices in a pair with multiplication facts	48–112	
Works on multiplication facts with a factor of 9	26–84	
Counts by 3 based on number patterns	93–105	
Writes the numbers for counting by 3 to 30	97–100	
Works on multiplication facts with a factor of 3	101–112	
Writes answers to multiplication facts with a factor of zero	105, 106	
Works addition, subtraction and multiplication problems that have a zero or a 1	109, 110	
DIVISION FACTS		
Writes the missing small number in families and writes or says the multiplication fact for some of those families	63–76	
Writes the missing small number in families, then applies the commutative property	77–81	
Writes the missing small number in families, then writes the related division fact	82–89	
Writes the missing small number in familes with a factor of 4	90–93	

Skills	Taught in these Lessons	Date Lessons Completed
Writes the missing small number in families with a small number of 9	94–96	
Writes answers to division facts based on multiplication and division number families	97–101	
Writes answers to division facts with a divisor of 5	102, 103	
Completes division facts, some of which have an answer of 5	104, 105	
Writes answers to division facts with a divisor of 3	106–117	
Writes answers to division facts, some of which have an answer of 3	108–119	
Practices in a pair with division facts	119, 120	
MENTAL ARITHMETIC		
Responds to mental addition problems that have 2-digit and 1-digit numbers	46–95	
Responds to mental addition problems that require renaming	102–120	
MORE/LESS		
Completes a greater-than or less-than sign between two numerals	21–25	
Makes greater-than and less-than statements from inequalities that have numbers and letters	26, 27	
Identifies numbers that are greater than or less than a given value	28–34	
NUMBER RELATIONSHIPS		
Writes addition problems for multiplication statements	37–40	
Writes addition problems to confirm the commutative property for multiplication	44	
Checks answers to subtraction facts by adding	45	
Identifies reasonable number families and writes column problems for them	49–51	

Level C Contents

Skills	Taught in these Lessons	Date Lessons Completed
Figures out multiple number families that have the same big number	50	
Uses an alternative strategy for figuring out the answers for subtraction facts	81–83	
PLACE VALUE		
Writes numerals from dictation	1, 2	
Answers place-value questions about the number of digits and how many hundreds, tens, or ones	1, 2	
Writes numerals in expanded notation, called place-value addition (for example: 37 is $\begin{smallmatrix}30\\+\,7\end{smallmatrix}$)	5, 6	
Reads 4-digit numerals	35	
Reads, then writes 4-digit numerals from dictation	36, 37	
Writes 4-digit numerals from descriptions	38, 39	
Reads 10- and 100-thousands numerals	42–46	
Writes numerals for 2-digit tens numbers	46–48	
Writes numerals for 2-digit hundreds numbers (for example: 14 hundreds)	49, 50	
Writes numerals for 2-digit tens numbers (23 tens) and 2-digit hundreds numbers (23 hundreds)	51–59	
COLUMN ADDITION		
Writes answers to column-addition problems that do not require renaming	1, 2	
Writes answers to column-addition problems that require renaming to the tens column	3, 4	
Writes answers to column-addition problems that require renaming to the hundreds column	5	
Writes answers to column-addition problems that require renaming to the tens and hundreds columns	6, 7	
Writes answers to column-addition problems that require renaming 2 tens (e.g., 7 + 7 + 9)	42	

Skills	Taught in these Lessons	Date Lessons Completed
COLUMN SUBTRACTION		
Writes answers to column-subtraction problems that do not require regrouping	4, 5	
Rewrites 2-digit numerals for regrouping	7, 8	
Writes answers to column-subtraction problems that have zero as the first digit in the answer	7	
Writes answers to subtraction problems, all or some of which require regrouping	9–14	
Identifies the last two digits of 3-digit numerals	14, 15	
Writes answers to regrouping problems with hundreds numbers	15–17	
Rewrites 3-digit numerals for regrouping	18–21	
Writes answers to regrouping problems that require rewriting the hundreds digit	20–23	
Writes answers to regrouping problems (ones or tens)	24–31	
Identifies subtraction problems that cannot be worked	33–35	
Rewrites the hundreds digit and the tens digit for regrouping twice	37, 38	
Writes answers to problems that require regrouping twice	38–40	
Writes answers to subtraction problems, some of which require regrouping twice	41–43	
Writes answers to regrouping problems with thousands numbers	44	

Level C Contents

Level C Contents

Skills	Taught in these Lessons	Date Lessons Completed
Sets up number families for comparison problems that ask for the difference	49, 50	
Solves comparison problems that ask for the difference	51–101	
Sets up number families for comparison problems that give the difference between the two things being compared	52, 53	
Solves comparison problems, some of which ask about a difference (how much more) and some of which ask about one of the values (how much)	53–71	
Puts values forward along the arrow or backward along the number-family arrow	54–56	
Solves action problems by first writing the values in a number family	57–72	
Solves word problems that require adding and subtracting fractions	90–116	
Solves word problems involving coins	92, 93	
Solves classification word problems such as, "There were 60 cars in all. 14 were red cars. The rest were blue cars. How many blue cars were there?"	93–97	
Sets up multiplication/division number families for sentences from word problems	94–96	
Solves multiplication and division word problems such as, "Each box holds 7 cans. You have 35 cans. How many boxes do you have?"	97–100	
Solves a variety of addition and subtraction problems	98, 99	
Solves multiplication/division word problems, some of which require writing a column multiplication problem	104, 105	
Solves multiplication/division word problems with variation in sentence order	108–114	
Solves comparison problems with complex syntax	113–116	

Skills	Taught in these Lessons	Date Lessons Completed
ANALYZING DATA: TABLES		
Writes the totals for the columns and rows in a table	15–19	
Answers questions based on a table	17–19	
Uses number families to fill in missing numbers in a table	44–59	
Writes and works problems based on vertical number families	56, 57	
Uses number-family analysis to fill in missing numbers in rows of one table and columns of a copy of that table	60–63	
Uses number-family analysis to fill in rows, then columns of a single table	65–68	
Uses number-family analysis to fill in missing numbers in tables and interprets the data to answer questions	69, 70	
Copies a table, figures out the missing numbers, and interprets the data to answer questions	72–75	
Fills in facts for a table, figures out the missing numbers, and interprets the data to solve the problem	76–83	
Solves a comparison problem using data from a table; inserts the answers in the table and then figures out the missing numbers	85–90	
Solves word and comparison problems using data from a table, fills in the missing numbers in the table, and interprets the data to answer questions	91–106	
Uses data from a table to solve comparison word problems	101–103	
Uses data from a table to solve problems involving time	111–114	
Solves problems based on tables that involve multiplication	112, 113	

Level C Contents

Skills	Taught in these Lessons	Date Lessons Completed
Solves multi-step problems based on a table	114–116	
Inserts data in a table involving time and then answers questions based on the table	115–117	
Solves for unit cost for items in a table	119, 120	
FRACTIONS		
Writes denominators that correspond to the whole-number portions of number lines	53, 54	
Writes the fraction for each inch marker on portions of number lines	55–60	
Writes the fraction for each inch marker and for some intermediate points on a number line	61–63	
Writes the fraction for each unit marker on a vertical number line	63–71	
Writes fractions from dictation	64	
Writes a fraction for the shaded portion of a number line	65–67	
Writes the bottom number of a fraction and then shades the number line to represent the fraction	65–99	
Writes a fraction for shaded regions of a geometric figure	68–70	
Indicates whether a fraction is more than 1 unit, less than 1 unit, or equal to 1 unit	73–83	
Reads numerical fractions	75–79	
Completes fractions that are equal to 1; then completes the greater-than/less-than sign between a fraction and 1	77–79	
Adds and subtracts fractions written with a single denominator (for example: $\frac{6 + 3}{2}$)	80–82	
Adds and subtracts only those fractions that have like denominators	83–89	

Skills	Taught in these Lessons	Date Lessons Completed
Completes the greater-than/less-than or equal sign between a fraction and 1	84, 85	
Relates multiplication/division number families to fractions	90–94	
Relates multiplication/division number families to fractions on a number line	94–102	
Relates fractions to multiplication/division number families	99–103	
Reduces fractions to whole numbers	103–107	
Relates fractions to division	106, 108	
Writes fractions as division problems	109–116	
Writes division problems as fractions	112–117	
Writes numerical fractions from descriptions	116–120	
COORDINATE SYSTEM		
Finds points on a coordinate system for X and Y values	38–40	
Writes the X and Y values for points shown on a coordinate system	41, 42	
GRAPHS		
Interprets graphs to answer questions	74–76	
AREA		
Figures out the area of rectangles	9–15	
Completes a rectangle, then figures out the area	15, 16	
Figures out the area of rectangles and writes the units in the answer	16–30	
Draws a rectangle, measures the sides, figures out the area	17, 18	
Draws a rectangle on a coordinate system and figures out the area	19–23	

Level C Contents

Skills	Taught in these Lessons	Date Lessons Completed
Applies the commutative property by writing two multiplication problems to represent the area of rectangles	25–32	
Solves area word problems by drawing a rectangle	35, 36	
VOLUME		
Multiplies three factors	115, 116	
Calculates the volume of various boxes	117–120	
TIME		
Writes the time for clocks to the nearest 5 minutes	13–37	
Writes the number of minutes for a partial clock	69–71	
Writes both the hour and exact minutes for clocks	79, 80	
Adds and subtracts times such as $\begin{array}{r} 5:15 \\ -12 \\ \hline \end{array}$	110, 111	
STATISTICS: RANGE		
Solves problems that require finding the longest distance and the shortest distance between two towns on a map	102–105	
Solves problems that require finding the range in values for a certain number of coins	111–118	

Skills	Taught in these Lessons	Date Lessons Completed
MONEY		
Reads and writes money amounts	9	
Works simple problems involving dollars and cents	10, 17	
Writes the number of cents for rows of like coins (nickels or dimes)	20, 21	
Identifies relevant information and then determines the total amount a person spends or the amount that is left after the purchase	24, 40	
Writes the number of cents for rows containing two types of coins	29, 30	
Rounds dollars and cents values to the nearest whole dollar	66, 67	
Rounds dollar amounts to estimate how much a person spends	68, 69	
Writes multiplication number families to represent groups of coins	86–88	
Writes multiplication number families for groups of coins, some of which show all the coins and some of which give the value for the group	89–91	
Counts out amounts such as $2.34 using dollar bills and coins	107–109	

For Level C Placement Test, see page 183.

Level C, Lesson 68 (Presentation Book)

Objectives

- Write the missing small number in multiplication/division number families and write the multiplication facts for some of those families. (Exercise 1)

- **Write fractions for shaded regions of geometric figures.** (Exercise 2)
  Note: In earlier activities, students wrote fractions for shaded portions of a number line. In this activity, they write fractions for different representations.

- **Round dollar amounts to estimate how much a person would spend.** (Exercise 3)

- Write answers to multiplication problems with a factor of 9. (Exercise 4)

- Use number-family analysis to fill in missing numbers in rows and columns in a single table. (Exercise 5)

- Solve action and comparison word problems. (Exercise 6)

- Practice in pairs with subtraction facts. (Exercise 7)

EXERCISE 1 NUMBER FAMILIES
Missing Factor

a. Open your workbook to lesson 68 and find part 1.
- These are multiplication number families with the second small number missing.
b. Your turn: Write the missing number in each family. Next to each family in the last column, write the multiplication fact that begins with the first small number. Raise your hand when you're finished. (Observe students and give feedback.)
c. Check your work.
- Family A: 1 times some number equals 8. What's the missing number? (Signal.) *8.*
- Family B: 3 times some number equals 30. What's the missing number? (Signal.) *10.*
- Family C: 5 times some number equals 50. What's the missing number? (Signal.) *10.*
- Family D: 2 times some number equals 10. What's the missing number? (Signal.) *5.*
- Family E: 2 times some number equals 12. What's the missing number? (Signal.) *6.*
- Family F: 2 times some number equals 14. What's the missing number? (Signal.) *7.*
- Family G: 2 times some number equals 8. What's the missing number? (Signal.) *4.*
- Family H: 2 times some number equals 4. What's the missing number? (Signal.) *2.*
- Family I: 7 times some number equals 70. What's the missing number? (Signal.) *10.*
- Family J: 10 times some number equals 100. What's the missing number? (Signal.) *10.*
- Family K: 1 times some number equals 7. What's the missing number? (Signal.) *7.*
- Family L: 2 times some number equals 6. What's the missing number? (Signal.) *3.*

d. Get ready to say the multiplication facts for the families in the last column.
- Family G. (Signal.) *2 times 4 equals 8.*
- Family H. (Signal.) *2 times 2 equals 4.*
- Family I. (Signal.) *7 times 10 equals 70.*
- Family J. (Signal.) *10 times 10 equals 100.*
- Family K. (Signal.) *1 times 7 equals 7.*
- Family L. (Signal.) *2 times 3 equals 6.*

EXERCISE 2 WRITING FRACTIONS
Based on Geometric Regions

a. (Draw on the board:)

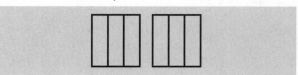

- You're going to write fractions for pictures that do not look like units on a number line, but they work the same way.
b. (Touch the first box.)
  Here's one unit. It's divided into parts.
- (Touch the second box.)
  Here's another unit divided into the same number of parts.
c. Let's write the bottom number of the fraction for these units. Look at each unit and figure out how many parts each unit is divided into.
- Everybody, how many parts? (Signal.) *3.*
- Yes, the first unit has 3 parts. The second unit has 3 parts. So **each** unit is divided into 3 parts. The bottom number of the fraction is 3.
- (Write $\overline{3}$:)

$$\overline{3}$$

d. I'll shade some of the parts.
(Shade 4 parts:)

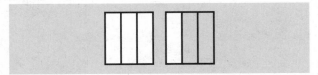

e. Now we can complete the fraction. We just count the shaded parts from the beginning.
- Everybody, how many shaded parts? (Signal.) *4.* That's the top number.
- (Complete the fraction:)

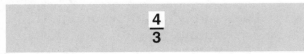

$$\frac{4}{3}$$

- Here's the fraction for the shaded parts.

Workbook Practice

a. Find part 2 in your workbook.
- Touch picture A.
Listen: First figure out how many parts each unit is divided into. Count the parts for each unit. Everybody, how many parts in each unit? (Signal.) *3.*
- That's the bottom number of the fraction. Now look at the number of shaded parts in A. Everybody, how many shaded parts? (Signal.) *2.*
- That's the top number of the fraction. Your turn: Write the fraction for A. √
- (Write on the board:)

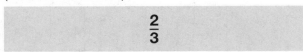

$$\frac{2}{3}$$

- Here's the fraction for A.
b. Touch B.
Look at the number of parts each unit is divided into and write the bottom number of the fraction. Then stop.
- Everybody, what's the bottom number? (Signal.) *3.*
- Each unit is divided into 3 parts, so the bottom number is 3. Now write the top number. √
- Everybody, what's the top number? (Signal.) *5.* There are 5 shaded parts, so the top number is 5.
c. Touch C.
First write the bottom number. Then write the top number. Raise your hand when you're finished. (Observe students and give feedback.)
- Everybody, what's the bottom number of the fraction for C? (Signal.) *4.*
- What's the top number? (Signal.) *6.*
d. Raise your hand if you got all the fractions right.

EXERCISE 3 ESTIMATION
Adding Rounded Dollar Amounts

a. Open your textbook to lesson 68 and find part 1.
- I'll read what it says in the box. Follow along: The price tags show the cost of different items. You're going to figure out **about** how much you'd spend if you bought more than one item. You do that by adding the dollar amounts that are close to the values on the price tags. If the price tag says 4 dollars and 10 cents, you add 4 dollars. If the price tag says 6 dollars and 95 cents you add 7 dollars.
b. Problem A: You want to buy items 1, 2 and 3. **About** how much will you spend? Here's how you figure out **about** how much you'll spend. You write the easy dollar amounts that are close to each value. Then you add them. You want to buy items 1, 2 and 3.
- Touch price tag 1.
2 dollars and 92 cents is close to a dollar amount. What amount? (Signal.) *3 dollars.*
- Touch price tag 2.
3 dollars and 10 cents is close to a dollar amount. What amount? (Signal.) *3 dollars.*
- Touch price tag 3.
95 cents is close to a dollar amount. What amount? (Signal.) *1 dollar.*
- (Write on the board:)

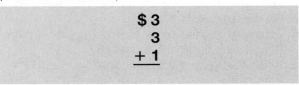

$$\begin{array}{r} \$\,3 \\ 3 \\ +\,1 \end{array}$$

- Here's the problem.
You add 3 plus 3 plus 1.
c. Your turn: Use lined paper for problem A. Write the 3, 3 and 1. Remember to write a dollar sign next to the first number you'll add. Then add the three numbers and write the total with a dollar sign. You don't need decimal points. Raise your hand when you're finished. (Observe students and give feedback.)
- Check your work. Everybody, what does 3 dollars plus 3 dollars plus 1 dollar equal? (Signal.) *7 dollars.*
- That's about how much you'd have to spend to buy items 1, 2 and 3.
d. Touch problem B: You want to buy items 2, 3 and 4. About how much would you spend? Figure out the close dollar amounts for items 2, 3 and 4. Add the close dollar amounts. Write a dollar sign in the answer. Raise your hand when you're finished. (Observe students and give feedback.)

- 8 dollars and 11 cents is the price for item 4. That's close to what dollar amount? (Signal.) *8 dollars.*
- So you added 3 dollars plus 1 dollar plus 8 dollars. Everybody, what's the answer? (Signal.) *12 dollars.*
- Yes, you'd spend about 12 dollars for those three items.
e. Your turn: Work the rest of the problems in part 1. Raise your hand when you're finished.
   (Observe students and give feedback.)
f. Check your work.
- Problem C: You want to buy items 1, 4 and 5. 5 dollars and 88 cents is the price for item 5. That's close to what dollar amount? (Signal.) *6 dollars.*
- Read the addition problem and the answer. (Signal.) *3 dollars plus 8 dollars plus 6 dollars equals 17 dollars.*
- Yes, you'd spend about 17 dollars for those items.
- Problem D: You want to buy items 3, 4 and 5. Read the addition problem and the answer. (Signal.) *1 dollar plus 8 dollars plus 6 dollars equals 15 dollars.*
- Yes, you'd spend about 15 dollars for those items.
g. Raise your hand if you got all the addition problems right.

EXERCISE 4 MULTIPLYING WITH 9

a. Find part 2 in your textbook.
   I'll read what it says in the box. Follow along:
   These are multiplication problems that have 9 as a small number. So the first digit of the answer is 1 less than the first small number.
- Remember, figure out the first digit. Then write the whole answer.
b. Problem A: **7** times 9. What's the first digit of the answer? (Signal.) *6.*
- Problem B: **4** times 9. What's the first digit of the answer? (Signal.) *3.*
- Problem C: **8** times 9. What's the first digit of the answer? (Signal.) *7.*
- Problem D: **6** times 9. What's the first digit of the answer? (Signal.) *5.*
   (Repeat step b until firm.)
c. Your turn: Write the letters A through H on your paper. Then write the answer to each problem. Don't copy the problem. Just write the answer. Remember, the answers are numbers you say when you count by 9.
   (Observe students and give feedback.)
d. Check your work.
- Problem A: 7 times 9. What's the answer? *63.*
- Problem B: 4 times 9. What's the answer? *36.*
- Problem C: 8 times 9. What's the answer? *72.*

- Problem D: 6 times 9. What's the answer? *54.*
- Problem E: 9 times 9. What's the answer? *81.*
- Problem F: 5 times 9. What's the answer? *45.*
- Problem G: 3 times 9. What's the answer? *27.*
- Problem H: 2 times 9. What's the answer? *18.*

EXERCISE 5 TABLES
Using Number Families

a. Find part 3 in your textbook.
   You're going to figure out all the missing numbers in this table. Remember, first work all the rows you can work. Then work all the columns that have two numbers.
b. Your turn: Copy the table. Figure out the missing numbers and put them in the table. Raise your hand when you're finished.
   (Observe students and give feedback.)
c. (Write on the board:)

	66	227
96		129
257		

- Here's the table you started with. You worked the rows first.
- Read the problem and the answer for the top row. (Signal.) *227 minus 66 equals 161.*
- (Write **161:**)

161	66	227
96		129
257		

- Read the problem and the answer for the middle row. (Signal.) *129 minus 96 equals 33.*
- (Write **33:**)

161	66	227
96	33	129
257		

d. Then you worked the columns.
- The first column has all its numbers.
- Read the problem and the answer for the second column. (Signal.) *66 plus 33 equals 99.*
- (Write **99:**)

161	66	227
96	33	129
257	99	

- Read the problem and the answer for the last column. (Signal.) *227 plus 129 equals 356.*
- (Write **356:**)

161	66	227
96	33	129
257	99	356

e. Raise your hand if you figured out all the missing numbers in the table.

EXERCISE 6 PROBLEM SOLVING
Action and Comparison Word Problems

a. Find part 4 in your textbook.
   Some of these problems tell what happened first and what happened next. Other problems tell who had more or who had less.
b. Your turn: Read each problem. Write the number family for each problem. Raise your hand when you have a number family for each problem. (Observe students and give feedback.)
c. (Write on the board:)

a. $\underline{118 \quad \square} \longrightarrow 142$

b. $\underline{718 \quad \overset{83}{\cancel{8}}} \longrightarrow P$

c. $\underline{147 \quad J} \overset{228}{\longrightarrow} \cancel{8}$

d. $\underline{\square \quad 406} \longrightarrow 906$

- Here's what you should have for each problem.
- Raise your hand if you got all of them right.

d. Now write the addition problem or subtraction problem for each number family and figure out the answer. Remember the unit name. Raise your hand when you're finished.
   (Observe students and give feedback.)
e. Check your work.
- Problem A: A woman weighed 142 pounds. She lost some weight. The woman ended up weighing 118 pounds. How many pounds did the woman lose? Say the number problem and the answer. (Signal.) *142 minus 118 equals 24.*
- What's the unit name? (Signal.) *Pounds.*
- How many pounds did the woman lose? (Signal.) *24 pounds.*
- Problem B: A plane traveled 718 miles farther than a car traveled. The car traveled 83 miles. How far did the plane travel? Say the number problem and the answer. (Signal.)
  718 plus 83 equals 801.
- What's the unit name? (Signal.) *Miles.*
- How far did the plane travel? (Signal.) *801 miles.*
- Problem C: Joe had 147 dollars less than Sue. Sue had 228 dollars. How much money did Joe have? Say the number problem and the answer. (Signal.) *228 minus 147 equals 81.*
- What's the unit name? (Signal.) *Dollars.*
- How much money did Joe have? (Signal.) *81 dollars.*
- Problem D: Sue had some money. She earned 406 dollars more. She ended up with 906 dollars. How much money did Sue have to begin with? Say the number problem and the answer. (Signal.) *906 minus 406 equals 500.*
- What's the unit name? (Signal.) *Dollars.*
- How much money did Sue have to begin with? (Signal.) *500 dollars.*
f. Raise your hand if you got all of them right.

EXERCISE 7 FACT REVIEW
Paired Practice

Note: **If time permits, conduct the paired practice now. If time is not available now, schedule it at another time or have students write answers to the problems on lined paper.**

a. Find part 5 in your textbook.
   We're going to work in pairs.
   Sit with your partners. Today B team goes first. B team, raise your hand.

b. A team, raise your hand. A team, find the section for lesson 68, part 5 in the back of your textbook. Those are the answers. Remember, for each mistake you'll tell the correct answer and you'll make a tally mark.

- B team, when I say go, say the letter of the item, then say the fact. Then go to the next item. You've got 1 minute. Remember, raise your hand if there's a question. No arguing.
- B members, are you ready? (Signal.) *Yes.*
- A members, are you ready? (Signal.) *Yes.*
- Get ready. Go.
  (Observe students and give feedback.)

c. (At the end of 1 minute:) Stop.
   A team, tell your partners the number of errors they made.

- B team, raise your hand if you did all the problems and made no more than 1 mistake. Those are stars.
  (Count students and write number on board: B team _____.)

d. Now, B members, find the section for lesson 68, part 5 in the back of your textbook. Those are the answers.

- A members, go to lesson 68, part 5 in your textbook. A members, get ready to say the letter and the fact for each item.

e. A members, are you ready? (Signal.) *Yes.*
- B members, are you ready? (Signal.) *Yes.*
- You've got 1 minute. Go.

f. (At the end of 1 minute:) Stop.

g. B team, tell your partners the number of errors they made.

- A team, raise your hand if you did all the problems and made no more than 1 mistake. Those are stars.
  (Count students and write number on board: A team _____.)

h. The _____ team won, but all students who made no more than 1 mistake are stars.

i. Raise your hand if you made no errors at all. Those students are superstars. Congratulations for remembering the facts.

EXERCISE 8 INDEPENDENT WORK

a. Do the independent work for lesson 68. First do the work in the textbook. Then do the exercise in the workbook.

b. (Assign **Connecting Math Concepts** *Independent Worksheet* 44 and *Math Facts Worksheet* 88 as classwork or homework. Before beginning the next lesson, check the students' independent work.)

Level C, Lesson 68 (Workbook)

Part 1 shows multiplication/division number families. A number family has two "small numbers" (factors) and a "big number" (product). Each family relates four multiplication/division facts. For example, family g relates the facts: $2 \times 4 = 8$; $4 \times 2 = 8$; $8 \div 2 = 4$; $8 \div 4 = 2$. Working with number families lightens the load for fact memorization.

In **part 1,** students fill in the missing factor for each family, then write a multiplication fact for families g through l ($2 \times 4 = 8$; $2 \times 2 = 4$, and so forth). Multiplication/division facts number families were introduced in lesson 32. Related families with factors of 1 or 10 were practiced in lessons 34–50. Related facts with a factor of 2 were practiced in lessons 41–50.

Writing division facts from number families will be introduced in lesson 86.

Starting in lesson 97, students solve multiplication/division story problems using a number-family strategy.

For example: Each box holds 7 cans. You have 35 cans. How many boxes do you have? Based on the statement: **Each box holds 7 cans,** students construct a number family with letters:

$$7 \overline{\smash{\big)}\ \overset{\textstyle B}{}}\ C$$

Then substitute:

$$7 \overline{\smash{\big)}\ \overset{\textstyle B\ 35}{}}\ ¢$$

The missing value is one of the factors, implying a division problem.

Each item in **part 2** requires students to write a fraction (2/3, 5/3, 6/4) for a geometric representation. Students have worked with fractional divisions on number lines since lesson 55. (See workbook, **part 3**).

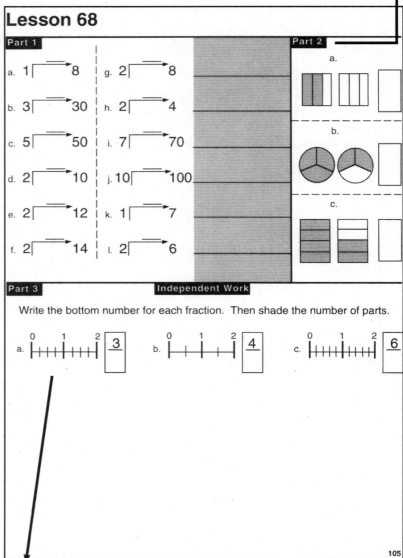

Students work **part 3** of the workbook independently, after the structured parts of the lesson have been completed.

Problems of the form shown in **part 3** appeared in lessons 65–67. Previously, students have written fractions for whole-number portions shown on a number line (lessons 55–60). Intermediate points were represented in lessons 61–63. Students have also worked with portions of vertical number lines (introduced in lesson 63).

Level C, Lesson 68 (Textbook)

This exercise introduces the concept of money estimation by working with values rounded to the nearest dollar. (In the two preceding lessons, students simply rounded values to the nearest dollar.)

Students estimate for each of the items in **part 1.** Addition problems involving exact money amounts were introduced in lesson 24.

In lesson 40, subtraction problems were introduced. For these problems, students figured out the amount remaining after a purchase. Problems of the type shown in **part 1** will also be practiced in lesson 69 and tested in test 7.

In lesson 72, students will work two sets of problems, one set requiring estimates, the other requiring exact amounts.

In lesson 76, students will be required to discriminate between the two problem types within one problem set. This discrimination is then required for independent-work exercises throughout the remainder of the program.

In **part 2,** students work times 9 problems. Before working multiplication problems with 9 as a factor, students learned to skip-count by 9. This skill was introduced in lessons 5–8. It was reviewed in three lessons prior to lesson 68. Students also worked with number families with a "small number" of 9, for example, $7 \overline{\smash{\big)}\ \overset{9}{63}}$. This type of number-family exercise occurred in lessons 62–65.

Students were first introduced to data tables in lesson 15.

Problems of the type shown in **part 3** have appeared since lesson 65.

Students add or subtract in any row or column that has two values in order to complete the table.

In the next lesson (69), students will work with tables that have labels for columns and rows. For example:

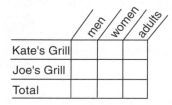

Starting in lesson 76, students will put numbers in a table based on written information (e.g., 94 women ate at Joe's Grill), complete the table and answer questions (e.g., How many more men ate at Kate's Grill than at Joe's Grill?)

Work on analyzing data in tables continues through the end of the program.

Part 4 requires students to discriminate between two types of addition/subtraction story problems: comparison and action. Comparison problems were introduced in lesson 43, action problems in lesson 57. For both types, students use a number-family strategy. For example, item c is a comparison problem. Joe has less than Sue, so Sue represents the "big number" in the family. Joe is a "small number," and the difference (147) is the other small number.

Part 2

- These are multiplication problems that have 9 as a small number.
- So the first digit of the answer is 1 less than the first small number.

Write the answer to each problem.

a. 7 x 9 = ■   b. 4 x 9 = ■   c. 8 x 9 = ■   d. 6 x 9 = ■

e. 9 x 9 = ■   f. 5 x 9 = ■   g. 3 x 9 = ■   h. 2 x 9 = ■

Part 3   Copy the table. Figure out the missing numbers.

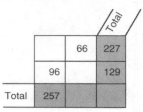

Part 4   Write the number family for each problem.
Then write the number problem and figure out the answer.

a. A woman weighed 142 pounds. She lost some weight. The woman ended up weighing 118 pounds. How many pounds did the woman lose?

b. A plane traveled 718 miles farther than a car traveled. The car traveled 83 miles. How far did the plane travel?

c. Joe had 147 dollars less than Sue. She had 228 dollars. How much money did Joe have?

d. Sue had some money. She earned 406 dollars more. She ended up with 906 dollars. How much money did Sue have to begin with?

Lesson 68 **167**

Students write:
$\overset{147 \quad J}{\underrightarrow{}}$ S . A number for Sue is given, so students substitute:

$\overset{147 \quad J}{\underrightarrow{}}$ S 228. Now students see they must subtract to find the missing number for Joe.

A third type of addition/subtraction story problem—classification—is introduced in lesson 93.

Students practice the subtraction facts in **part 5** with a partner. One student has an answer key. The other student reads each problem in **part 5** and says the answer. Paired practice for subtraction facts occurs in 12 lessons (27–96), on the average once every six lessons.

Facts appear in a paired-practice exercise after they have been introduced and practiced in a number-family context. For example, several problems in **part 5** subtract 4 or have an answer of 4. The number families that correspond to items a and b are: $\xrightarrow{4 \quad 9} 13$, $\xrightarrow{4 \quad 6} 10$.

Part 5 **Paired Practice**

a. $13 - 9 = \blacksquare$ b. $10 - 4 = \blacksquare$ c. $12 - 6 = \blacksquare$ d. $11 - 7 = \blacksquare$

e. $8 - 4 = \blacksquare$ f. $9 - 3 = \blacksquare$ g. $11 - 6 = \blacksquare$ h. $10 - 5 = \blacksquare$

i. $12 - 8 = \blacksquare$ j. $10 - 6 = \blacksquare$ k. $9 - 6 = \blacksquare$ l. $9 - 5 = \blacksquare$

m. $9 - 4 = \blacksquare$ n. $10 - 6 = \blacksquare$ o. $8 - 6 = \blacksquare$ p. $14 - 10 = \blacksquare$

Independent Work

Parts 6 through 8 of the textbook (and **part 3** of the workbook) are the independent work for lesson 68. These parts review problem types that were practiced in a structured form in earlier lessons.

Part 6 **Copy the problems and figure out the answers.**

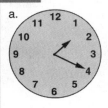

a. 700 b. 10 c. 50 d. 2 e. 400
   x 2   x 9   x 6   x 8   x 4

Column multiplication with 2-digit numbers on top was introduced in lesson 59. Students worked problems with 3-digit numbers on top (e.g., items a, e) starting at lesson 61.

Mixed sets such as the one in **part 6** were introduced in lesson 63 and appeared for four lessons through lesson 67.

Lesson 68 is the first lesson in which students work a mixed set independently.

Part 7 **Write the time for each clock.**

a.   b.   c.

Telling time to the nearest five minutes was taught in Level B. In Level C, it is reviewed in lessons 13–15, and in lesson 37. Telling time is also practiced independently in 14 lessons prior to lesson 68.

Part 8 **Write all the numbers for counting by 4 to 40.**

4 ■ ■ ■ ■ ■ ■ ■ ■ 40

Do the independent work for lesson 68 in your workbook.

168 *Lesson 68*

Counting by 4 to 40 was introduced in lesson 42. Students practiced for three consecutive lessons, and again in lesson 48. Starting in lesson 49, counting by 4 was applied to multiplication problems with a factor of 4.

Level C

Sample Track: Problem Solving

Level C of *Connecting Math Concepts* provides an intensive treatment of problem solving. The major topics include the following:

- word problems
- classification
- comparison
- table problems about time, weight, and money
- graphs
- area of rectangles
- "range" problems that require eliminating possibilities

Problem-solving activities are presented in almost every lesson, carefully integrated with the computational skill tracks. For example, as soon as students can add and subtract fractions, they are introduced to word problems requiring those operations.

Work with problem solving always starts with simple problems, but it progresses to problems that are very sophisticated for third-grade students.

WORD PROBLEMS

The strategy for solving most word problems in Level C is to use a number family to determine the calculation required. The main types of addition/subtraction word problems in Level C include comparison, classification, and temporal sequence. Multiplication/division problems involve the words *each* or *every*.

COMPARISON

Work on comparison problems begins in Lesson 25 of Level C. Students learn how to relate letters and other symbols to sentences about *more* or *less*.

EXERCISE 7 WORD PROBLEMS
Comparison

a. (Write on the board:)

You're going to work word problems that are just like number problems. But they have letters.

- Listen to this sentence: A is more than B. That sentence tells about two numbers—A and B in a number family. You don't know whether A is 20 or 17 or 56. But you do know that A is **more than** B. So if A is 20, B is less than 20.

- Listen again: A is more than B. Which is more, A or B? (Signal.) *A.*
- Here's a rule about A and B. One of these numbers is the big number in the number family. Which is the big number? (Signal.) *A.*
- So I write A for the big number and B for a small number.
- (Write to show:)

- That family shows us that the number for A is more than the number for B.
- (Erase letters:)

b. New problem. Listen: C is less than D. One of these numbers is the big number.
- Listen again and think about which letter is the big number and which is a small number. C is less than D.
- Is C a small number or the big number? (Signal.) *A small number.*
  Yes, C is less. So it must be the small number. D is the big number.
- (Write to show:)

- That family shows us that the number for C is less than the number for D.
- (Erase letters:)

c. One more. R is smaller than T.
  Listen again and think about the number family. R is smaller than T.
- Is R a small number or the big number? (Signal.) *A small number.*
  Yes, R is smaller. It's a small number, so T must be the big number.
- (Write:)

- Here's what you write for R is smaller than T.

a. J is less than M.

b. R is more than P.

c. P is more than J.

d. W is less than J.

WORKBOOK PRACTICE

a. Your turn: Open your workbook to Lesson 25 and find part 1.
- Sentence A: J is less than M.
- Write the letters in the number family. Write the small number close to the big number. Raise your hand when you're finished. √
b. Check your work.
- (Write on the board:)

- Everybody, what's the big number for sentence A? (Signal.) *M.*
- And J is a small number.
c. Sentence B: R is more than P.
- Write the letters in the number family. √
d. Check your work.
- (Write on the board:)

- Everybody, what's the big number for sentence B? (Signal.) *R.*
What's the small number? (Signal.) *P.*
e. Work the rest of the problems in part 1. Raise your hand when you're finished.
(Observe students and give feedback.)
- (Write on the board:)

f. Check your work.
Here's what you should have for problems C and D. Raise your hand if you got both of them right.

Starting in Lesson 29 students work from statements containing a circled number and construct families that have three values. When the sentence is read without saying the circled number, it tells about the two values that are being compared. The circled letter is the first small number in the family.

Part 1   Make a number family for each problem.
First put the two values in the number family.
Then put the circled number in the family.

a. T   45

97

a. R is ⑫ larger than V.   b. F is ㊶ less than W.
c. F is ⑫ less than 31.   d. 70 is ⑫ less than P.
e. R is ㊶ more than 280.

EXERCISE 1 COMPARISON

a. Open your textbook to Lesson 29 and find part 1. I'll read the instructions: Make a number family for each problem. First put the two values in the number family. Then put the circled number in the family.
- Remember, read the problem without reading the circled number. That tells you where the letters go in the family. Then the circled number is always the first small number.
b. Problem A: R is 12 larger than V.
- Your turn: Use lined paper. Put the two letters in the number family. Then put the 12 in the family. Raise your hand when you're finished.
(Observe students and give feedback.)
c. (Write on the board:)

- Check your work. Here's what you should have. R is larger than V, so R is the big number. V is a small number. 12 is the other small number.
d. Problem B: F is 56 less than W. Your turn: First put the two letters in the number family. Then put the circled number in the family. Raise your hand when you're finished.
(Observe students and give feedback.)
e. (Write on the board:)

- Check your work. Here's what you should have. F is less than W, so F is a small number. W is the big number. 56 is the other small number.

f. Problem C works just like the problems you've worked, but it has two numbers and a letter.
• Listen: F is 12 less than 31.
Say the problem without the circled number. (Signal.) *F is less than 31.*
• Put those values in the family. Then put the circled number in the family. Raise your hand when you're finished.
(Observe students and give feedback.)
g. (Write on the board:)

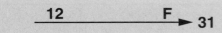

• Check your work. Here's what you should have for problem C. F is less than 31, so F is a small number. 31 is the big number. 12 is the first small number.
h. Problem D. 70 is 12 less than P. Say it without the circled number. (Signal.) *70 is less than P.*
• Problem E. R is 56 more than 280. Say it without the circled number. (Signal.) *R is more than 280.*
(Repeat step h until firm.)
i. Your turn: Make the families for D and E. Remember to first put in the values that are not circled. Then put in the circled number. Raise your hand when you're finished.
(Observe students and give feedback.)
j. (Write on the board:)

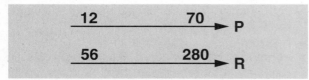

• Check your work. Here's what you should have for problems D and E.
• Raise your hand if you got both of them right.
k. You can write the addition problem or the subtraction problem for families that have two numbers and a letter. You can't work the number problems for families that have only one number.
l. Your turn: Circle each number family you can work. Remember, those have two numbers. Raise your hand when you're finished.
• Check your work. You should have circled families C, D, and E. Those are the problems you can work.
• Do it. Figure out the missing number in families C, D, and E. Write the column problem and the answer. Then cross out the letter in the family and write the missing number. Raise your hand when you're finished.
m. Check your work.
• Problem C. Read the problem and the answer. (Signal.) *31 minus 12 equals 19.*

• So what number is F? (Signal.) *19.*
• Problem D. Read the problem and the answer. (Signal.) *12 plus 70 equals 82.*
• So what number is P? (Signal.) *82.*
• Problem E. Read the problem and the answer. (Signal.) *56 plus 280 equals 336.*
• So what number is R? (Signal.) *336.*
• Raise your hand if you got the missing numbers for families C, D, and E correct.

Beginning in Lesson 38, students solve the prototype of a comparison word problem. The first sentence is a comparison of two letters. The next sentence gives a numerical value for one of the letters. Students make the number family for the first sentence; then, using information from the second sentence, they cross out one of the letters and write its value. The family then has two known numbers, so the missing number can be calculated:

Part 2   Make the number family.
Then write the addition problem or subtraction problem.
Then answer the question the problem asks about.

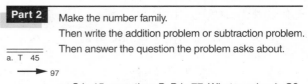

    a. S is 15 more than B. B is 77. What number is S?
    b. F is 66 less than T. F is 399. What number is T?
    c. J is 185 more than M. J is 276. What number is M?
    d. L is 207 less than R. R is 288. What number is L?

EXERCISE 2 COMPARISON
Substitution

a. Find part 2 in your textbook.
These are really hard problems because they have two letters. You're going to figure out the number for one of those letters.
b. Touch problem A.
Listen to the whole problem: S is 15 more than B. B is 77. What number is S?
• Listen to the first sentence again: S is 15 more than B.
• Your turn: Make the number family for that sentence. Raise your hand when you're finished.
(Observe students and give feedback.)
c. (Write on the board:)

• Here's what you should have for the first sentence. It shows that S is 15 more than B.
d. The next sentence in the problem says: B is 77. If B is 77, I can cross out B and write 77. Watch.

- (Write to show:)

- The last sentence in the problem says: What number is S? That's the number we don't know.
- Now we can work the problem and figure out what number S is.
- Your turn: Fix up your number family with the number for B. Then work the problem and figure out what number S is. Raise your hand when you're finished.
(Observe students and give feedback.)
e. Check your work.
- Everybody, what number is S? (Signal.) *92.*
- (Write to show:)

f. Problem B. Here's the first sentence. F is 66 less than T.
- Write the number family for that sentence. Raise your hand when you're finished.
(Observe students and give feedback.)
- (Write on the board:)

- Here's the number family.
- Now read the next sentence of the problem. It tells you a number for one of the letters. Cross out the letter it tells about and write the number for that letter. Raise your hand when you're finished.
(Observe students and give feedback.)
- (Write to show:)

- Here's what you should have.
- The last sentence asks: What number is T? Figure out what number T is. Raise your hand when you're finished.
(Observe students and give feedback.)
- Check your work.
- Everybody, what number is T? (Signal.) *465.*
g. Problem C. Here's the first sentence. J is 185 more than M.
- Write the number family for that sentence. Raise your hand when you're finished.
(Observe students and give feedback.)

- (Write on the board:)

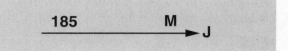

- Here's the number family.
- Now read the next sentence of the problem. It tells you a number for one of the letters. Cross out the letter it tells about and write the number for that letter. Raise your hand when you're finished.
(Observe students and give feedback.)
- (Write to show:)

- Here's what you should have.
- The last sentence asks: What number is M? Figure out what number M is. Raise your hand when you're finished.
(Observe students and give feedback.)
- Check your work.
- Everybody, what number is M? (Signal.) *91.*
h. Your turn: Work the last problem in part 2. Raise your hand when you're finished.
(Observe students and give feedback.)
- (Write on the board:)

- Check your work. L is 81.
- Raise your hand if you got everything right.

In Lesson 40, students make families for statements containing names. The names work just like the letters. These sentences tell about relationships other than more/less and bigger/smaller: "John is *shorter* than Mary." "Paul is *older* than Barbara." "Ann has *fewer* coins than Tracy."

The rule used to solve these problems is: The name that has the bigger number is the big number in the family. For example, "Paul is older than Barbara." Who has the bigger number of years, Paul or Barbara? Paul is the bigger number.

In Lesson 43, students work complete problems. They write two letters for the names in the problem and make a number family for the first sentence.

Then students read the next sentence and replace one of the letters with a number. Finally, they calculate the missing number:

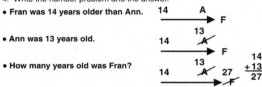

- Here's how to work the problems:
1. Read the first sentence and make the number family with two letters and a number.
2. Then read the next sentence. That sentence gives a number for one of the letters. Cross out the letter and write the number.
3. Figure out the number for the other letter.
4. Write the number problem and the answer.

- Fran was 14 years older than Ann.
- Ann was 13 years old.
- How many years old was Fran?

Write the complete number family. Then write the addition problem or subtraction problem and the answer.

a. Jane was (17) years younger than Bill. Bill was 56 years old. How many years old was Jane?

b. Sam was 52 years younger than Ginger. Sam was 31 years old. How many years old was Ginger?

c. Fran was 11 years older than Ron. Fran was 31 years old. How many years old was Ron?

d. Jan was 14 years younger than Al. Jan was 34 years old. How many years old was Al?

EXERCISE 5 PROBLEM SOLVING
Comparing Age

a. Find part 4 in your textbook.
These are rules for working word problems with names. You work them just like the problems with two letters.

b. I'll read what it says in the box. Follow along: Here's how to work these problems. Read the first sentence and make the number family with two letters and a number.

- Then read the next sentence. That sentence gives a number for one of the letters. Cross out the letter and write the number.
- Figure out the number for the other letter.
- Write the number problem and the answer.

c. Here's a problem. Its says: Fran was 14 years older than Ann. Ann was 13 years old. How many years old was Fran?

- Your textbook shows the steps for working the problem.
- The first sentence of the problem says: Fran was 14 years older than Ann. You can see the number family for that sentence. What letters stands for Fran? (Signal.) *F.*
- What letter stands for Ann? (Signal.) *A.*
- Who is older, Fran or Ann? (Signal.) *Fran.*

- That's why Fran is the big number. Fran is 14 more. So 14 is the other small number.
- The next sentence of the problem says Ann was 13 years old. Ann is **A** in the number family. So you cross out A and write her number, 13.
- The question asks: How many years old was Fran? You do the addition problem and figure out that Fran was 27 years old. All done.

d. Touch problem A.
I'll read it: Jane was 17 years younger than Bill. Bill was 56 years old. How many years old was Jane?

- Go back to the first sentence. 17 is circled. So the rest of the sentence says: Jane was years younger than Bill.

e. Your turn: Make the number family. Put J and B in the family. Put in the circled number. Then stop. Raise your hand when you're finished.
(Observe students and give feedback.)

- (Write on the board:)

- Here's what you should have. √

f. The next sentence says: Bill was 56 years old. That gives a number for B. So cross out B and write the number. √

- (Cross out **B** and write **56.**)

a.   17   J   56 / B̶

- Here's what you should have.

g. The next sentence asks the question: How old was Jane?

- Which letter does that question ask about? (Signal.) *J.*
- Do you add or subtract to figure out Jane's number? (Signal.) *Subtract.*
- You'll do that later.

h. Touch problem B.
We'll set up the number family for that problem. I'll read the first sentence: Sam was 52 years younger than Ginger.

- Your turn: Write the number family for that sentence. Remember to use the first letter of each name. Raise your hand when you're finished.
(Observe students and give feedback.)
- (Write on the board:)

b.   52   S   G

- Here's what you should have for the first sentence.

i. Here's the next sentence: Sam was 31 years old. Replace one of the letters in the family with its number. Raise your hand when you're finished.
• (Cross out **S** and write **31**:)

b. 52 —————→ 31 ̶S̶ → G

• Here's what you should have for the second sentence.
j. Here's the last sentence: How many years old was Ginger? That sentences tells you which letter you'll figure out. Which letter? (Signal.) *G.*
• Do you add or subtract to figure out the number for G? (Signal.) *Add.*
k. I'll read the rest of the problems. Follow along:
• Problem C. Fran was 11 years older than Ron. Fran was 31 years old. How many years old was Ron?
• Problem D. Jan was 14 years younger than Al. Jan was 34 years old. How many years old was Al?
l. Your turn: For the rest of the problems in part 4, write the number family with two letters. Then replace one of the letters with a number. Raise your hand when you're finished.
(Observe students and give feedback.)
m. (Write on the board:)

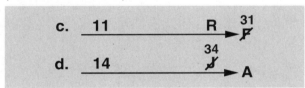

c. 11 —————→ R → 31 ̶F̶

d. 14 —————→ 34 ̶J̶ → A

• Check your work.
Here's what you should have for each problem.
n. Your turn again: Write the addition problem or subtraction problem for each family and figure out how old the people in the problems were. Raise your hand when you're finished.
(Observe students and give feedback.)

o. Check your work.
Read each number problem and the answer.
• Problem A. (Signal.) *56 minus 17 equals 39.*
• Problem B. (Signal.) *52 plus 31 equals 83.*
• Problem C. (Signal.) *31 minus 11 equals 20.*
• Problem D. (Signal.) *14 plus 34 equals 48.*
p. Raise your hand if you figured out how old all the people were.

TABLE PROBLEMS

Level C presents three types of table problems: addition/subtraction, multiplication/division, and graphs. The solution strategy is to treat rows and columns of a table as number families and figure out the missing numbers. Sometimes information is given about where numbers go in a table. Information may be in the form of comparisons, as in Lesson 91:

Part 2	Cars	Trucks	Total vehicles
Elm Street			100
Maple Street			35
Total for both streets		75	

Fact 1: There were 25 cars on Elm Street.
Fact 2: There were 10 more cars on Maple Street than there were on Elm Street.

a. How many cars were on Maple Street? _____
b. How many trucks were there in all? _____
c. Were there more cars or trucks? _____
d. Were there more trucks on Elm Street or on Maple Street? _____

EXERCISE 3 TABLES
Completing and Interpreting Data

a. Find part 2 in your workbook.
This table shows the number of cars and trucks on Elm Street and on Maple Street. The table has a lot of numbers missing. But the facts next to the table give you information about numbers that go in the table.

b. Fact 1: There were 25 cars on Elm Street.
Fact 2: There were 10 more cars on Maple Street than there were on Elm Street. You'll make a number family for that fact.
- Listen: Put the number for Fact 1 in the table. Then make a number family for Fact 2, figure out how many cars were on Maple street, and put that number in the table. Then figure out the rest of the missing numbers in the table. Raise your hand when you're finished.

(Observe students and give feedback.)

c. (Write on the board:)

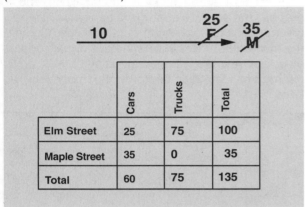

- Check your work. Here's the number family for Fact 2 and all the numbers you should have in your table.
- Raise your hand if you got everything right.

d. Check your work. I'll read each question. You tell me the answer.
- Question A: How many cars were on Maple Street? (Signal.) *35.*
- Question B: How many trucks were there in all? (Signal.) *75.*
- Question C: Were there more cars or trucks? (Signal.) *Trucks.*
- Question D: Were there more trucks on Elm Street or on Maple Street? (Signal.) *Elm Street.*

Also in this level are table problems about time. These involve the time a person left, the duration of the trip, and the time the person arrived at the destination. The number-family strategy applies to these tables as well.

GRAPHS

Problems with bar graphs and pictographs are introduced in Lesson 74. Information represented in graphs is related to information in tables.

- You can use numbers to show the values in a column. Or you can use pictures to show the same values.

- Here are numbers that show how many pounds of berries were picked on Monday and on Tuesday.

Day	Pounds of Berries Picked on 2 days
Monday	4
Tuesday	2
Total for both days	6

- Here is a picture graph that shows the same values. Each berry represents one pound of berries.

Day	Pounds of Berries Picked on 2 Days
Monday	🍓🍓🍓
Tuesday	🍓🍓
Total for both days	🍓🍓🍓🍓🍓🍓

- Here's another kind of graph. It's called a bar graph. The bars on the graph start in the same place.

Day	Pounds of Berries Picked on 2 Days
	1 2 3 4 5 6
Monday	████████
Tuesday	███
Total for both days	████████████

- The bar for Monday is 4 units long. The end of that bar is at the line for 4 units. Each unit represents one pound of berries.

- The bar for Tuesday is 2 units long.

- The bar for the total is 6 units long.

A. Inches of Rainfall in 2 Cities

City	Inches
River City	🜁🜁🜁🜁🜁🜁🜁🜁🜁
Mountain City	🜁🜁🜁🜁🜁
Total for both cities	🜁🜁🜁🜁🜁🜁🜁 🜁🜁🜁🜁🜁🜁🜁

1. Did more inches of rain fall in River City or in Mountain City?

2. How many inches of rain fell in River City?

3. How many inches fell in both cities?

B. Trucks Travelling on 2 Streets

Street	Number of Trucks
	1 2 3 4 5 6 7 8 9 10 11 12 13 14 15
River Street	████████████
Mountain Street	████████████████
Total for both streets	██████████████████████████████

1. Did more trucks go down River Street or Mountain Street?

2. How many total trucks went down both streets?

3. How many trucks went down Mountain Street?

C. Trees Planted in 2 Parks

Parks	Trees
River Park	🌳🌳🌳
Mountain Park	🌳🌳🌳🌳
Total for both Parks	🌳🌳🌳🌳🌳🌳🌳

1. How many trees were planted in both parks?

2. In which park were more trees planted?

3. How many trees were planted in River Park?

EXERCISE 5 GRAPHS
Interpreting Bar and Picture Graphs

a. Find part 2 in your textbook.
   I'll read what it says in the box. Follow along: You can use numbers to show the values in a column. Or you can use pictures to show the same values.

- Here are numbers that show how many pounds of berries were picked on Monday and on Tuesday.
- Everybody, how many pounds of berries were picked on Monday? (Signal.) *4.*
- How many pounds on Tuesday? (Signal.) *2.*
- How many pounds were picked on both days? (Signal.) *6.*
- Here is a picture graph that shows the same values. Each berry represents one pound of berries.
- Touch the berries for Monday. How many berries? (Signal.) *4.*
- So how many pounds? (Signal.) *4.*
- Touch the berries for Tuesday. How many berries? (Signal.) *2.*
- So how many pounds? (Signal.) *2.*
- The total for both days is 6 berries. That's 6 pounds.
- Here's another kind of graph. It's called a bar graph. The bars on the graph start in the same place. The bar for Monday is 4 units long. Each unit represents one pound of berries. The end of that bar is at the line for 4 units. The bar for Tuesday is 2 units long. The bar for the total is 6 units long.

b. Find the graphs on the next page.
   These are picture graphs and bar graphs that show things you've worked with in tables. The title of each graphs tells what it shows.
- The title for A is: Inches of Rainfall in 2 Cities.
- The title for B is: Trucks Traveling on 2 Streets.
- The title for C is: Trees Planted in 2 Parks.

c. You're going to use lined paper and answer the questions.
- Picture A shows the rainfall for 2 cities: River City and Mountain City. Each drop represents 1 inch of rain.
- I'll read the questions: Did more inches of rain fall in River City or in Mountain City? How many inches of rain fell in River City? How many inches fell in both cities?
- Write answers to those questions. Raise your hand when your finished. (Observe students and give feedback.)

d. Check your work.
- Question 1: Did more inches of rain fall in River City or in Mountain City? (Signal.) *River City.*
- Question 2: How many inches of rain fell in River City? (Signal.) *10.*

- Question 3: How many inches fell in both cities? (Signal.) *16.*

e. B is a graph that shows the number of trucks that went down River Street and Mountain Street. The length of each bar show how many trucks went down that street.
- I'll read the questions: Did more trucks go down River Street or Mountain Street? How many total trucks went down both streets? How many trucks went down Mountain Street?
- Write the answers. Raise your hand when you're finished. (Observe students and give feedback.)

f. Check your work.
- Question 1: Did more trucks go down River Street or Mountain Street? (Signal.) *Mountain Street.*
- Question 2: How many total trucks went down both streets? (Signal.) *15.*
- Question 3: How many trucks went down Mountain Street? (Signal.) *9.*

g. Graph C shows pictures of the trees planted in River Park and Mountain Park. But those are bundles of trees. Each bundle has ten little trees in it. So remember to count 10 for each bundle of trees.
- I'll read the questions: How many trees were planted in both parks? In which park were more trees planted? How many trees were planted in River Park?
- Write the answers. Raise your hand when you're finished. (Observe students and give feedback.)

h. Check your work.
- Question 1: How many trees were planted in both parks? (Signal.) *70.*
- Question 2: In which park were more trees planted? (Signal.) *Mountain Park.*
- Question 3: How many trees were planted in River Park? (Signal.) *30.*

NUMBER FAMILIES AND EQUATIONS

Level C includes problem-solving activities that require the application of knowledge about number families and equations. For example, several problems require students to use number-family logic to determine whether the number families presented are reasonable. Students are also required to make inferences about equations in which signs or numbers are missing.

Scope and Sequence for
Connecting Math Concepts, Level D

Connecting Math Concepts, Level D extends students' mathematical power and understanding. Building on the strong foundation of Levels A–C, Level D extends whole-number skills to include multiplication and

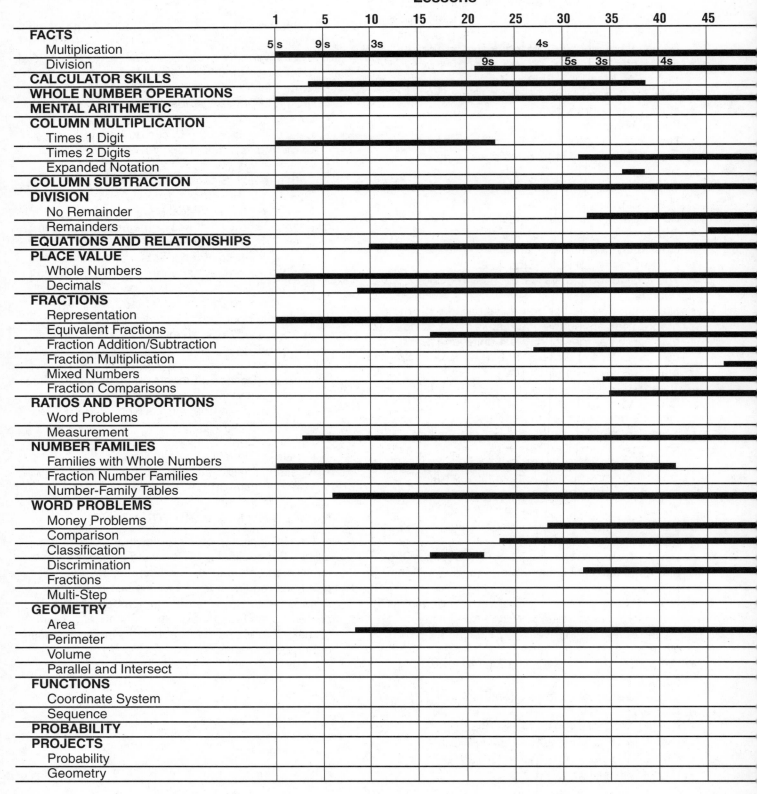

Lessons

	1	5	10	15	20	25	30	35	40	45
FACTS										
Multiplication	5s	9s	3s				4s			
Division					9s		5s 3s		4s	
CALCULATOR SKILLS										
WHOLE NUMBER OPERATIONS										
MENTAL ARITHMETIC										
COLUMN MULTIPLICATION										
Times 1 Digit										
Times 2 Digits										
Expanded Notation										
COLUMN SUBTRACTION										
DIVISION										
No Remainder										
Remainders										
EQUATIONS AND RELATIONSHIPS										
PLACE VALUE										
Whole Numbers										
Decimals										
FRACTIONS										
Representation										
Equivalent Fractions										
Fraction Addition/Subtraction										
Fraction Multiplication										
Mixed Numbers										
Fraction Comparisons										
RATIOS AND PROPORTIONS										
Word Problems										
Measurement										
NUMBER FAMILIES										
Families with Whole Numbers										
Fraction Number Families										
Number-Family Tables										
WORD PROBLEMS										
Money Problems										
Comparison										
Classification										
Discrimination										
Fractions										
Multi-Step										
GEOMETRY										
Area										
Perimeter										
Volume										
Parallel and Intersect										
FUNCTIONS										
Coordinate System										
Sequence										
PROBABILITY										
PROJECTS										
Probability										
Geometry										

division algorithms. Concepts and operations with fractions and mixed numbers are carefully presented and applied, and decimals are introduced. Extensive problem-solving activities emphasize strategies with tables, number families, and ratios. Other topics include perimeter, area, functions, and probability. The Scope and Sequence Chart shows where each track or major topic begins and where it ends.

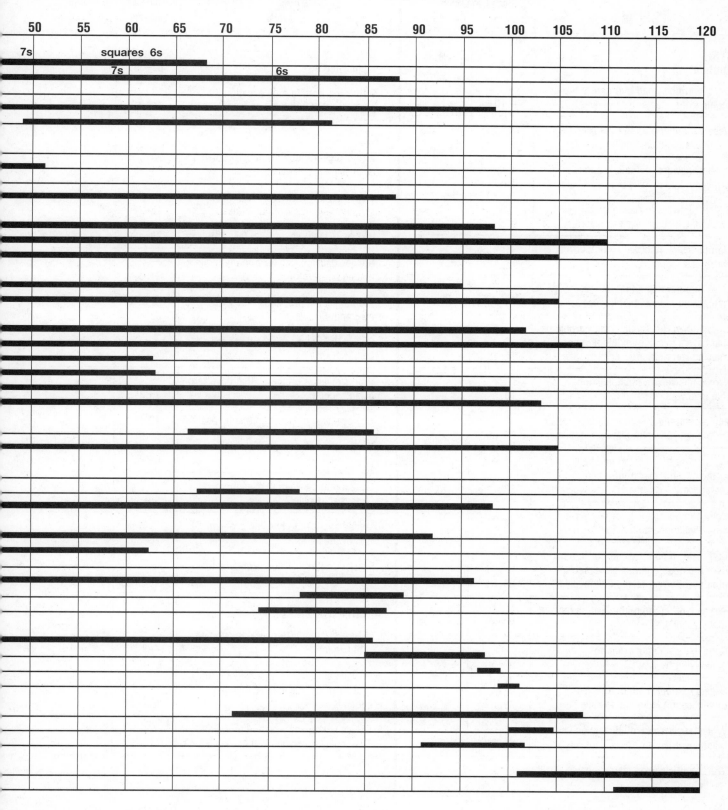

Level D Contents

Skills	Taught in these Lessons	Date Lessons Completed
FACTS		
Multiplication		
Uses a number map to organize the multiplication facts that involve 5.	1–10	
Uses a number map to organize the multiplication facts that involve 9.	5–9	
Writes answers to multiplication problems that involve 9.	8–13	
Writes answers to multiplication facts, some of which have a 1 or a zero.	9	
Completes numbers in a number map for threes.	11, 12	
Uses number maps to organize multiplication facts that involve 3.	13–19	
Says and works multiplication problems that have a missing middle number or a missing last number.	14–18	
Writes answers to multiplication facts that involve 3.	18	
Figures out the missing middle number for multiplication problems that have 9.	23–25	
Figures out the missing middle number or the missing first number for multiplication problems that involve 9.	26	
Uses number maps to organize the multiplication facts that involve 4.	28	
Completes a number map for fours and uses the map to write answers to multiplication problems that involve 4.	29–31	
Writes answers to multiplication facts that involve 4.	32–56	
Completes a number map for multiplying by 7.	48–50	
Uses a number map to organize multiplication facts that involve 7.	49–52	
Writes answers to multiplication facts that involve 7.	55–57	
Works with "square" facts for multiplying.	58, 59	

Skills	Taught in these Lessons	Date Lessons Completed
Completes a number map for multiplying by 6.	63–66	
Writes answers to multiplication problems that involve 6.	65–68	
Division		
Writes algebra multiplication problems as division problems.	21–73	
Writes division problems from statements that tell about "times."	25–27	
Writes answers to division fact problems.	28–48	
Applies division rule for 5 to numerals that end in zero or 5.	31, 32	
Works a set of problems that divide by 5 and 9.	33	
Solves division problems that divide by 3.	34–38	
Works division problems that have zero as a dividend.	35	
Solves division problems that involve 4.	42–56	
Writes and solves dictated division-fact problems.	55, 56	
Uses a number map to organize division facts that involve 7.	58–60	
Writes answers to division problems that divide by 6.	76–86	
Works a set of division problems that divide by 7, 6, 4 and 3.	87	
CALCULATOR SKILLS		
Uses a calculator to check answers to problems.	4–8	
Uses a calculator to check addition problems that have more than two addends.	6	
Solves column subtraction problems. Then checks answers with a calculator.	12–17	

Level D Contents

Skills	Taught in these Lessons	Date Lessons Completed
Writes and solves column subtraction problems from row problems. Then checks answers with a calculator.	13, 14	
Solves column multiplication problems. Then checks answers with a calculator.	38	
WHOLE NUMBER OPERATIONS		
Writes and solves column addition problems.	1	
Works a set of problems that calls for different operations: addition, subtraction, multiplication.	5	
Solves multiplication problems that involve a money amount and a whole number.	89–91	
Estimates the sums of addition problems involving hundreds or thousands numbers.	97, 98	
MENTAL ARITHMETIC		
Writes answers to orally presented addition problems that have a 2-digit and a 1-digit addend.	49	
Works mental addition problems that require renaming.	55–57	
Solves mental addition problems of the form: 56 plus what number equals 60?	62–64	
Solves problems of the form: Some number plus 1 equals 600.	78–82	
COLUMN MULTIPLICATION **Times 1 Digit**		
Solves column multiplication problems that multiply 2-digit numerals by 1-digit numerals.	1–5	
Solves column multiplication problems that multiply 3-digit numerals by 1-digit numerals.	6–8	
Solves column multiplication problems that have a zero.	15, 16	
Solves multiplication problems that have a 5-digit value times a 1-digit value.	23	

Skills	Taught in these Lessons	Date Lessons Completed
Times 2 Digits		
Solves row problems that multiply a 1-digit value by a tens number.	32, 33	
Solves column problems that multiply a 1-digit value by a tens number.	34, 35	
Solves column problems that multiply a 2-digit value by a tens value.	36	
Solves column multiplication problems. Then checks answers with a calculator.	38	
Solves 2-digit-times-2-digit multiplication problems that require no carrying or carrying for the tens only.	41–44	
Solves 2-digit-times-2-digit multiplication problems that require carrying for the ones and carrying for the tens.	45–48	
Solves column problems that multiply a 3-digit value by a 2-digit value.	49–51	
Expanded Notation		
Writes statements of "expanded notation" for 2-digit values.	37–39	
COLUMN SUBTRACTION		
Writes and solves subtraction problems that require one renaming.	1–4	
Writes and solves column subtraction problems that require more than one renaming.	8–11	
Solves column subtraction problems. Then checks answers with a calculator.	12–17	
Writes and solves column subtraction problems from row problems. Then checks answers with a calculator.	13, 14	
Solves subtraction problems that involve items with price tags.	32–46	
Solves subtraction problems that involve zero(s) and require renaming.	82–87	

Level D Contents

Skills	Taught in these Lessons	Date Lessons Completed
DIVISION **No Remainder**		
Solves division problems that have a 3-digit dividend and a 3-digit answer.	33–35	
Solves division problems that have a 3-digit dividend and a 2-digit answer.	36, 37	
Works division problems by first underlining the first digit or the first two digits of the dividend to determine where to write the first digit of the answer.	38–42	
Solves division problems, some of which have 4-digit dividends.	44	
Solves division problems that have zero(s) in the dividend.	45–53	
Identifies answers to division problems that do not have a sufficient number of digits in the answer.	45	
Works division problems that have 3-digit, 4-digit or 5-digit dividends.	50–56	
Corrects wrong answers to division problems.	57, 58	
Completes division equations of the form: 24 ÷ 6.	97, 98	
Remainders		
Completes equations that involve both multiplication and addition.	45–63	
Works division problems in which the first digit of the answer has a remainder.	68–76	
Works division problems in which the last digit of the answer has a remainder.	106–110	
EQUATIONS AND RELATIONSHIPS		
Completes equations that have a missing sign or a missing number.	10–15	
Says and works multiplication problems that have a missing middle number or a missing last number.	14–18	
Completes equations for fractions that equal whole numbers.	16–22	

Skills	Taught in these Lessons	Date Lessons Completed
Writes and completes equations with a missing number from verbal descriptions.	19–26	
Writes multiplication and addition problems from descriptions that tell about what number.	20–26	
Writes algebra multiplication problems as division problems.	21–73	
Completes inequalities for whole numbers.	21, 22	
Copies fractions that equal whole numbers and writes the equations for these fractions.	23–34	
Writes addition or multiplication equations using three compatible numbers.	27–32	
Completes equations to show the fraction that equals a whole number.	35–60	
Rewrites equations of the form: number = number, sign, number.	37, 38	
Writes the missing operation sign in equations.	46	
Writes division problems and answers for fractions that equal whole numbers.	56–88	
Completes a table that has division problems and equations involving fractions and whole numbers.	63–65	
Completes a table that has rows for multiplication problems and corresponding division problems.	66–69	
Completes equations that tell about the multiplication and addition needed to reach a number.	68, 69	
Completes a table that shows corresponding multiplication facts, division facts and fraction-to-whole-number equations.	78	
Writes equations that show the fraction that equals a hundredth decimal number.	89–91	
Writes mixed numbers equal to decimals or decimals equal to mixed numbers.	91–93	

Level D Contents

Skills	Taught in these Lessons	Date Lessons Completed
Writes fractions for division problems that use the sign: ÷.	95	
Completes an equation that shows a division problem, the equivalent fraction and the equivalent whole number.	96	
Completes a table with columns for decimal values, mixed numbers and fractions.	96, 97	
Rewrites fractions as equivalent decimal values.	98–105	
PLACE VALUE **Whole Numbers**		
Reads 4-digit thousands numerals.	1, 2	
Writes 4-digit thousands numerals.	3–5	
Reads thousands numerals that have more than 4 digits.	7–9	
Reads thousands numerals that have 4, 5 or 6 digits.	12	
Writes 5-digit thousands numerals.	13	
Writes 4- and 5-digit thousands numerals.	14	
Writes 4-, 5- and 6-digit thousands numerals.	15–17	
Writes 4-, 5- and 6-digit thousands numerals from verbal descriptions.	16–21	
Rounds thousands numerals to the nearest thousand.	91	
Rounds thousands numerals to the nearest hundred.	92–95	
Decimals		
Writes dollar-and-cents amounts from written descriptions.	8–13	
Aligns and computes dollar-and-cents amounts.	24–26	
Writes hundredths decimal values from descriptions.	87, 88	
Writes equations that show the fraction that equals a hundredth decimal number.	89–91	

Skills	Taught in these Lessons	Date Lessons Completed
Orders whole numbers, some of which have a decimal point and zeros after the decimal.	92–95	
Completes a table with columns for decimal values, mixed numbers and fractions.	96, 97	
Rewrites fractions as equivalent decimal values.	98–105	
FRACTIONS **Representation**		
Writes fractions for pictures of fractions.	1–34	
Writes fractions from pictures, then indicates which fractions are more than 1.	3–5	
Writes fractions for separate groups and for number lines.	6–9	
Writes fractions from descriptions that tell about the numbers or that tell about the picture.	7–34	
Writes equations for pictures of fractions that show whole numbers.	11–15	
Writes fractions for whole numbers on a number line.	22–24	
Writes fractions for zero on number lines.	25	
Writes fractions that have a denominator of 1 for a "whole number" number line.	27	
Indicates verbally whether fractions equal 1 or do not equal 1.	33, 34	
Completes fractions for whole numbers on number lines that show no fractional divisions.	37–41	
Indicates where fractions that do not equal whole numbers go on a number line.	46–48	
Identifies numerators and denominators of fractions.	81	
Compares fractions with like numerators.	99–101	

Level D Contents

Skills	Taught in these Lessons	Date Lessons Completed	Skills	Taught in these Lessons	Date Lessons Completed
Equivalent Fractions			Works a set of fraction problems that requires addition, subtraction and multiplication.	51–63	
Completes equations for fractions that equal whole numbers.	16–22		Solves multiplication problems that have a fraction and a whole number.	53–55	
Completes equations to show various fractions that equal whole numbers.	29–43		Solves multiplication problems that have a whole number and a fraction that equals 1.	54, 55	
Identifies pictures that show equivalent fractions and write the equation.	42–44		Completes equations by figuring out the fraction the first value is multiplied by.	59–61	
Completes equations that show a whole number and an equivalent fraction.	55, 56		Determines parts of two different fractions to complete equations that multiply fractions.	62	
Solves problems that multiply by a fraction, then writes a simple equation for problems that multiply by 1.	56–58		**Mixed Numbers**		
Completes equations that involve multiplying fractions, then writes simple equations for problems that multiply by 1.	59–64		Indicates where mixed numbers go on a number line for fifths.	34	
			Indicates the appropriate number line for mixed numbers.	35–37	
Writes equations for pairs of pictures of equivalent fractions, then identifies the fractions that equal 1.	65–73		Writes addition equations for mixed numbers.	38–70	
Completes equations involving equivalent fractions by indicating the fraction that equals 1 and completing the fraction after the equal sign.	66–75		Adds or subtracts to work problems that involve either a whole number and a fraction or two fractions.	42–47	
Uses division to figure out the missing fraction that equals 1.	73		Adds or subtracts to work problems that involve a whole number and a fraction.	43–47	
Writes $=$ or $\neq$ between pairs of fractions.	80–96		Writes equations that show mixed numbers for fractions on a number line.	49–54	
Solves equivalent-fraction problems to determine whether a decimal number or a fraction is larger.	106, 107		Writes fractions for mixed numbers with 2-digit whole numbers or denominators.	52	
Fraction Addition/Subtraction			Completes equations to show the mixed numbers that equal fractions.	57–59	
Identifies and works fraction addition and subtraction problems that can be worked without rewriting.	27–34		Writes equations that show the mixed numbers improper fractions equal.	61–65	
Works a set of fraction problems that require addition, subtraction and multiplication.	51–63		Writes the whole number or mixed number a fraction equals.	66, 67	
Fraction Multiplication			Follows instructions involving the word **denominator** to work mixed-number problems.	74	
Solves problems that multiply a fraction by a fraction.	46–49				

Level D Contents

Skills	Taught in these Lessons	Date Lessons Completed
Writes fractions for mixed numbers of the form: 4 + 36/100.	95	
Writes fractions that equal mixed numbers written without a plus sign.	100	
Fraction Comparison		
Indicates whether fractions are more, less or equal to 1 from verbal descriptions.	35–57	
Identifies whether a value is multiplied by more than 1 or less than 1.	71–73	
Compares fractions with unlike denominators to determine which is larger.	72	
Compares fractions with like or unlike denominators to determine which is larger.	74	
Identifies whether a fraction is multiplied by more than 1 or less than 1.	74–80	
Indicates whether the answer to a fraction-multiplication problem is more than or less than the starting fraction.	81, 82	
Identifies whether a value is multiplied by more than 1, less than 1 or 1.	83, 84	
Uses equivalent-fraction equations to compare fractions.	101–103	
RATIOS AND PROPORTIONS **Word Problems**		
Writes names and fractions for sentences that give ratio information.	64, 65	
Writes names and fractions for sentences that tell about **each** or **every**.	68, 69	
Works complete ratio word problems.	71–78	
Writes names and fractions for sentences that use the wording: The ratio of . . .	81	
Measurement		
Solves ratio problems involving length by using the table of measurement facts.	83, 84	

Skills	Taught in these Lessons	Date Lessons Completed
Solves ratio problems involving units of time by referring to the table of measurement facts.	85	
Solves ratio problems involving capacity by using the table of measurement facts.	86	
Works a mixed set of ratio problems involving units of time, weight and capacity.	87, 88	
Solves ratio problems involving metric units of length by using the table of measurement facts.	89	
Works ratio problems involving time.	94	
Works ratio problems that involve dollar amounts.	95–97	
Writes fractions for sentences that refer to **per**.	99	
Compares two or three ratios.	102–105	
NUMBER FAMILIES **Families with Whole Numbers**		
Constructs addition and subtraction problems from number families that have one missing number.	1–5	
Writes and solves addition and subtraction problems from vertical number families.	6, 7	
Solves number-family problems based on data.	39–42	
Fraction Number Families		
Completes number families that show two fractions.	66	
Completes number families that show a fraction and a whole number.	67–71	
Completes number families that show a fraction with a 2-digit or 3-digit denominator and the whole number 1.	76	
Writes fraction number-families for different diagrams of fractions.	77, 78	

Level D Contents

Skills	Taught in these Lessons	Date Lessons Completed
Number-Family Tables		
Computes the missing number in each row of a 3-by-3 table.	6, 7	
Computes the missing number in each column of a 3-by-3 table.	9	
Completes two number-family tables, one by working rows, the other by working columns.	11–14	
Figures out all the missing numbers in a table by first working all the columns that have two numbers, then working all the rows that have two numbers.	17–21	
Answers questions by referring to a completed number-family table.	18–23	
Uses number-family analysis to figure out all the missing numbers in a table.	22–25	
Answers comparison questions by referring to a completed number-family table.	24–26	
Writes missing numbers in a table, then answers questions.	27–29	
Completes a number-family table that gives only four numbers.	48	
Completes a table that involves times for when a person leaves, how long the trip takes and when the person arrives.	51, 52	
Uses facts to put needed numbers in a 3-by-3 table.	53–59	
Uses comparative information and number-family analysis to put a number in a 3-by-3 table.	61–65	
Uses facts including comparative information to put numbers in a 3-by-3 table.	66, 67	
Uses information displayed in a bar graph to generate numbers for a 3-by-3 table.	98, 99	

Skills	Taught in these Lessons	Date Lessons Completed
WORD PROBLEMS **Money Problems**		
Writes addition problems to determine the cost of specified items that are displayed with price tags.	29–31	
Solves multiplication word problems that tell about a dollar amount and the number of items purchased.	92	
Comparison		
Makes number families with two names to show comparison.	24	
Makes families with three names and a difference number from comparison sentences.	25–27	
Solves comparison word problems.	28–31	
Solves word problems that ask about the difference.	43, 44	
Solves word problems, some of which ask about the difference and some of which tell about the difference.	45, 46	
Solves price-tag problems that ask about the difference.	47, 48	
Solves price-tag problems, some of which ask about the difference and some of which tell about the difference.	52–60	
Uses numerical answers to price-tag problems to identify "mystery items."	53	
Uses price-tag information to work a set of comparison problems that ask about the name of objects or the difference number.	54–59	
Makes number families for price-tag comparison sentences.	61	
Works variations of comparison problems involving price tags.	62, 63	
Classification		
Solves word problems that require classification inferences.	16–22	

Level D Contents

Skills	Taught in these Lessons	Date Lessons Completed
Discrimination		
Makes number families for sentences, some of which compare and some of which classify.	33–35	
Solves number-family problems, some of which compare and some of which classify.	36, 37	
Works a mixed set of number-family word problems.	88, 89	
Works a mixed set of word problems involving dollar amounts.	93, 94	
Fractions		
Writes fraction number-families from word problems.	79	
Makes fraction number-families to solve word problems.	81–83	
Solves fraction number-family word problems that give numbers, not fractions.	84–86	
Works a mixed set of fraction number-family word problems.	87	
Solves fraction number-family word problems that ask questions about **numbers** and about **fractions.**	88, 89	
Multi-Step		
Works problems that involve given information about amounts **in,** amounts **out** and amounts **ended up** with.	74–78	
Works "stacking" problems that give more than one value for in or for out.	79–87	
GEOMETRY **Area**		
Computes the area of rectangles, first by repeated addition, then by multiplication.	9–12	
Computes the area of rectangles by multiplication.	13	
Computes the area of rectangles and writes abbreviations for the appropriate unit names in the answers.	14–18	

Skills	Taught in these Lessons	Date Lessons Completed
Draws diagrams from descriptions of rectangles and computes the area.	19–22	
Works area-of-rectangle problems that require multiplication or division.	79–84	
Perimeter		
Computes the perimeter of rectangles by addition.	85	
Computes both the perimeter and area of rectangles.	86, 87	
Computes perimeters of figures that are not rectangles.	88, 89	
Figures out the length of a side by using a number family.	90–92	
Works a set of problems that asks about the length of an unmarked side or about the perimeter.	93	
Works a mixed set of area word problems, some of which ask about the length of a side, some of which ask about the number of square units.	96, 97	
Volume		
Computes the volume of a box.	98, 99	
Parallel & Intersect		
Identifies pairs of lines that intersect and that are parallel.	99, 100	
FUNCTIONS		
Coordinate System		
Uses information about X and Y coordinates to identify points.	72–74	
Writes X and Y values for points on a coordinate grid.	75, 76	
Completes a function table that gives values for X and the function rule.	77–82	
Uses information about X and Y values to plot points and draws a line on a coordinate grid.	83, 84	
Completes a function table and graphs the function.	85–87	

Level D Contents

Skills	Taught in these Lessons	Date Lessons Completed
Writes two functions for specified X and Y values.	88–92	
Selects the appropriate function rule and completes a function table.	93–96	
Completes a function table and determines a function rule given a graph of the function.	97, 98	
Plots equivalent fractions on a coordinate system.	105	
Plots equivalent ratios on a coordinate system.	106	
Uses a graph of equivalent ratios on a coordinate grid to answer questions.	107, 108	
Sequence		
Writes a function to express the pattern in a sequence.	100–105	
PROBABILITY		
Ranks fractions for the probability of picking a winner.	91–93	
Translates fractions into statements of probability involving winners and losers.	93, 94	
Conducts an experiment that compares probability predictions with actual outcomes.	94	
Makes a fraction number-family based on a description of winners and losers in a set.	95–97	
Solves problems that ask about the probability of winners or expected trials.	98–102	
PROJECTS		
Project: Conducts an experiment to test a prediction of the number of trials needed to get 20 winners when flipping one coin.	101	
Project: Conducts an experiment to test a prediction of the number of needed trials to get 20 winners flipping two coins simultaneously.	102	

Skills	Taught in these Lessons	Date Lessons Completed
Project: Conducts an experiment to determine the number of cards that are winners.	103–105	
Project: Conducts an experiment to verify whether the probability of three coins being all heads is 1 out of 6 or 1 out of 8.	106	
Project: Determines the probability of 4 out of 4 coins being heads and 5 out of 5 coins being heads.	107	
Project: Determines the ratio of winners to total possibilities of a die; then conducts experiments to confirm the fraction 1-sixth.	108	
Project: Predicts the probability of two dice both showing 1 and conducts an experiment to verify or refute the prediction.	109	
Project: Conducts an experiment to determine the number of cards that are winners; then plots the ratios on a coordinate grid and answers questions.	110	
Project: Verifies that the area of a triangle is 1-half the area of a rectangle with the same base and height.	111	
Project: Verifies that the equation for the area of a triangle works for right triangles of different shapes.	112	
Project: Demonstrates that the equation for the area of a triangle works for triangles that do not have a 90-degree angle.	113	
Project: Figures the area and perimeter of a room; then computes the cost of carpeting the room and installing baseboard molding.	114	
Project: Figures out the "rules" for the relationship between perimeter and area of a square.	115	
Project: Demonstrates that the equation for the area of a triangle works for a range of triangles that have the same base and same height.	116	

Level D Contents

Skills	Taught in these Lessons	Date Lessons Completed	Skills	Taught in these Lessons	Date Lessons Completed
Project: Figures out the dimensions of a "mystery" rectangle by using clues that tell about the (a) relationship of its width and height; (b) range of its area; (c) relationship between its area and perimeter.	117		Project: Creates a function table for converting a cake recipe that serves 4 into a recipe that serves 12.	120	
Project: Conducts a sighting experiment to arrange cards of different heights so they appear to be the same height; then uses ratio equations to confirm the distances between cards and spotter.	118		Project: (This exercise is optional.) Conducts a survey; uses the results as a basis for projecting the results of a survey that involves a larger number of respondents; then combines data with those from other small-scale surveys on the same topic.	120	
Project: Graphs data from the experiment in lesson 118 to show the general function for the relationship between the height of an object and its distance from the spotter.	119				

For Level D Placement Test, see page 186.

Level D, Lesson 46 (Presentation Book)

Objectives

- Solve subtraction problems that involve items with price tags. (Exercise 1)
- **Solve problems that multiply a fraction by a fraction.** (Exercise 2)
- Solve word problems, some of which ask about the difference and some of which tell about the difference. (Exercise 3)
- Complete equations that involve both multiplication and addition. (Exercise 4)
- Solve 2-digit times 2-digit multiplication problems that require carrying for the ones and carrying for the tens. (Exercise 5)
- **Indicate where fractions that do not equal whole numbers go on a number line.** (Exercise 6)
  Note: Students first complete the number line to show the fractions for whole numbers. Then they indicate placement of fractions that do not equal whole numbers.
- **Write the missing operation sign in equations (for example: 12 = 4 ■ 3). (Exercise 7)**

EXERCISE 1 MONEY
Price-Tag Subtraction

a. Open your textbook to lesson 46 and find part 1. √
- These problems tell how much the person started out with and how much the person spent. You have to figure out how much the person ended up with. You do that by subtracting the amount the person spent.
b. Work problem A. Make a box around the answer. Raise your hand when you're finished.
   (Observe students and give feedback.)
- (Write on the board:)

$$\text{a.} \quad \$\ \cancel{3}^2\cancel{5}.\cancel{8}^7\cancel{0}^{10}$$
$$-\ 16.29$$
$$\boxed{\$\ 19.51}$$

- Check your work. Here's what you should have for problem A. Tim ended up with $19.51.
c. Work problem B. Raise your hand when you're finished. (Observe students and give feedback.)
- (Write on the board:)

$$\text{b.} \quad \$\ 2\cancel{4}^3 1.00$$
$$-\ 134.00$$
$$\boxed{\$\ 107.00}$$

- Here's what you should have for problem B. Tina ended up with $107.00.
d. Work problem C. Raise your hand when you're finished. (Observe students and give feedback.)

- (Write on the board:)

$$\text{c.} \quad \$\ \cancel{2}^1 0.75$$
$$-\ 12.34$$
$$\boxed{\$\ 8.41}$$

- Here's what you should have for problem C. Reggie ended up with $8.41.

EXERCISE 2 FRACTIONS
Multiplication

a. Find part 2.
   You've learned to add and subtract fractions. The rules in the box show how to **multiply** fractions. I'll read what it says. Follow along: When you multiply fractions, you multiply the top numbers and write the answer on top. Then you multiply the bottom numbers and write the answer on the bottom.
b. You can see the problem 3-fourths times 2-fifths.
- The multiplication problem for the top is 3 times 2. That's 6. You write 6 on top.
- The multiplication problem for the bottom is 4 times 5. That's 20. You write 20 on the bottom. I'll read the whole equation: 3-fourths times 2-fifths equals 6-twentieths.
c. Your turn: Use lined paper. Copy problem A and write the answer. Remember, multiply the top numbers and write that answer on top. Then multiply the bottom numbers and write that answer on the bottom. Raise your hand when you've worked problem A.

- (Write on the board:)

$$a. \ \frac{2}{9} \times \frac{4}{2} = \frac{8}{18}$$

- Check your work. You multiplied the top numbers, 2 times 4, and got 8 on the top. Then you multiplied 9 times 2 and got 18 on the bottom. 2-ninths times 4-halves equals 8-eighteenths. Raise your hand if you got everything right.

d. Your turn: Copy problem B and work it. Raise your hand when you're finished.
   (Observe students and give feedback.)

- Everybody, what does 2-thirds times 4 over 1 equal? (Signal.) *8-thirds.*
- Raise your hand if you got it right.

e. Your turn: Copy problem C and work it. Raise your hand when you're finished.
   (Observe students and give feedback.)

- Everybody, what does 7-halves times 2-tenths equal? (Signal.) *14-twentieths.*
- Raise your hand if you got it right.

f. Your turn: Copy and work the rest of the problems in part 2. Raise your hand when you're finished.
   (Observe students and give feedback.)

g. Check your work.
- Problem D. What does 1-third times 5-halves equal? (Signal.) *5-sixths.*
- Problem E. What does 2-eighths times 4 over 1 equal? (Signal.) *8-eighths.*
- That's 1.

h. Raise your hand if you got everything right.

EXERCISE 3 WORD PROBLEMS
Comparison/Difference Discrimination

a. Find part 3.
   All these problems compare. Some tell the difference number. Some ask about the difference.

b. Problem A: An oak tree is 345 years old. A pine tree is 178 years old. How much younger is the pine tree than the oak tree?

- Work the complete problem. Remember the unit name in the answer. Raise your hand when you're finished.
   (Observe students and give feedback.)

- (Write on the board:)

difference	pine	oak
a. ——— 178 ——→		345

- Here's what you should have. The big number is for **oak**. The number is **345**. A small number is for **pine**. The number is **178**. To find the answer you subtracted 178 from 345. The answer is 167. Raise your hand if you wrote that answer.

c. Problem B: An oak tree is 167 years old. Mr. Brown is 134 years younger than the oak tree. How old is Mr. Brown?

- Make the number family and figure out the answer. Raise your hand when you're finished.
   (Observe students and give feedback.)

- (Write on the board:)

difference	Mr. Brown	oak
b. ——— 134 ——→		167

- Check your work. Here's what you should have. The big number is for **oak**. That's **167** years. The difference number is **134**. To find the answer, you subtracted 134 from 167. The answer is 33 years. Raise your hand if you wrote that answer.

d. Your turn: Work the rest of the problems in part 3. Raise your hand when you're finished.
   (Observe students and give feedback.)

e. (Write on the board:)

difference	Fran	Jill
c. ——— 333 ——→ 7891		

difference	Jill	Fran
d. ——— 3601 ——→		4012

f. Check your work. Here's what you should have for problems C and D.

- For problem C, you worked the number problem: 333 plus 7891. The answer is 8224.
- How far did Jill run? (Signal.) *8224 yards.*
- For problem D, you worked the number problem: 4012 minus 3601. The answer is 411.
- How many days older than Jill was Fran? (Signal.) *411.*

g. Raise your hand if you got everything right for problems C and D.

EXERCISE 4 EQUATIONS
Two Operations

a. Open your workbook to lesson 46 and find part 1. √
• Each problem shows a number that is not a number for counting by 5. The number map shows the numbers for counting by 5. You'll tell how to get to the number for 5 that comes just before the number in the problem. Then you'll tell how many you have to add.
b. The number in problem A is 13. That is not a number for 5. Touch the number on the map that comes just before 13.
• Everybody, what number are you touching? (Signal.) *10.*
• How many times do you count by 5 to get to 10? (Signal.) *2.*
• 5 times 2 is 10. We have to add to get 13. How many do we add? (Signal.) *3.*
c. Complete equation A. Raise your hand when you're finished.
(Observe students and give feedback.)
• (Write on the board:)

> **a. 13 = 5 × 2 + 3**

• Here's equation A. 13 equals 5 times 2 plus 3.
d. Problem B. What's the number? (Signal.) *24.*
• That's not a number for counting by 5. What's the number for 5 that comes just before 24? (Signal.) *20.*
• How many times do you count to get to 20? (Signal.) *4.*
• Yes, 5 times 4 is 20. You want to get to 24. How many do you add? (Signal.) *4.*
• Complete equation B. Raise your hand when you're finished. √
• (Write on the board:)

> **b. 24 = 5 × 4 + 4**

• Here it is. 24 equals 5 times 4 plus 4.
e. Problem C. What's the number? (Signal.) *33.*
• That's not a number for counting by 5. What's the correct number? (Signal.) *30.*
• How many times do you count to get to 30? (Signal.) *6.*
• Yes, 5 times 6 is 30. You want to get to 33.
• Your turn: Complete the equation for C. Raise your hand when you're finished. √
• (Write on the board:)

> **c. 33 = 5 × 6 + 3**

• Here's what you should have: 33 equals 5 times 6 plus 3.
f. Your turn: Work the rest of the problems in part 1. Find the number just before the number in the problem. Write the number of times. Then write how many you add. Raise your hand when you're finished.
(Observe students and give feedback.)
g. Check your work. Read the equation for each problem.
• Problem D. (Signal.) *6 equals 5 times 1 plus 1.*
• Problem E. (Signal.) *47 equals 5 times 9 plus 2.*
• Problem F. (Signal.) *19 equals 5 times 3 plus 4.*
h. Raise your hand if you got everything right.

EXERCISE 5 COLUMN MULTIPLICATION
Two Renamings

a. Find part 2.
For these problems, you'll do a lot of carrying. Remember, when you work the first problem, write the number you carry very lightly. Then cross it out or erase it before you work the next problem.
b. Problem A. Everybody, read the whole problem. (Signal.) *57 times 93.*
c. Say the first problem you'll work. (Signal.) *57 times 3.*
• Say the next problem you'll work. (Signal.) *57 times 90.*
(Repeat step c until firm.)
d. Work problem A. After you work the first problem, remember to cross out or erase the number you carried. Raise your hand when you're finished.
(Observe students and give feedback.)
• (Write on the board:)

$$
\begin{array}{r}
\overset{\displaystyle 6}{\overset{\displaystyle \not{2}}{5\,7}} \\
\times\,\underset{\scriptstyle 1}{9\,3} \\
\hline
1\,7\,1 \\
+\,5\,1\,3\,0 \\
\hline
5\,3\,0\,1
\end{array}
$$

a.

• Check your work. Here's what you should have. I've shown the carried number crossed out. 57 times 3 equals 171. 57 times 90 equals 5130. 57 times 93 equals 5301. Raise your hand if you got it right.
e. Problem B. Everybody, read the whole problem. (Signal.) *28 times 15.*
• Read the problem you'll work first. (Signal.) *28 times 5.*
• Read the problem you'll work next. (Signal.) *28 times 10.*

- Work problem B. Raise your hand when you're finished. (Observe students and give feedback.)
- (Write on the board:)

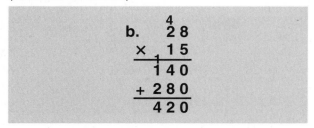

- Check your work. Here's what you should have. 28 times 5 equals 140. 28 times 10 equals 280. 28 times 15 equals 420. Raise your hand if you got everything right.
f. Problem C. Everybody, read the whole problem. (Signal.) *68 times 29.*
- Read the problem you'll work first. (Signal.) *68 times 9.*
- Read the problem you'll work next. (Signal.) *68 times 20.*
- Work problem C. Raise your hand when you're finished. (Observe students and give feedback.)
- (Write on the board:)

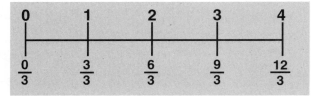

- Check your work. Here's what you should have. 68 times 9 equals 612. 68 times 20 equals 1360. 68 times 29 equals 1972. Raise your hand if you got everything right.

EXERCISE 6 WRITING FRACTIONS
Number Lines

a. Find part 3.
You're going to write fractions for whole numbers on the number line. Then you're going to draw lines to show where some other fractions go on the number line.
b. Write fractions for the whole numbers on the number line. Raise your hand when you're finished. (Observe students and give feedback.)
- (Draw on the board:)

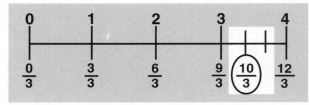

- Here's what you should have. The bottom number is **3** for all the fractions.
c. (Write on the board:)

d. Here's 10-thirds. 10-thirds is not a whole number. It goes between whole numbers. It goes at the tenth mark from the beginning of the number line. You can figure out exactly where it goes by starting at the beginning of the number line and counting 10 parts. Or you can start at 9-thirds and count 1 mark.
- Find the mark for the tenth part. Below that mark, write the fraction 10-thirds in a circle with a line to show exactly where it belongs on the number line. Raise your hand when you're finished. (Observe students and give feedback.)
- (Write to show:)

- Here is where 10-thirds belongs. It is 1 place after 9-thirds.
e. (Write on the board:)

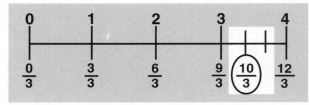

- Here's another fraction that is not a whole number.
- What's the top number? (Signal.) *5.*
- So it's 5 parts from the beginning of the number line. 5-thirds is 2 marks past 3-thirds. Write 5-thirds in a circle with a line to show exactly where it goes. Raise your hand when you're finished. (Observe students and give feedback.)
- (Write to show:)

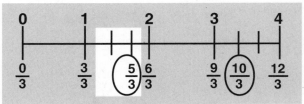

- Here's what you should have. 5-thirds is 2 parts more than the whole number 1. It's just before the whole number 2.

EXERCISE 7 EQUATIONS
Missing Signs

a. Find part 4.
Each equation has the number you end up with as the first number. A sign is missing in each equation.

b. Problem A. The first number is 30. That's the number you end up with. The numbers on the other side of the equal sign are 5 and 6.
- What's the missing sign? (Signal.) *A times sign.*
- Yes, the equation should say: 30 equals 5 **times** 6.
- Problem B. What's the first number? (Signal.) *40.*
- That's the number you end up with. The numbers on the other side of the equal sign are 42 and 2.
- What's the missing sign? (Signal.) *A minus sign.*
- Yes, the equation should say: 40 equals 42 **minus** 2.

c. Your turn: Write the missing sign in each equation. Raise your hand when you're finished. (Observe students and give feedback.)

d. Check your work. I'll read what you should have for each equation.
- Equation A: 30 equals 5 times 6.
- Equation B: 40 equals 42 minus 2.
- Equation C: 19 equals 4 plus 15.
- Equation D: 45 equals 40 plus 5.
- Equation E: 45 equals 9 times 5.
- Equation F: 45 equals 50 minus 5.

EXERCISE 8 INDEPENDENT WORK

a. Find part 5.
You'll work part 5 independently.

b. Find part 4 in your textbook.
You'll work parts 4 through 9 independently.

c. (Assign **Connecting Math Concepts** *Independent Worksheet* 24 as classwork or homework. Before beginning the next lesson, check the students' independent work.)

Level D, Lesson 46 (Textbook)

For each item in **part 1,** students work a column subtraction problem to figure out how much money each person had after the purchase. Problems of this form also appeared in lessons 32 and 33.

Students first learned how to write dollar-and-cents amounts in lessons 8 and 9. In lessons 24 and 26, students aligned dollar-and-cents amounts for addition/subtraction problems. Price-tag addition problems were introduced in lesson 29.

After lesson 46, students will work a variety of more sophisticated addition/subtraction price-tag problems involving a difference. For example: After Larry buys the skateboard, he'll still have $13.45. How much money does he have now? **or:** Hank had $35.99. He bought one of the items. He still had $23.15. Which item did he buy?

The work with price-tag problems continues through lesson 63.

Lesson 46

Part 1

a. Tim had $35.80. He bought the helmet. How much did he end up with?

b. Tina had $241.00. She bought the bike. How much did she end up with?

c. Reggie had $20.75. He bought the backpack. How much did he end up with?

Part 2

- When you multiply fractions, you multiply the top numbers and write the answer on top. Then you multiply the bottom numbers and write the answer on the bottom.

  Here's: $\frac{3}{4} \times \frac{2}{5}$

- The multiplication problem for the top is 3 × 2. That's 6. You write 6 on top. $\frac{3}{4} \times \frac{2}{5} = \boxed{\frac{6}{}}$

- The multiplication problem for the bottom is 4 × 5. That's 20. You write 20 on the bottom. $\frac{3}{4} \times \frac{2}{5} = \boxed{\frac{6}{}}$

a. $\frac{2}{9} \times \frac{4}{2} = \boxed{}$ b. $\frac{2}{3} \times \frac{4}{1} = \boxed{}$ c. $\frac{7}{2} \times \frac{2}{10} = \boxed{}$

d. $\frac{1}{3} \times \frac{5}{2} = \boxed{}$ e. $\frac{2}{8} \times \frac{4}{1} = \boxed{}$

144   *Lesson 46*

Part 2 introduces the steps for solving problems that multiply fractions. Problems of this form appear for three consecutive lessons.

In earlier lessons (27–34), students learned how to work addition or subtraction problems with like denominators. Starting in lesson 51, students will work a mixed set of problems that add, subtract or multiply fractions. In lessons 53–55, students will solve problems that multiply a fraction and a whole number. In lessons 61–63, students will work a mixed set of problems that adds, subtracts or multiplies a whole number and a fraction (e.g., $\frac{4}{5} + 9$, $3 - \frac{4}{3}$, $3 \times \frac{4}{3}$).

Some of the items in **part 3** ask about a difference number (e.g., item a); others tell a difference number (e.g., item b). Students construct a number family to determine whether the problem calls for addition or subtraction. For item a, students know that the pine tree is younger than the oak tree, so the oak tree is the "big number" (total) and the pine tree is a "small number." The other "small number" is always the difference.

Here is the family for item a:

dif pine oak
☐   178 ➔ 345 . Students add to find a

missing big number and subtract to find a missing small number. In this case, students subtract.

Students make this family for item c:

dif Fran Jill
333 7891 ➔ ☐ . The big number is missing,

so students add to find the number of yards for Jill.

Comparison number families were first introduced in Level C, and reviewed in lessons 24–31 of Level D. Problems that ask about the difference are a new problem type, not taught in Level C. Comparison number families are later applied to money problems (lessons 61–63).

Parts 4 through 9 (and **part 5** of the workbook) are the independent work for lesson 46. These parts review problem types that were practiced in a structured form in earlier lessons.

In **part 4,** students divide by 3 or by 4. Facts dividing by 3 were introduced in lessons 34–38. Facts dividing by 4 were introduced in lessons 42–45. Division is taught as the inverse of multiplication. All basic multiplication/division facts are covered by the end of Level D.

Part 5 combines what students have learned about addition/subtraction of fractions with like denominators (taught in lessons 27–34) and what they know about fractions that equal whole numbers (lessons 11–24). Mixed sets similar to the one shown in **part 5** appeared in lessons 44 and 45.

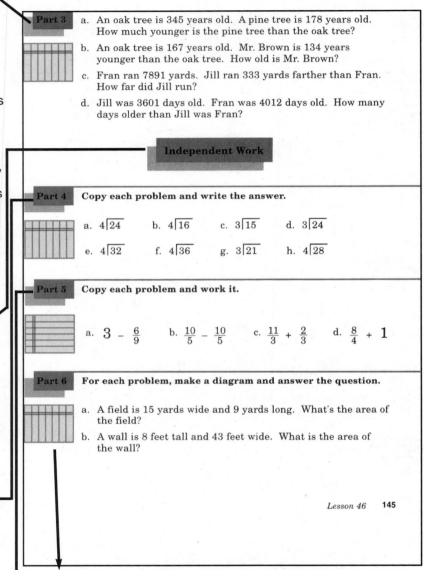

Part 3
a. An oak tree is 345 years old. A pine tree is 178 years old. How much younger is the pine tree than the oak tree?

b. An oak tree is 167 years old. Mr. Brown is 134 years younger than the oak tree. How old is Mr. Brown?

c. Fran ran 7891 yards. Jill ran 333 yards farther than Fran. How far did Jill run?

d. Jill was 3601 days old. Fran was 4012 days old. How many days older than Jill was Fran?

Independent Work

Part 4 Copy each problem and write the answer.

a. $4\overline{)24}$ b. $4\overline{)16}$ c. $3\overline{)15}$ d. $3\overline{)24}$

e. $4\overline{)32}$ f. $4\overline{)36}$ g. $3\overline{)21}$ h. $4\overline{)28}$

Part 5 Copy each problem and work it.

a. $3 - \frac{6}{9}$ b. $\frac{10}{5} - \frac{10}{5}$ c. $\frac{11}{3} + \frac{2}{3}$ d. $\frac{8}{4} + 1$

Part 6 For each problem, make a diagram and answer the question.

a. A field is 15 yards wide and 9 yards long. What's the area of the field?

b. A wall is 8 feet tall and 43 feet wide. What is the area of the wall?

Lesson 46 **145**

The area of a rectangle was introduced in lesson 9, and practiced in five consecutive lessons from lesson 12 to lesson 16. In lessons 19–22, students draw diagrams from descriptions, as they do in **part 6.** Lesson 46 is the ninth lesson in which area problems have appeared in the independent work.

Reading and writing 4-digit numerals was taught and practiced in lessons 1-5. 5-digit and 6-digit numerals were introduced in lessons 7-17. Written descriptions (such as those shown in **part 7**) first appeared in lesson 15. Similar independent work activities have appeared in seven other lessons prior to lesson 46.

Short division was introduced in lesson 33 and continued for nine consecutive lessons through lesson 42. More difficult types (e.g., with 4-digit answers or with zeros in the answer) were introduced in lessons 44 and 45.

The problems in **part 8** represent a range of division types introduced before this point in the program, including problems for which the first digit of the answer is over the second digit of the dividend (e.g., items a, d). If the first digit of the dividend is smaller than the divisor, students underline two digits:

$3\overline{|15}06$ and place the first digit of the answer over the last underlined digit: $3\overline{|1\overset{5}{5}}06$.

If the first digit is as big as the divisor, the students underline one digit: $5\overline{|5}005$ and place the first digit of the answer above the underlined digit: $5\overline{|\overset{1}{5}}005$.

In later lessons (68-76), students will solve problems in which the first digit of the answer has a "remainder" (e.g., $4\overline{|\overset{8}{34}_2}4$). Problems in which the last digit of the answer has a remainder (e.g., $4\overline{|7_3 27}^{\,181R3}$) are taught in lessons 106-110.

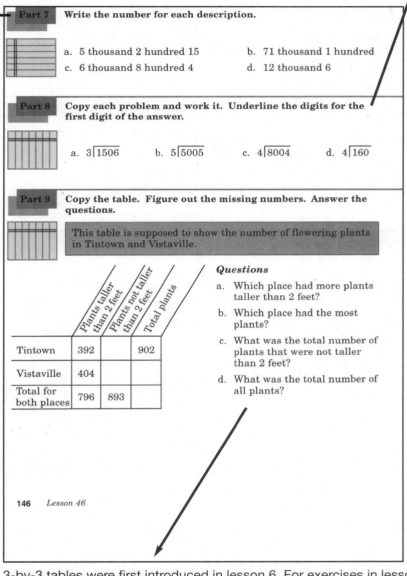

Part 7 Write the number for each description.

a. 5 thousand 2 hundred 15   b. 71 thousand 1 hundred
c. 6 thousand 8 hundred 4   d. 12 thousand 6

Part 8 Copy each problem and work it. Underline the digits for the first digit of the answer.

a. $3\overline{)1506}$ b. $5\overline{)5005}$ c. $4\overline{)8004}$ d. $4\overline{)160}$

Part 9 Copy the table. Figure out the missing numbers. Answer the questions.

This table is supposed to show the number of flowering plants in Tintown and Vistaville.

	Plants taller than 2 feet	Plants not taller than 2 feet	Total plants
Tintown	392		902
Vistaville	404		
Total for both places	796	893	

Questions

a. Which place had more plants taller than 2 feet?

b. Which place had the most plants?

c. What was the total number of plants that were not taller than 2 feet?

d. What was the total number of all plants?

146   *Lesson 46*

3-by-3 tables were first introduced in lesson 6. For exercises in lessons 6 through 21, students analyzed the position of missing numbers in columns/rows of a table and figured out all the missing numbers by addition or subtraction. In lesson 18, students were required to answer questions based on a completed table. In lesson 27, students filled in missing numbers in a table and also answered questions, as they do in **part 9.** This type of problem has appeared independently in six lessons prior to lesson 46.

In later lessons, students will put numbers in a table based on written facts (lessons 53-59) and use comparative information (lessons 61-67) or information from a bar graph (lessons 98, 99) to complete a table before answering questions about the data.

Level D, Lesson 46 (Workbook)

Note: **Parts 1-4 of the workbook are teacher-directed (worked after part 3 of the textbook). Students work part 5 independently.**

The problems in **part 2** require carrying both for the ones and for the tens. This is the second lesson in which this problem type occurs. It will appear in two more consecutive lessons before 3-digit times 2-digit problems are introduced in lesson 49.

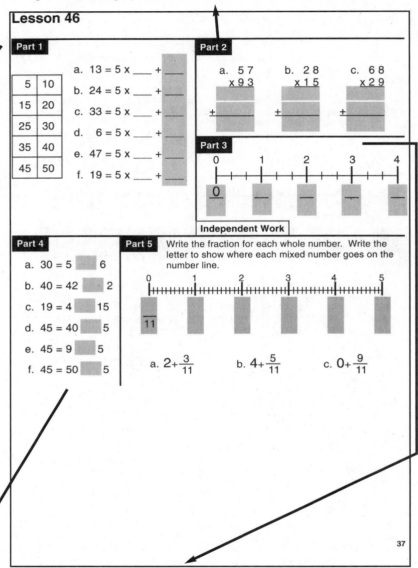

For each item in **part 1,** students figure a number in the count-by-5 series that comes just before the number to the left of the equal sign, figure out the number of times they count by 5, and how many to add to complete the equation. For example, for item a, students write:

$13 = 5 \times 2 + 3$. Lesson 46 is the second lesson in which this type of task occurs. It occurs in three subsequent consecutive lessons.

The task prepares students to work division problems with remainders.

For example: $5\overline{)135}$. Students figure the first digit in the answer is 2:

$5\overline{)135}$ with 2 above. To figure the remainder, students work the same steps as in **part 1:**
5×2 is 10, $+ 3$ is 13. So the remainder is 3:

$5\overline{)13_35}$. This type of division problem will be introduced in lesson 68.

For each item in **part 4,** students figure out the missing operational sign. Equations with a value alone on the left side of the equal sign were introduced in lesson 37.

To work problems in **part 3,** students first complete the fractions for the whole numbers shown on the number line. (This activity has occurred in nine lessons prior to lesson 46.) Next, students indicate where fractions that do not equal whole numbers (5/3 and 10/3) go on the number line. This new component continues for three consecutive lessons after lesson 46.

Students work **part 5** of the workbook independently, after the structured parts of the lesson have been completed. Placing mixed numbers on a number line was introduced in lesson 34. Students have also written fraction equations for mixed numbers (lesson 38-41). For: $2 + \frac{3}{11}$, students write: $\frac{22}{11} + \frac{3}{11} = \frac{25}{11}$. In later lessons (49, 52-54, 56) students will write mixed-number equations (e.g., $\frac{14}{3} = 4 + \frac{2}{3}$) for fractions based on a number line. This work strengthens the relationship between fractions, whole numbers, and mixed numbers.

Note: In Level D, mixed numbers are shown as addition expressions (e.g., $2 + \frac{3}{11}$) to convey the meaning of the traditional notation (e.g., $2\frac{3}{11}$). From lesson 100, students will see all mixed numbers written traditionally.

Level D

Sample Track: Equivalent Fractions

In Level D, students work on multiplying a fraction by a fraction, multiplying a fraction by a whole number, and relating fractions that are involved in multiplication equations.

Students learn the following rules about multiplying: If you multiply a value by more than 1, you end up with more than the starting value. If you multiply by 1, you end up with a value that's equivalent to the starting value. If you multiply by less than 1, you end up with less than the starting value.

This understanding of multiplying by 1 is extremely important for the understanding of equivalent fractions, simplifying fractions, and ratios.

The work with multiplication begins in Lesson 46. Students learn the basic steps of multiplying on the top and writing the answer on the top, and multiplying on the bottom and writing the answer on the bottom.

Part 2

- When you multiply fractions, you multiply the top numbers and write the answer on top. Then you multiply the bottom numbers and write the answer on the bottom.

  Here's: $\frac{3}{4} \times \frac{2}{5}$

- The multiplication problem for the top is 3 × 2. That's 6. You write 6 on top. $\quad \frac{3}{4} \times \frac{2}{5} = \boxed{\frac{6}{}}$

- The multiplication problem for the bottom is 4 × 5. That's 20. You write 20 on the bottom. $\quad \frac{3}{4} \times \frac{2}{5} = \boxed{\frac{6}{20}}$

a. $\frac{2}{9} \times \frac{4}{2} = \boxed{}$ b. $\frac{2}{3} \times \frac{4}{1} = \boxed{}$ c. $\frac{7}{2} \times \frac{2}{10} = \boxed{}$

d. $\frac{1}{3} \times \frac{5}{2} = \boxed{}$ e. $\frac{2}{8} \times \frac{4}{1} = \boxed{}$

EXERCISE 2 FRACTIONS
Multiplication

a. Find part 2.
You've learned to add and subtract fractions. The rules in the shaded box show how to **multiply** fractions. I'll read what it says. Follow along: When you multiply fractions, you multiply the top numbers and write the answer on top. Then you multiply the bottom numbers and write the answer on the bottom.

b. You can see the problem 3-fourths times 2-fifths.

- The multiplication problem for the top is 3 times 2. That's 6. You write 6 on top.

- The multiplication problem for the bottom is 4 times 5. That's 20. You write 20 on the bottom. I'll read the whole equation: 3-fourths times 2-fifths equals 6-twentieths.

c. Your turn: Use lined paper. Copy problem A and write the answer. Remember, multiply the top numbers and write that answer on top. Then multiply the bottom numbers and write that answer on the bottom. Raise your hand when you've worked problem A.

- (Write on the board:)

  a. $\frac{2}{9} \times \frac{4}{2} = \frac{8}{18}$

- Check your work. You multiplied the top numbers, 2 times 4, and got 8 on the top. Then you multiplied 9 times 2 and got 18 on the bottom. 2-ninths times 4-halves equals 8-eighteenths. Raise your hand if you got everything right.

d. Your turn: Copy problem B and work it. Raise your hand when you're finished.
(Observe students and give feedback.)

- Everybody, what does 2-thirds times 4 over 1 equal? (Signal.) *8-thirds.*

- Raise your hand if you got it right.

e. Your turn: Copy problem C and work it. Raise your hand when you're finished.
(Observe students and give feedback.)

- Everybody, what does 7-halves times 2-tenths equal? (Signal.) *14-twentieths.*

- Raise your hand if you got it right.

f. Your turn: Copy and work the rest of the problems in part 2. Raise your hand when you're finished.
(Observe students and give feedback.)

g. Check your work.

- Problem D. What does 1-third times 5-halves equal? (Signal.) *5-sixths.*

- Problem E. What does 2-eighths times 4 over 1 equal? (Signal.) *8-eighths.*

- That's 1.

h. Raise your hand if you got everything right.

After students have practiced working multiplication problems in Lessons 47 and 49, they work with mixed sets of fraction problems. Some call for addition or subtraction; some require multiplication.

Here's an activity from Lesson 51:

Part 4

a. $\frac{3}{4} \times \frac{8}{4} = \boxed{}$ b. $\frac{3}{4} + \frac{8}{4} = \boxed{}$ c. $\frac{7}{2} - \frac{3}{2} = \boxed{}$

d. $\frac{8}{2} \times \frac{3}{5} = \boxed{}$ e. $\frac{1}{6} + \frac{4}{6} = \boxed{}$ f. $\frac{4}{3} \times \frac{5}{2} = \boxed{}$

EXERCISE 4 FRACTIONS
Consolidation

a. Find part 4.
   Some of these problems add or subtract fractions. Some multiply. Remember, when you add or subtract, you just copy the bottom number and work on top. When you multiply, you multiply on top **and** on the bottom.
b. Copy and work the problems in part 4. Raise your hand when you're finished.
   (Observe students and give feedback.)
c. Check your work. Read each problem and the answer.
- Problem A. (Signal.) *3-fourths times 8-fourths equals 24-sixteenths.*
- Problem B. (Signal.) *3-fourths plus 8-fourths equals 11-fourths.*
- Problem C. (Signal.) *7-halves minus 3-halves equals 4-halves.*
- Problem D. (Signal.) *8-halves times 3-fifths equals 24-tenths.*
- Problem E. (Signal.) *1-sixth plus 4-sixths equals 5-sixths.*
- Problem F. (Signal.) *4-thirds times 5-halves equals 20-sixths.*
d. Raise your hand if you got all the problems right.

In Lesson 53, students are taught a procedure for multiplying a whole number by a fraction. They write a "simple" fraction for the whole number—the whole number over 1.

The key discrimination for fraction operations comes after students have worked for several lessons on fraction-multiplication problems that have a whole number. In Lesson 61, students work a mixed set of problems that require multiplication, addition, or subtraction. Each problem has a whole number and a fraction. Students apply the rule for changing the whole number into an appropriate fraction. If the problem multiplies, they write the whole number over 1. If the problem adds or subtracts, they write the whole number as an equivalent fraction with the same denominator as the other fraction in the problem.

Part 1

a. $3 \times \dfrac{4}{3} =$ b. $3 - \dfrac{4}{3} =$ c. $6 + \dfrac{3}{7} =$

d. $8 \times \dfrac{5}{9} =$ e. $\dfrac{4}{5} \times 9 =$ f. $\dfrac{4}{5} + 9 =$

EXERCISE 1 FRACTIONS
Discrimination

a. Open your workbook to Lesson 61 and find part 1. √
- All these problems have a whole number and a fraction. For some problems, you'll add or subtract. For other problems, you'll multiply. Remember, when you add or subtract, you must change the whole number into a fraction that has the same bottom number as the other fraction. When you multiply, you can make a simple fraction with 1 as the bottom number.
b. Problem A: 3 times 4-thirds. You're multiplying. Does 3 have to have the same bottom number as 4-thirds? (Signal.) *No.*
- Problem B. 3 minus 4-thirds. Does 3 have to have the same bottom number as 4-thirds? (Signal.) *Yes.*
- Problem C. 6 plus 3-sevenths. Does 6 have to have the same bottom number as 3-sevenths? (Signal.) *Yes.*
- Problem D. 8 times 5-ninths. Does 8 have to have the same bottom number as 5-ninths? (Signal.) *No.*
- You can write 8 as 8 over 1.
c. Your turn: In the space below each problem, write the problem with the correct fraction for the whole number and write the answer. Raise your hand when you're finished.
   (Observe students and give feedback.)
d. Check your work. Read the whole equation for each problem.
- Problem A. (Signal.) *3 over 1 times 4-thirds equals 12-thirds.*
- Problem B. (Signal.) *9-thirds minus 4-thirds equals 5-thirds.*
- Problem C. (Signal.) *42-sevenths plus 3-sevenths equals 45-sevenths.*
- Problem D. (Signal.) *8 over 1 times 5-ninths equals 40-ninths.*
- Problem E. (Signal.) *4-fifths times 9 over 1 equals 36-fifths.*
- Problem F. (Signal.) *4-fifths plus 45-fifths equals 49-fifths.*

The rule for multiplying by 1 generates procedures for working with ratios, proportions, and equivalent fractions. That rule is presented in Lesson 54. Here's the first part of the exercise:

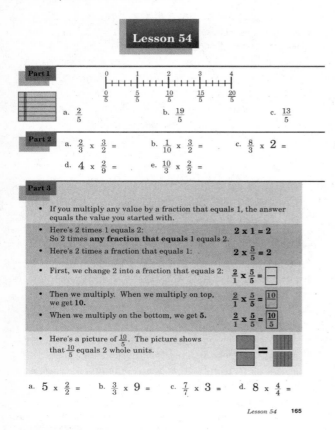

EXERCISE 5 EQUIVALENT FRACTIONS
Multiplying by 1

a. Find part 3.
I'll read what it says in the box. Follow along: If you multiply any value by a fraction that equals 1, the answer equals the value you started with.

- You can see the equation: 2 times 1. That equals 2.
- So 2 times **any fraction that equals 1** equals 2. You can see the equation: 2 times 5-fifths equals 2.
- Here's how to show that 2 times 5-fifths equals 2.
- First, we change 2 into a fraction that equals 2. That's 2 over 1.
- Then we multiply. When we multiply on top, we get **10**. 2 times 5 equals 10.
- When we multiply on the bottom, we get **5**. 1 times 5 equals 5.
- You can see a picture below the last equation. The picture shows the fraction for 2 over 1 and for 10-fifths. Both of these fractions equal 2 whole units.
- So 2 times 5-fifths **does** equal 2 wholes.
- Remember, any value times 1 equals that value. That's true for whole numbers and for all fractions.

b. Find the problems for part 3.
All these problems have whole numbers multiplied by fractions. All the fractions equal 1. So the answer to all the problems will be the same as the whole number in the problem.

c. Problem A: 5 times 2-halves. When you multiply, you'll end up with a fraction that equals the whole number 5.

d. Your turn: Copy the problem and work it. Remember to change 5 into a simple fraction. Raise your hand when you're finished. **(Observe students and give feedback.)**

- (Write on the board:)

$$\text{a. } \frac{5}{1} \times \frac{2}{2} = \frac{10}{2}$$

- Here's what you should have. 5 over 1 times 2-halves equals 10-halves.

e. Problem B: 3-thirds times 9. You're multiplying a whole number and a fraction that equals 1. So you'll end up with a fraction that equals the whole number.

- Copy the problem and work it. Remember to change the whole number into a simple fraction. Raise your hand when you're finished. **(Observe students and give feedback.)**

- (Write on the board:)

$$\text{b. } \frac{3}{3} \times \frac{9}{1} = \frac{27}{3}$$

- Here's what you should have. 3-thirds times 9 over 1 equals 27-thirds.

Beginning in Lesson 56, students work a problem set that requires them to discriminate whether the first value in the problem and the ending fraction are equivalent. The test is whether the first value is multiplied by 1. Students first work a set of problems, some of which are multiplied by a fraction that equals 1. Students then identify the problems that have equivalent fractions. Next to these problems, students write a simple equation showing only the two equivalent fractions:

$$\frac{5}{4} \times \frac{10}{10} = \boxed{\frac{50}{40}} \qquad \frac{5}{4} = \frac{50}{40}$$

Starting in Lesson 59, students work problem sets that show the starting and ending fractions. Students figure out the missing middle fraction. If the fraction equals 1, students write out the simple equation.

Here's part of the exercise from Lesson 59:

Part 2

a. $\frac{2}{5} \times \boxed{} = \frac{10}{15}$ b. $\frac{4}{9} \times \boxed{} = \frac{12}{27}$ c. $\frac{5}{3} \times \boxed{} = \frac{15}{21}$

d. $6 \times \boxed{} = \frac{30}{5}$ e. $\frac{1}{4} \times \boxed{} = \frac{4}{36}$

WORKBOOK PRACTICE

a. Find part 2 in your workbook.
b. Problem A: 2-fifths times some fraction equals 10-fifteenths. You're going to figure out the missing fraction. Say the problem for the bottom numbers. Get ready. (Signal.) *5 times what number equals 15?*
- What's the answer? (Signal.) *3.*
- Say the problem for the top numbers. Get ready. (Signal.) *2 times what number equals 10?*
- What's the answer? (Signal.) *5.*
- Write the missing fraction. Raise your hand when you're finished.
  (Observe students and give feedback.)
- You figured out what to multiply 2-fifths by to get 10-fifteenths. What did you multiply by? (Signal.) *5-thirds.*
c. Problem B: 4-ninths times some fraction equals 12-twenty-sevenths.
- Say the problem for the bottom numbers. (Signal.) *9 times what number equals 27?*
- What's the answer? (Signal.) *3.*
- Say the problem for the top numbers. Get ready. (Signal.) *4 times what number equals 12?*
- What's the answer? (Signal.) *3.*
- Write the missing fraction. Raise your hand when you're finished.
  (Observe students and give feedback.)
- Everybody, 4-ninths times some fraction equals 12-twenty-sevenths. What's the missing fraction? (Signal.) *3-thirds.*
- That's 1.
d. Your turn: Write the missing fraction for problem C. Raise your hand when you're finished.
  (Observe students and give feedback.)
- (Write on the board:)

c. $\frac{5}{3} \times \boxed{\frac{3}{7}} = \frac{15}{21}$

- The missing fraction is 3-sevenths. 5-thirds times 3-sevenths equals 15-twenty-firsts.
e. Write the missing fractions for the rest of the problems in part 2. Raise your hand when you're finished.
  (Observe students and give feedback.)

- (Write on the board:)

d. $\frac{6}{1} \times \boxed{\frac{5}{5}} = \frac{30}{5}$

e. $\frac{1}{4} \times \boxed{\frac{4}{9}} = \frac{4}{36}$

f. Here's what you should have for problems D and E.
- Problem D. Read the equation. (Signal.) *6 over 1 times 5-fifths equals 30-fifths.*
- Problem E. Read the equation. (Signal.) *1-fourth times 4-ninths equals 4-thirty-sixths.*
g. Raise your hand if you got everything right.
h. For some of these problems you multiplied by 1. So you ended up with the same value you started with. If you multiplied by 1, write the number you started with and the fraction it equals in the shaded box after the problem. Write the equations only for the problems you multiplied by 1.
i. (Write on the board:)

b. $\frac{4}{9} = \frac{12}{27}$

d. $6 = \frac{30}{5}$

j. Here's what you should have.
- For problem B, you multiplied by 3-thirds. The equation you wrote is 4-ninths equals 12-twenty-sevenths.
- For problem D, you multiplied by 5-fifths. The equation you wrote is 6 equals 30-fifths.

The final set of problems that require the discrimination of multiplying by 1 or not 1 begins in Lesson 62. Students are presented with problems of the form:

$$\frac{6}{2} \times \frac{}{7} = \frac{24}{}$$

$$\frac{3}{5} \times \frac{4}{} = \frac{}{20}$$

These problems provide a superb review of everything students have learned about equivalent fractions as they relate to multiplication. The problems also set the stage for the work that students will do with ratio and proportion problems.

To work the first problem, students work a division problem on top: 24 ÷ 6. Students then work a multiplication problem on the bottom: 2 × 7.

They determine whether the fractions are equivalent by attending to whether the middle fraction equals 1. That fraction ($\frac{4}{7}$) does not equal 1 so $\frac{6}{2}$ and $\frac{24}{14}$ are not equal.

In Lesson 66, students are introduced to the basic "ratio equation":

$$\frac{3}{5} \times \frac{\square}{\square} = \frac{\square}{20}$$

The fractions are equivalent. Therefore, the first fraction must be multiplied by 1.

To figure out that fraction and to complete the fraction after the equals sign, students first figure out whether they can work on the top or on the bottom. They can work on the bottom because there are two numbers on the bottom. (There's only one number on the top.)

When students work the problem on the bottom (20 ÷ 5), they have the bottom number of the missing fraction:

$$\frac{3}{5} \times \frac{\square}{\boxed{4}} = \frac{\square}{20}$$

Students know that two fractions in the original equation are equivalent; therefore, 4 is the denominator of a fraction that equals 1. Students complete the fraction, then multiply on top to complete the fraction after the equal sign:

$$\frac{3}{5} \times \frac{\boxed{4}}{\boxed{4}} = \frac{\boxed{12}}{20}$$

After students receive an explanation and a board demonstration with the problem shown above, students apply the problem-solving steps to other problems.

Here's the first part of the workbook practice:

Part 3

In each problem, the fraction you start with and the fraction you end up with are equal.

a. $\dfrac{3}{5} \times \dfrac{\ \ }{\ \ } = \dfrac{}{20}$

b. $\dfrac{7}{2} \times \dfrac{\ \ }{\ \ } = \dfrac{}{18}$

c. $\dfrac{3}{4} \times \dfrac{\ \ }{\ \ } = \dfrac{21}{}$

d. $\dfrac{6}{5} \times \dfrac{\ \ }{\ \ } = \dfrac{60}{}$

WORKBOOK PRACTICE

a. Find part 3. You're going to work some of these hard problems.

b. Problem A is the problem on the board. The first thing you do is figure out the fraction that equals 1. You can't start on top because there's only one number on top. You can start on the bottom.
- Say the question for the bottom numbers. (Signal.) *5 times what number equals 20?*
- What's the answer? (Signal.) *4.*
- So what's the fraction that equals 1? (Signal.) *4-fourths.*
- Write the fraction that equals 1. Then multiply on top and complete the last fraction. Raise your hand when you're finished.
  (Observe students and give feedback.)

c. Problem B: 7-halves times a fraction equal to 1 equals some fraction with 18 on the bottom. The first thing you do is figure out the fraction that equals 1.
- Can you say the question for the top numbers of the fraction? (Signal.) *No.*
- There's only one top number so you can't say the question.
- Can you say the question for the numbers on the bottom? (Signal.) *Yes.*
- Say the question. (Signal.) *2 times what number equals 18?*
- What's the answer? (Signal.) *9.*
- Write the fraction that equals 1. Raise your hand when you're finished.
  (Observe students and give feedback.)
- (Write on the board:)

$$\text{b.} \quad \frac{7}{2} \times \frac{9}{9} = \frac{\square}{18}$$

- Here's what you should have so far. Say the problem for the top numbers. (Signal.) *7 times 9 equals what number?*
- Write the answer. Raise your hand when you're finished. √
- (Write to show:)

$$\text{b.} \quad \frac{7}{2} \times \frac{9}{9} = \frac{\boxed{63}}{18}$$

- Here's what you should have. You figured out a fraction that equals 7-halves. That fraction is 63-eighteenths. You had to multiply 7-halves by 9-ninths.

Students practice working problems of this type through Lesson 70. The work provides students with all the prerequisite skills needed to work ratio problems.

RATIOS AND PROPORTIONS

Starting in Lesson 64, students practice writing names and the fraction for sentences that express proportional relationships. The sentences are of the type: There are 4 fleas for every 3 dogs. Students write the names in the same order they occur in the sentence: **fleas** and **dogs.**

They write the fraction showing the number for fleas and the number for dogs:

$$\frac{\textit{fleas}}{\textit{dogs}} = \frac{4}{3}$$

This is the first step that students will later take when they work ratio word problems.

Here's the first part of the exercise from Lesson 64:

EXERCISE 6 RATIOS

a. Open your textbook to Lesson 64 and find part 1. √
- You're going to write fractions and names for sentences. Learning to do this is very important because you'll need it later when you solve hard word problems. Each sentence tells you about a fraction.
b. Touch sentence A.
  The sentence says: There were 3 girls for every 4 boys. The words **girls** and **boys** are underlined. So here's what you write.
- (Write on the board:)

> a. $\frac{girls}{boys}$

- Now you write the number for girls and the number for boys. What's the number for girls? (Signal.) *3.*
- So I write **3** on top.
- What's the number for boys? (Signal.) *4.*
- So I write **4** on the bottom.
- (Write to show:)

> a. $\frac{girls}{boys}$ $\boxed{\frac{3}{4}}$

- The names and the fraction show that there are 3 girls for every 4 boys.
- Your turn: Copy the names and the fraction for sentence A. Raise your hand when you're finished. (Observe students and give feedback.)

In Lesson 68, students learn that **each** box or **each** house refers to **1** box or **1** house. For this sentence: There were 8 shoes in each box, students write:

a. $\frac{shoes}{boxes}$ $\boxed{\frac{8}{1}}$

In Lesson 71, students work word problems. Students combine what they have learned about equivalent fractions with the skill of writing names and fractions for sentences that tell about proportions.

Here's the first part of the exercise from Lesson 71:

EXERCISE 4 RATIOS
Word Problems

a. Find part 2.
  You're going to work ratio problems. They are difficult, and many high school students have trouble with ratios. But you already know how to work them. They are just equivalent-fraction problems with names. You have to figure out a missing number in the equivalent-fraction equation.
b. Touch problem A.
  Here's the first sentence: There are 4 boys for every 7 girls. I'll write the names and the fraction for that sentence.
- What are the names? (Signal.) *Boys and girls.*
- What's the fraction? (Signal.) *4-sevenths.*
- (Write on the board:)

> a. $\frac{boys}{girls} = \frac{4}{7}$

c. We've done the first sentence. Before we do the second sentence, I'll write an equal sign.
- (Write =, leaving space between the fraction and =:)

> a. $\frac{boys}{girls}$ $\frac{4}{7}$ $\qquad =$

- The next sentence will tell about one of the names. If the sentence tells about boys, I write the number on top. That's where any number for **boys** belongs.
- Where would I write a number for girls? (Signal.) *On the bottom.*
d. Listen to the next sentence: There are 21 girls.
- Does that sentence give a number for boys or a number for girls? (Signal.) *A number for girls.*
- So do I write **21** on top or on the bottom? (Signal.) *On the bottom.*

- (Write to show:)

$$\text{a.} \quad \frac{\textbf{boys}}{\textbf{girls}} \quad \frac{4}{7} \quad = \frac{}{\boxed{21}}$$

e. The last sentence asks: How many boys are there? So I make a box for boys.
- Does the box go on top or on the bottom? (Signal.) *On top.*
- (Write to show:)

$$\text{a.} \quad \frac{\textbf{boys}}{\textbf{girls}} \quad \frac{4}{7} \quad = \frac{\boxed{}}{21}$$

- Now we just work the equivalent-fraction problem and find the missing number. 4-sevenths equals the fraction after the equal sign, so 4-sevenths is multiplied by a fraction that equals 1.
- (Write to show:)

$$\text{a.} \quad \frac{\textbf{boys}}{\textbf{girls}} \quad \frac{4}{7} \boxed{\times \ \underline{\ \ }} = \frac{\boxed{}}{21}$$

f. Now we have a problem that you can work. Can you work the problem on the bottom or on the top? (Signal.) *On the bottom.*
- Say the problem for the bottom numbers. (Signal.) *7 times what number equals 21?*
- What number? (Signal.) *3.*
- So what's the fraction that equals 1? (Signal.) *3-thirds.*
- (Write to show:)

$$\text{a.} \quad \frac{\textbf{boys}}{\textbf{girls}} \quad \frac{4}{7} \times \boxed{\frac{3}{3}} = \frac{\boxed{}}{21}$$

g. Now you multiply on top to find the number of boys. 4 times 3. What's the answer? (Signal.) *12.*
- (Write to show:)

$$\text{a.} \quad \frac{\textbf{boys}}{\textbf{girls}} \quad \frac{4}{7} \times \frac{3}{3} = \frac{\boxed{12}}{21}$$

- The number 12 is on top. Are the top numbers for boys or for girls? (Signal.) *Boys.*
- So we answered the question: How many boys are there?
- If there are 21 girls, there are 12 boys.
- Your turn: Copy the work for problem A.
- Then write the answer on the line. Raise your hand when you're finished. √

Work with ratios continues in every lesson through 78. In Lesson 75, students work problems that involve large numbers.

For example: There were 7 perch for every 9 bass. There were 963 bass. How many perch were there?

Students set up the problem:

$$\frac{\textbf{perch}}{\textbf{bass}} \quad \frac{7}{9} \times \underline{\ \ } = \frac{\boxed{}}{963}$$

To work the problem on the bottom, students divide:

$$\begin{array}{r} 1\,0\,7 \\ 9\,\overline{\smash{)}\,9\,6\,3} \end{array}$$

Then they complete the fraction that equals 1 and figure out the number that goes in the box:

$$\frac{\textbf{perch}}{\textbf{bass}} \quad \frac{7}{9} \times \frac{107}{107} = \frac{\boxed{749}}{963}$$

There were 749 perch.

In Lesson 81, students are introduced to sentences that refer to the ratio: The ratio of dogs to cats is 6 to 11.

Students write:

$$\frac{\textbf{dogs}}{\textbf{cats}} \quad \frac{6}{11}$$

Students use a variation of the ratio analysis to work problems that involve measurement equivalences (starting in Lesson 83).

Students also work ratio problems that refer to time and to dollar amounts. (3 pounds of nuts costs $4.56. How much do 12 pounds cost?) Students are taught the meaning of **per**. (The car got 23 miles per gallon of gas.) Finally, students work "price-list" problems. (The list shows prices for 2 pounds of nuts. Students figure out how much 8 pounds would cost, or how many pounds of nuts they could buy for $10.00.)

The final type of ratio-related problem involves probability, and begins in Lesson 91. (See **Probability** on page 125 of *Presentation Book 2*.)

FRACTION COMPARISONS

For students to understand the relationship of one fraction to another, they must have some basis for comparison. If the fractions have the same denominator, the fraction with the larger numerator is the larger fraction. If the numerators are the same, the fraction with the smaller denominator is the larger fraction. Students also use information about whether fractions are more than 1 or less than 1 to compare their size. This analysis is taught in Lessons 72 through 102.

Another important basis for comparing fractions involves **multiplication.** The idea is that it is possible to go from one fraction to the other fraction using multiplication:

If $\frac{10}{16}$ equals $\frac{5}{8}$, you can multiply $\frac{5}{8}$ by 1 to get $\frac{10}{16}$.

If $\frac{9}{16}$ is less than $\frac{5}{8}$, you multiply $\frac{5}{8}$ by less than 1 to get $\frac{9}{16}$.

If $\frac{11}{16}$ is more than $\frac{5}{8}$, you multiply $\frac{5}{8}$ by more than 1 to get $\frac{11}{16}$.

The hardest part of this concept for students to understand is that if you multiply by less than 1, you end up with less than you start with.

Work with this idea begins in Lesson 71. After the introduction, students indicate whether a concealed value is more than 1 or less than 1.

Here's the workbook practice exercise from Lesson 71:

Part 1

a. $3 \times \blacksquare = 1$
more than 1
less than 1

b. $3 \times \blacksquare = 5$
more than 1
less than 1

c. $5 \times \blacksquare = 4$
more than 1
less than 1

d. $2 \times \blacksquare = 3$
more than 1
less than 1

e. $11 \times \blacksquare = 14$
more than 1
less than 1

WORKBOOK PRACTICE

a. Open your workbook to Lesson 71 and find part 1. √

• For each problem, you'll indicate whether you multiply by more than 1 or less than 1.

b. Problem A: 3 times some fraction equals 1. Do you end up with more than you start with or less than you start with? (Signal.) *Less than you start with.*

• So what do you know about the number you multiply by? (Signal.) *It's less than 1.*

c. Circle **less than 1.** Then work problem B. Remember, if you end up with **less** than you start with, you're multiplying by **less than 1.** If you end up with **more** than you start with, you're multiplying by **more than** 1. Raise your hand when you've finished problem B.
(Observe students and give feedback.)

• Check your work.

• Problem B: 3 times some fraction equals 5. What do you start with in that problem? (Signal.) *3.*

• What do you end up with? (Signal.) *5.*

• Do you end up with more than you start with or less than you start with? (Signal.) *More than you start with.*

• So what do you know about the number you multiply by? (Signal.) *It's more than 1.*

d. Work the rest of the problems in part 1. Raise your hand when you've finished. (Observe students and give feedback.)

e. Check your work.

• Problem C: 5 times some fraction equals 4. Do you end up with more than you start with or less than you start with? (Signal.) *Less than you start with.*

• So what do you know about the number you multiply by? (Signal.) *It's less than 1.*

• Problem D: 2 times some fraction equals 3. Do you end up with more than you start with or less than you start with? (Signal.) *More than you start with.*

• So what do you know about the number you multiply by? (Signal.) *It's more than 1.*

• Problem E: 11 times some fraction equals 14. Do you end up with more than you start with or less than you start with? (Signal.) *More than you start with.*

• So what do you know about the number you multiply by? (Signal.) *It's more than 1.*

f. Remember the rule about multiplying by more than 1 or less than 1.

In Lesson 74, students work problems that show the larger fraction in a multiplication equation circled. Students figure out whether the first fraction in the problem is multiplied by more than 1 or less than 1.

Here's the set of problems from Lesson 74:

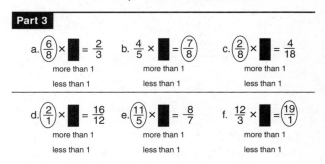

Part 3

a. $\left(\frac{6}{8}\right) \times \blacksquare = \frac{2}{3}$
more than 1
less than 1

b. $\frac{4}{5} \times \blacksquare = \left(\frac{7}{8}\right)$
more than 1
less than 1

c. $\left(\frac{2}{8}\right) \times \blacksquare = \frac{4}{18}$
more than 1
less than 1

d. $\left(\frac{2}{1}\right) \times \blacksquare = \frac{16}{12}$
more than 1
less than 1

e. $\left(\frac{11}{5}\right) \times \blacksquare = \frac{8}{7}$
more than 1
less than 1

f. $\frac{12}{3} \times \blacksquare = \left(\frac{19}{1}\right)$
more than 1
less than 1

For problem A, the first fraction is circled. That means the fraction is less. To end up with a value that is less, you multiply by less than 1.

For problem B, the last fraction is circled. To end up with a fraction that is larger, you multiply by more than 1.

In Lesson 81, students work a variation of the problem that gives information about the value after the times sign. For instance:

$$\frac{11}{17} \times \blacksquare = \blacksquare$$

more than 1 $\quad \dfrac{}{}$ than $\square$

Given that $\frac{11}{17}$ is multiplied by more than 1, the answer must be more than $\frac{11}{17}$.

Here's the exercise from Lesson 81:

Part 1

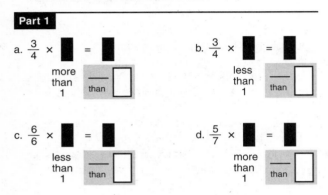

a. $\frac{3}{4} \times \blacksquare = \blacksquare$

more than 1 $\quad$ than $\square$

b. $\frac{3}{4} \times \blacksquare = \blacksquare$

less than 1 $\quad$ than $\square$

c. $\frac{6}{6} \times \blacksquare = \blacksquare$

less than 1 $\quad$ than $\square$

d. $\frac{5}{7} \times \blacksquare = \blacksquare$

more than 1 $\quad$ than $\square$

EXERCISE 7 FRACTION MULTIPLICATION
More or Less Than 1

a. Open your workbook to Lesson 81 and find part 1. √
- This is a new kind of problem. The problem shows the value you start with. It doesn't show what you multiplied by, but it tells you whether that value is more than 1 or less than 1. You have to tell about the value you **end up with.** If you multiply by less than 1, that value is less than you start with. If you multiply by more than 1, that value is more than you start with.
b. Problem A. What are you starting with? (Signal.) *3-fourths.*
- What do you know about the number you multiply by? (Signal.) *It's more than 1.*
- So, the number you end up with is more than 3-fourths. What do you know about the number you end up with? (Signal.) *It's more than 3-fourths.*
- Problem B. What are you starting with? (Signal.) *3-fourths.*
- What do you know about the number you multiply by? (Signal.) *It's less than 1.*
- So what do you know about the number you end up with? (Signal.) *It's less than 3-fourths.*
- Problem C. What are you starting with? (Signal.) *6-sixths.*

- What do you know about the number you multiply by? (Signal.) *It's less than 1.*
- So what do you know about the number you end up with? (Signal.) *It's less than 6-sixths.*
c. Go back to problem A.
- Do you end up with more than 3-fourths or less than 3-fourths? (Signal.) *More than 3-fourths.*
- Complete the statement under the box you end up with to say **more than 3-fourths.** Then complete the words for the rest of the problems in part 1. Raise your hand when you're finished. (Observe students and give feedback.)
d. Check your work.
- Problem A. Tell me about the number you end up with. (Signal.) *It's more than 3-fourths.*
- You should have written **more** than **3-fourths.**
- Problem B. Tell me about the number you end up with. (Signal.) *It's less than 3-fourths.*
- Problem C. Tell me about the number you end up with. (Signal.) *It's less than 6-sixths.*
- Problem D. Tell me about the number you end up with. (Signal.) *It's more than 5-sevenths.*

In Lesson 83, students work a problem set that requires them to apply several of the discriminations they have learned.

Each problem shows the starting value and the ending value:

$$\frac{2}{9} \times \blacksquare = \frac{5}{9}$$

more than 1
= 1
less than 1

Students first compare the values that are shown to determine which is larger. They circle the larger fraction.

Now they can figure out whether the missing value is more than 1, equal to 1, or less than 1. $\frac{5}{9}$ is more than $\frac{2}{9}$. Therefore, $\frac{2}{9}$ is multiplied by more than 1.

In Lesson 101, students learn how to compare fractions like $\frac{5}{4}$ and $\frac{15}{11}$. The procedure is to start with the fraction that has smaller numbers: $\frac{5}{4}$. Then use one of the numbers from the other fraction. Select the number that can be reached by multiplying:

$$\frac{5}{4} \times - = \frac{15}{\square}$$

Work the problem to find out what the second fraction would be if it equaled the first fraction.

$$\frac{5}{4} \times \frac{3}{3} = \frac{15}{\boxed{12}}$$

Compare the fraction you end up with ($\frac{15}{12}$) and tell whether it's more or less. Because $\frac{15}{12}$ is less than $\frac{15}{11}$, $\frac{5}{4}$ is less than $\frac{15}{11}$.

This procedure permits students to compare a wide range of fractions.

Here's part of the textbook practice from the introductory exercise in Lesson 101:

Part 1

a. $\frac{12}{5}$? $\frac{3}{2}$ b. $\frac{2}{3}$? $\frac{7}{9}$ c. $\frac{5}{3}$? $\frac{9}{6}$

EXERCISE 3 FRACTIONS
Comparison

b. Find the problems for part 1.
Each item shows two fractions you'll compare.

c. Item A: You'll compare 12-fifths and 3-halves. To compare these fractions, you start with the fraction that has smaller numbers. Which fraction? (Signal.) *3-halves.*

- Write that fraction with an equal sign after it. Leave a space for the fraction that equals 1. Raise your hand when you're finished.
- (Write on the board:)

a. $\frac{3}{2}$ =

- Now we'll write a fraction that equals 3-halves. That fraction will have one of the numbers from 12-fifths.
- (Write to show:)

a. $\frac{3}{2} = \frac{12}{\square}$

$\frac{3}{2} = \frac{\square}{5}$

- Here are two choices. 3-halves equals 12 over some number or 3-halves equals some number over 5. You can't work one of those problems.
- Copy the problem you can work. Raise your hand when you've done that much.

- You should have the equation: 3-halves equals 12 over some number. You can work that problem. Do it and figure out what 3-halves equals. Then write whether that fraction is more or less than 12-fifths. Write **more** or **less** after the equation. √
- Everybody, what does 3-halves equal? (Signal.) *12-eighths.*
- Is that fraction more or less than 12-fifths? (Signal.) *Less.*
- So **3-halves** is less that **12-fifths.**

d. Problem B: You'll compare 2-thirds and 7-ninths. Start with the fraction that has the smaller numbers. Write the equation that has one of the numbers in the other fraction. Pick the number you can get to by multiplying.
Raise your hand when you have that much.

- (Write on the board:)

b. $\frac{2}{3} = \frac{\square}{9}$

- Here's the problem you should have written. Figure out the fraction. Then write whether that fraction is more or less than 7-ninths. Raise your hand when you're finished.
- (Write to show:)

b. $\frac{2}{3} = \frac{\boxed{6}}{9}$ **less**

- Here's what you should have. The fraction that equals 2-thirds is 6-ninths. That fraction is less than 7-ninths, so 2-thirds is less than 7-ninths.

Another comparison type begins in Lesson 104. Problems give information about ratios. For instance: At Joe's, 4 pounds of rice cost $3. At Fran's, 18 pounds of rice cost $15.

Students write the information for each store:

Joe's pounds / Joe's $	$\frac{4}{3}$
Fran's pounds / Fran's $	$\frac{18}{15}$

Students pick the ratio with the smaller numbers and complete the equation, using the number from the other fraction. (They select the number they can reach through multiplication.)

$$\frac{\text{Joe's pounds}}{\text{Joe's \$}} \quad \frac{4}{3} = \frac{}{15}$$

When they complete the equation, they'll know how many pounds of rice you could buy for $15 at Joe's.

The answer is 20. Students then compare the fractions $\frac{18}{15}$ and $\frac{20}{15}$. The best deal is at Joe's.

The last type of comparison problem students work involves fractions and decimal values.

For example: Which is more, $\frac{2}{3}$ or .66?

Students write the decimal value as a fraction with a denominator of 100 ($\frac{66}{100}$). Then they write this problem:

$$\frac{2}{3} = \frac{66}{}$$

The completed equation is:

$$\frac{2}{3} \times \frac{33}{33} = \frac{66}{99}$$

$\frac{66}{99}$ is larger than $\frac{66}{100}$. So $\frac{2}{3}$ is more than .66.

Connecting Math Concepts, Level E

Connecting Math Concepts, Level E is a 125-lesson program that extends the concepts and skills taught in earlier levels. Students analyze and solve

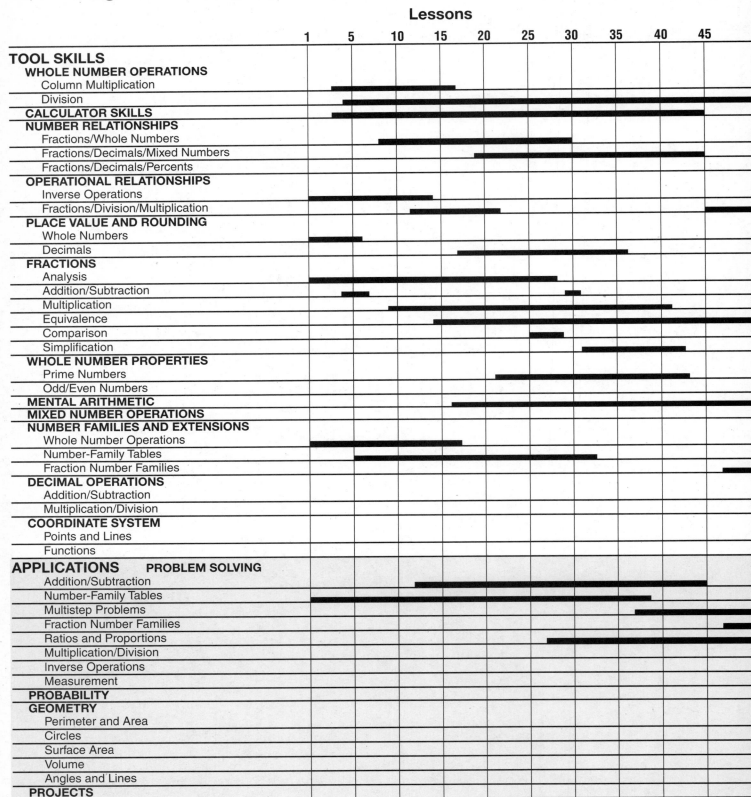

Lessons

1 5 10 15 20 25 30 35 40 45

TOOL SKILLS
- **WHOLE NUMBER OPERATIONS**
  - Column Multiplication
  - Division
- **CALCULATOR SKILLS**
- **NUMBER RELATIONSHIPS**
  - Fractions/Whole Numbers
  - Fractions/Decimals/Mixed Numbers
  - Fractions/Decimals/Percents
- **OPERATIONAL RELATIONSHIPS**
  - Inverse Operations
  - Fractions/Division/Multiplication
- **PLACE VALUE AND ROUNDING**
  - Whole Numbers
  - Decimals
- **FRACTIONS**
  - Analysis
  - Addition/Subtraction
  - Multiplication
  - Equivalence
  - Comparison
  - Simplification
- **WHOLE NUMBER PROPERTIES**
  - Prime Numbers
  - Odd/Even Numbers
- **MENTAL ARITHMETIC**
- **MIXED NUMBER OPERATIONS**
- **NUMBER FAMILIES AND EXTENSIONS**
  - Whole Number Operations
  - Number-Family Tables
  - Fraction Number Families
- **DECIMAL OPERATIONS**
  - Addition/Subtraction
  - Multiplication/Division
- **COORDINATE SYSTEM**
  - Points and Lines
  - Functions

APPLICATIONS   PROBLEM SOLVING
- Addition/Subtraction
- Number-Family Tables
- Multistep Problems
- Fraction Number Families
- Ratios and Proportions
- Multiplication/Division
- Inverse Operations
- Measurement
- **PROBABILITY**
- **GEOMETRY**
  - Perimeter and Area
  - Circles
  - Surface Area
  - Volume
  - Angles and Lines
- **PROJECTS**

increasingly complex problems, using ratios and proportions, tables, graphs, calculators, and other techniques. Work with fractions, decimals, measurement, geometry and functions, and

factorization is also included. The Scope and Sequence Chart shows where each track or major topic begins and where it ends.

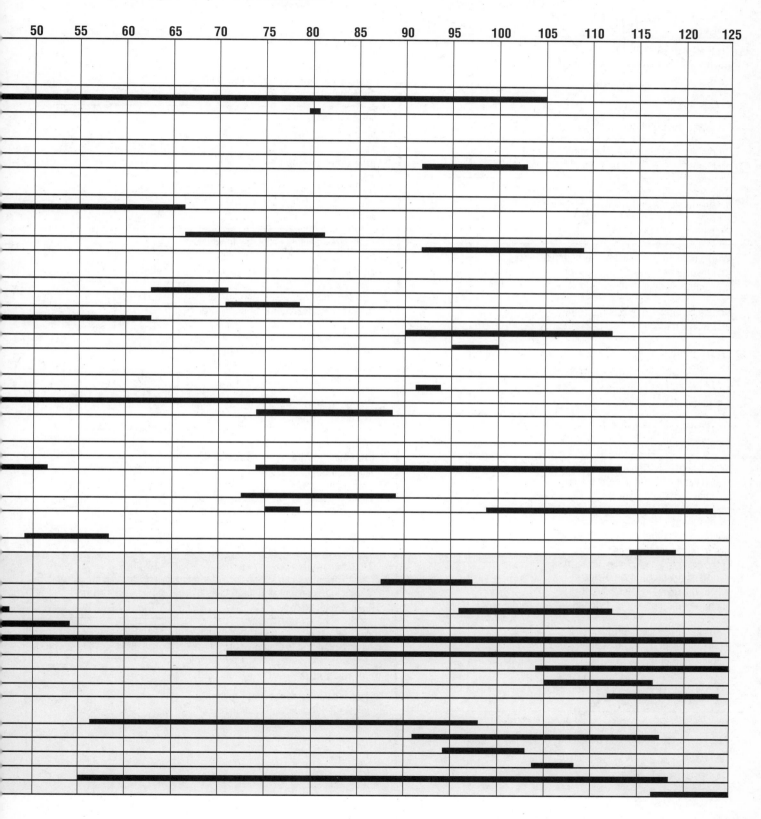

Level E Contents

WHOLE NUMBER OPERATIONS

Skills	Taught in these Lessons	Date Lessons Completed
Column Multiplication		
Works multiplication problems that have a tens number. Problems are of the form: $\begin{array}{r}18\\ \times\,50\end{array}$	2	
Works a mixed set of multiplication problems.	3	
Solves multiplication problems that involve two 2-digit values. Problems are of the form: $\begin{array}{r}53\\ \times\,42\end{array}$.	5, 6	
Works column-multiplication problems that involve carrying for both the ones digit and tens digit of the multiplier.	7–10	
Copies column multiplication problems and works them.	15	
Short Division		
Completes division problems to show the correct fact number and the remainder.	4–7	
Works division problems that have a single-digit answer and a remainder.	8–19	
Works short-division problems in which each digit of the dividend is a multiple of the divisor.	21	
Works short-division problems in which not all digits of the dividend are multiples of the divisor.	22–24	
Works short-division problems in which the divisor may be larger than the first digit of the dividend.	25–28	
Works short-division problems, some of which have zero as the middle digit of the answer.	29, 31	
Rewrites the answer to a division problem as a mixed number.	32–35	
Works short-division problems and writes the answers as mixed numbers.	36, 37	

Skills	Taught in these Lessons	Date Lessons Completed
Long Division		
Completes division problems by multiplying, subtracting, and writing the remainder as a fraction.	43–46	
Works partially-completed division problems that have 2-digit divisors; for example: $42\overline{)389}$ with 9 above.	46, 47	
Completes division problems, some of which have a 2-digit divisor and some of which have a 1-digit divisor.	48	
Completes division problems in which the whole-number part of the initial answer is either correct or too large.	49–57	
Corrects answers to division problems that have a remainder that is too large.	58–61	
Reworks long division problems in which the whole-number part of the answer shown is either too large or too small.	62–65	
Works division problems by saying the estimation problem for the tens.	66, 67	
Works division problems (for example: $68\overline{)364}$ by using rounding and estimating.	68–72	
Works division problems in which the estimation problem does not give the correct quotient.	86, 89	
Works long division problems that have 2-digit answers.	97–99	
Works long division problems that have 1- or 2-digit answers.	101–103	
Works a set of division problems that have 1-digit and 2-digit divisors.	104, 105	
Calculator Skills		
Uses a calculator to work problems involving addition, subtraction and multiplication.	3	

Level E Contents

Skills	Taught in these Lessons	Date Lessons Completed
Works division problems of the form: $4\overline{)616}$ using a calculator.	4	
Uses a calculator to figure out missing numbers in number families.	8, 9	
Uses a calculator to determine if numbers are prime numbers.	21, 22	
Uses a calculator to find the two prime factors of a larger composite number.	24, 25	
Uses a calculator to figure out the decimal value for any fraction or mixed number.	41–80	
Uses a calculator to figure out the fraction that equals 1 for equivalent fraction problems of the form: $\frac{5}{7}\left(-\right) = \frac{185}{259}$.	43–45	

NUMBER RELATIONSHIPS
Fractions/Whole Numbers

Skills	Taught in these Lessons	Date Lessons Completed
Writes division problems and answers for fractions that equal whole numbers.	8–11	
Writes equations that show a fraction and the whole number it equals. Problems are of the form: $\frac{\blacksquare}{7} = 6$.	14–18	
Completes an equation to show various fractions that equal a whole number.	25–27	
Completes equations to show the whole number a fraction equals.	23–30	

Fractions/Decimals/Mixed Numbers

Skills	Taught in these Lessons	Date Lessons Completed
Writes fractions for mixed numbers.	19–21	
Completes a table to show decimal values and equivalent fractions.	22, 23	
Writes equations that show a mixed number and the fraction it equals.	23, 24	

Skills	Taught in these Lessons	Date Lessons Completed
Completes a table to show decimal values and the corresponding mixed numbers.	24, 25	
Writes decimal values for fractions that have denominators of 10, 100, and 1000.	28–31	
Writes fractions with denominators of 10, 100, or 1000 for decimal values.	32, 33	
Completes a table to show decimal values and equivalent fractions with denominators of 10, 100, or 1000.	34	
Completes a table to show decimal numbers and mixed numbers for fractions with denominators of 10 or 100.	37, 38	
Rewrites fractions as mixed numbers.	39, 41	
Completes a table to show fractions with denominators of 10 or 100 and equivalent decimals and mixed numbers.	39–42	
Completes equations that show a fraction or mixed number and the decimal value it equals.	40	
Completes a table to show fractions and equivalent mixed numbers.	44, 45	
Completes inequality statements involving decimal values and fractions.	103	
Completes a table to show hundredths fractions and their equivalent decimal and percent values.	92–94	
Writes equations to show the decimal value for a specified percent value.	95	
Writes equations to show percents that equal specified decimal values.	96	
Writes equations for a mixed set of percent, decimal, and fractional values.	97, 98	

Level E Contents

Skills	Taught in these Lessons	Date Lessons Completed
Rewrites fractions as hundredths.	99	
Writes equations that show fractions and equivalent percent values.	101, 103	
OPERATIONAL RELATIONSHIPS **Inverse Operations**		
Writes division problems for multiplication problems of the form: $9 \times \blacksquare = 63$.	1–3	
Rewrites and solves problems of the form: $4 \times \blacksquare = 816$.	4	
Completes multiplication and division facts that have zero.	11	
Checks answers to addition problems by subtracting.	11, 12	
Checks answers to subtraction problems by adding.	13	
Checks answers to addition and subtraction problems by using the opposite operation.	14	
Fractions/Division/Multiplication		
Completes rows of a table to show the whole number a fraction equals and the corresponding division fact.	12, 13	
Completes a table to show the division fact for a fraction that equals a whole number.	17, 18	
Completes a table that has multiplication problems and corresponding fraction equations.	19–22	
Writes the missing middle value as a fraction for multiplication problems of the form: $3 (\blacksquare) = 369$.	45–51	
Completes equations of the form: $5 (\blacksquare) = 6$.	102	
PLACE VALUE AND ROUNDING **Whole Numbers**		
Rewrites equations of the form: $18 = 10 + 8$.	1, 2	
Completes equations to show place-value addition for 2-digit numbers (for example: $56 = 50 + 6$).	2–4	

Skills	Taught in these Lessons	Date Lessons Completed
Writes place-value addition equations for 3-digit numerals (for example: $357 = 300 + 50 + 7$).	5	
Writes place-value addition equations for 2-digit and 3-digit numerals.	6	
Rounds 2-digit values to the nearest ten.	66, 67	
Identifies the place of digits through millions (7-digit numerals).	71, 72	
Identifies the value of arrowed digits through millions (7-digit numerals).	73, 74	
Identifies the value of arrowed digits by subtraction.	75	
Rounds values to the nearest thousand, hundred, or ten.	76, 77	
Follows directions to round numerals to the nearest ten through nearest million.	78, 79	
Uses rounding to estimate the answers to problems.	81, 82	
Expresses numbers that are multiples of 10, 100, or 1000 as factors.	94	
Decimals		
Reads and write decimal values that end in tenths, hundredths, and thousandths.	17, 18	
Writes decimal values for tenths, hundredths, and thousandths, some of which have zero(s) before the last digit.	19–21	
Simplifies decimal values that end in zero(s).	35, 36	
Rounds decimal values to tenths or hundredths.	90, 91	
Rounds decimal values to tenths, hundredths, or thousandths.	92	
Orders decimal values.	102–104	
Converts amounts for cents into amounts for dollars and cents.	108, 109	

Level E Contents

Skills	Taught in these Lessons	Date Lessons Completed
FRACTIONS **Analysis**		
Writes fractions for pictures, then circles fractions that are more than 1.	1, 2	
Identifies fractions that are more than 1.	2	
Writes fractions from descriptions, then circles fractions that are more than 1.	3–6	
Writes fractions for values shown on a number line.	5, 6	
Writes fractions for whole numbers from descriptions.	7–9	
Writes equations from descriptions that give information about a fraction and the whole number it equals.	10, 11	
Classifies fractions as more than 1, less than 1, or equal to 1.	10, 11	
Writes fractions for whole numbers on a number line.	12	
Writes fractions for whole numbers on an undivided number line.	13–15	
Writes fractions from descriptions, some of which tell the number of whole units. (For example: The bottom number of the fraction is 5. The fraction equals 3 whole units.)	16	
Writes fractions from descriptions.	19	
Identifies numerators of fractions.	28	
Addition/Subtraction **(Like Denominators)**		
Identifies and solves problems involving addition and subtraction of fractions that do not need to be rewritten.	4–7	
Works column problems that add or subtract like-denominator fractions.	61, 62	

Skills	Taught in these Lessons	Date Lessons Completed
Addition/Subtraction (Unlike Denominators)		
Works addition and subtraction problems that have a whole number and a fraction, for example: $\frac{15}{4} + 1$; $9 - \frac{3}{12}$.	29, 31	
Works column addition and subtraction problems that have a whole number and a fraction.	63, 64	
Works column addition and subtraction problems that have either a whole number and a fraction or two fractions with the same denominator.	65	
Works problem pairs to show the least common multiple.	65–67	
Works addition and subtraction problems that have two fractions with unlike denominators.	67–71	
Works unlike-denominator problems, some of which require rewriting only one of the fractions.	69, 70	
Multiplication		
Multiplies two fractions.	9, 11	
Identifies the fraction problems in a mixed set (addition, subtraction, multiplication) that can be worked as written and works them.	12–16	
Determines whether the answer to a fraction-multiplication problem is more or less than the starting value in the problem.	31–35	
Works a set of addition, subtraction and multiplication problems that have a whole number and a fraction.	32–34	
Works fraction-multiplication problems in which the starting and ending values equal whole numbers.	36, 37	

Level E Contents

Skills	Taught in these Lessons	Date Lessons Completed
Works fraction-multiplication problems and indicates whether the starting value or ending value is greater.	38–41	
Solves multiplication problems by interpreting the phrase "a fraction **of** a value" as "a fraction **times** a value."	71–73	
Works column problems involving addition, subtraction, and multiplication of fractions.	73, 74	
Rewrites and works row problems involving fraction operations as column problems.	75, 78	
Equivalence		
Writes equations to show fractions that are equivalent.	14, 15	
Works fraction-multiplication problems to determine whether two fractions are equivalent.	16	
Figures out the fraction that equals 1 for a given pair of equivalent-fraction pictures.	17	
Writes equations for equivalent fractions and figures out the fraction that equals 1.	18, 19	
Uses multiplication to determine whether pairs of fractions are equivalent.	21–23	
Solves equivalent-fraction problems of the form: $\frac{3}{7}\left(-\right) = \frac{15}{\blacksquare}$.	24–26	
Uses a calculator to figure out the fraction that equals 1 for equivalent-fraction problems of the form: $\frac{5}{7}\left(-\right) = \frac{185}{259}$.	43–45	
Uses the sign $=$ or $\neq$ to indicate whether pairs of fractions are equivalent.	44	

Skills	Taught in these Lessons	Date Lessons Completed
Works equivalent-fraction problems with fractions that have 3-digit values; for example: $\frac{11}{10} = \frac{264}{\boxed{}}$.	46–48	
Uses division to determine whether pairs of fractions are equivalent.	48, 49	
Completes equations to determine whether two fractions are equivalent.	54–56	
Works equivalent-fraction problems by expressing the fraction that equals 1 as a fraction over a fraction.	55–58	
Works a mixed set of equivalent-fraction problems, some of which involve a complex fraction equal to 1.	59, 60	
Completes a series of equivalent fractions by referring to the first fraction in the series (for example: $\frac{2}{3} = \frac{\blacksquare}{18} = \frac{10}{\blacksquare} = \frac{4}{\blacksquare}$).	59–62	
Works equivalent-fraction problems in which one of the values is 1; for example: $\frac{3}{270} = \frac{1}{\square}$.	90	
Rewrites inequality statements for items that show more than one value on a side.	101, 102	
Comparison		
Converts two fractions into whole numbers and identifies the greater fraction.	25, 26	
Compares fractions, not all of which equal whole numbers.	27	
Compares fractions using $>, <,$ or $=$.	28, 29	
Completes inequality statements involving whole numbers and fractions.	90, 91	
Compares fractions with unlike denominators.	111, 112	

Level E Contents

Skills	Taught in these Lessons	Date Lessons Completed
Simplification		
Uses prime factors to simplify fractions.	31	
Simplifies fractions, some of which result in a numerator of 1.	32–37	
Simplifies fractions, some of which equal a whole number.	38	
Uses prime-factor analysis to determine whether fractions can be simplified.	41, 42	
Simplifies fractions and writes mixed numbers for fractions that are more than 1.	43	
Simplifies fractions in which the numerator and denominator are multiples of 10, 100, or 1000.	95–98	
Simplifies equivalent fractions in which the numerator and denominator end with one or more zeros.	99, 100	
WHOLE NUMBER PROPERTIES **Prime Numbers**		
Uses a calculator to determine if numbers are prime numbers.	21, 22	
Multiplies prime factors.	23	
Shows the prime factors for composite values.	24	
Uses a calculator to find the two prime factors of a larger composite number.	24, 25	
Writes equations for composite values to show only prime factors.	25–29	
Rewrites equations to show prime factors for two composite factors.	26, 27	
Shows the prime factors for composite values.	44	
Odd/Even Numbers		
Determines whether numbers are odd or even by dividing by 2.	91, 92	

Skills	Taught in these Lessons	Date Lessons Completed
Refers to the last digit of larger numbers to determine whether they are odd or even.	93	
Mental Arithmetic		
Works single-digit division problems mentally (for example: $3\overline{)23}$).	16–18	
Converts mixed numbers into fractions using mental math.	22	
Uses mental math to solve subtraction problems that have a difference of less than 10.	38, 39	
Works single-digit division problems mentally and writes the remainder as a fraction.	41	
Works problems mentally that require rewriting fractions as mixed numbers.	42, 43	
Determines the missing value for orally-presented problems; for example: 7 times some fraction equals 9. What's the fraction?	52–61	
Works problems of the form: $4x = 7; x = \blacksquare$.	62–64	
Works problems of the form: $4x = 7; 1x = \blacksquare$.	65, 66	
Identifies the missing factor for orally presented problems that tell about more than one object and ask about 1.	77	
MIXED NUMBER OPERATIONS		
Works column problems that add or subtract mixed numbers having like-denominator fractions.	74, 75	
Works addition and subtraction problems that have a whole number and a mixed number.	76, 77	
Simplifies mixed numbers that have fractions that equal 1.	79	

Level E Contents

Skills	Taught in these Lessons	Date Lessons Completed
Works column problems that add mixed numbers having like-denominator fractions and simplifies the answers.	80, 81	
Works subtraction problems in which the minuend is a whole number and the subtrahend is a mixed number.	84, 85	
Works column problems that add and subtract whole numbers and mixed numbers.	86, 87	
Works addition and subtraction problems involving mixed numbers that are in a ratio-table context.	88, 89	

NUMBER FAMILIES AND EXTENSIONS
Whole Number Operations

Skills	Taught in these Lessons	Date Lessons Completed
Writes column problems to find missing numbers in number families.	1–4	
Translates addition-subtraction problems into number-family problems and solves.	15–17	
Analyzes and solves addition-subtraction equations that do not have the missing value after the equal sign.	90–92	

Number-Family Tables

Skills	Taught in these Lessons	Date Lessons Completed
Computes the missing number in each row of a 3-by-3 table.	5–7	
Computes the missing number in each column of a 3-by-3 table.	7	
Figures out missing numbers in 3-by-3 tables by working rows and columns, respectively.	8	
Works the same 3-by-3 table twice, first using the columns as number families, then using the rows as number families.	9	
Works the same 3-by-3 table twice, first using the rows as number families, then using the columns as number families.	11, 12	

Skills	Taught in these Lessons	Date Lessons Completed
Completes a 3-by-3 table by first working rows with two numbers, then columns that have two numbers.	13–16	
Completes a 3-by-3 table.	33	

Fraction Number Families

Skills	Taught in these Lessons	Date Lessons Completed
Completes fraction number families that show a fraction and a big number of 1; for example: $\frac{\blacksquare}{\blacksquare} \; \frac{5}{8} \rightarrow 1$.	46, 47	
Completes fraction number families of the form: $\frac{3}{\blacksquare} \; \frac{7}{\blacksquare} \rightarrow \frac{\blacksquare}{\blacksquare}$.	51	
Makes fraction number families for statements of the form: M is $\frac{2}{5}$ of 1.	74, 75	
Makes number families for statements of the form: J is $\frac{3}{4}$ of B.	76	
Makes fraction number families for sentences that compare two values.	77–79	
Makes fraction number families for sentences that compare and sentences that classify.	84–86	
Makes fraction number families for sentences that refer to parts of a whole group.	93	
Writes fraction number families for sentences that tell about percents or about fractions.	112, 113	
Makes fraction number families based on illustrations of Xs in a bag.	113	

DECIMAL OPERATIONS
Addition/Subtraction

Skills	Taught in these Lessons	Date Lessons Completed
Writes and solves column addition and subtraction problems involving dollar-and-cent amounts.	31	
Writes row problems involving dollar-and-cent values as column problems.	73	

Level E Contents

Skills	Taught in these Lessons	Date Lessons Completed
Adds decimal values.	85	
Subtracts decimal values.	86	
Adds and subtracts decimal values.	87	
Adds and subtracts whole numbers and decimal values.	89	
Multiplication/Division		
Works problems that multiply a dollar-and-cent amount by a whole number.	75	
Works a mixed set of problems involving dollar-and-cent amounts.	78	
Multiplies a whole number and a decimal value.	99, 101	
Works multiplication problems that have two decimal values.	102	
Multiplies decimal values.	103–105	
Works division problems that have a decimal value in the dividend.	123	
COORDINATE SYSTEM **Points and Lines**		
Writes the X and Y values for points shown on the coordinate system.	49, 51	
Graphs points on the coordinate system given their X and Y values.	52, 53	
Completes a table to show X and Y values of points shown on a coordinate system.	54, 55	
Identifies incorrectly-plotted points on a coordinate system.	56, 57	
Relates a line on the coordinate system to values in a table.	56–58	
Functions		
Completes a function table that indicates X values for points on a line, and graphs those points.	114, 115	
Figures out a function and completes a function table.	117	
Generates possible functions for a given set of X and Y values and completes a function table.	118	

Skills	Taught in these Lessons	Date Lessons Completed
PROBLEM SOLVING **Addition/Subtraction**		
Makes number families for comparison sentences.	12, 13	
Uses number families to solve addition and subtraction comparison word problems.	14–16	
Uses number families to solve word problems that tell what happened first and next.	18–23	
Works number-family problems that refer to **in, out,** and **end up**.	34–36	
Uses number families to solve comparison word problems that ask about the difference number.	45	
Works number-family problems that tell about **goals** and **difference**.	87–89	
Makes vertical number families for word problems that tell about either **in** or **out**.	93–95	
Works a mixed set of word problems which require horizontal or vertical number families.	96, 97	
Number-Family Tables		
Answers questions by referring to a 3-by-3 table.	1	
Answers questions about comparative amounts by referring to a 3-by-3 table.	2–4	
Completes a 3-by-3 table and answers questions by referring to the table.	17	
Uses comparison facts to figure out numbers needed in a 3-by-3 table.	26–29	
Constructs and uses a 3-by-3 table with column and row headings.	33–35	
Constructs a 3-by-3 table using a comparison fact to figure out a needed number.	36–39	
Multi-Step Problems		
Works number-family problems that give more than one number for **in** and/or **out**.	37, 38	

Level E Contents

Skills	Taught in these Lessons	Date Lessons Completed
Works word problems that imply number families with more than one value for **in** or **out**.	39–44	
Works word problems that have two vertical number families (one for **in** and one for **out**).	45–48	
Works number-family problems involving dollar amounts and change.	81–83	
Works a mixed set of word problems that require vertical number families.	84	
Works horizontal goal problems that require vertical number families for **goal, now** or **both**.	96–98	
Works average problems by dividing.	111, 112	
Fraction Number Families		
Constructs fraction number families to solve word problems. (For example: $\frac{3}{5}$ of the children were girls. What fraction of the children were boys?)	47–49	
Uses fraction number families to solve word problems that tell about numbers and ask about fractions. (For example: 7 of the berries are ripe. 2 are not ripe. What fraction of the berries are not ripe?)	51, 52	
Works a mixed set of fraction number family problems.	53, 54	
Ratios and Proportions (Equations)		
Writes and solves ratio equations for word problems.	27–32	
Solves word problems and writes the answers as a number and a unit name.	40	
Works picture problems that show ratios and proportions.	42, 43	

Skills	Taught in these Lessons	Date Lessons Completed
Works proportion problems that involve 3- and 4-digit numbers.	49–51	
Answers questions by referring to complex ratios.	58–60	
Solves proportion problems, some of which require multiplying by a complex fraction equal to 1.	61–63	
Uses facts to complete a table that shows equivalent ratios.	63–66	
Graphs a line on the coordinate system for a set of equivalent ratios and answers questions based on the line.	71–77	
Works a set of problems that tell about more than 1 and ask a question.	78, 79	
Works a mixed set of word problems that require multiplication, division, or a ratio equation.	89, 101	
Works proportion word problems that have numbers that end in zeros.	101	
Computes averages.	108, 109	
Works a mixed set of multiplication and proportion problems that tell about 1 and ask about more than 1.	121–123	
Ratios and Proportions (Tables)		
Completes ratio tables.	52–55	
Solves word problems using ratio tables.	56–63	
Works ratio-table problems that give information for fraction number families.	64–66	
Works ratio-table problems, some of which require fraction number families.	67–69	
Uses facts to complete a table that shows equivalent ratios and checks work by graphing points on the coordinate system.	68, 69	

Level E Contents

Skills	Taught in these Lessons	Date Lessons Completed
Works ratio-table problems that have a comparison statement involving fractions. For example: The sand weighed $\frac{2}{5}$ as much as the cement.	82–84	
Works a mixed set of ratio-table problems, some of which compare.	87, 88	
Works ratio-table problems in which the second column contains two mixed numbers.	91, 92	
Makes fraction number families and ratio tables for problems that do not provide fraction information.	94, 95	
Discriminates between problems that require a ratio table and those that require only a ratio equation.	105, 106	
Works ratio-table problems that involve percents.	106–109	
Uses a ratio table to work word problems that give two or three names.	107	
Works ratio-table problems that compare percents.	110, 111	
Works a mixed set of ratio-table problems that include fractions and percents.	114	

Multiplication/Division

Skills	Taught in these Lessons	Date Lessons Completed
Works word problems of the form: 4 cakes = 7 pounds, 1 cake = ■.	71, 72	
Identifies the missing factor for problems that tell about more than one object and ask about 1. For example: 3 toys weigh 16 ounces. What does 1 toy weigh?	73, 76	
Works multiplication word problems that tell about 1 and ask about more than 1.	81	
Works multiplication and division word problems.	82–85	

Skills	Taught in these Lessons	Date Lessons Completed
Works a mixed set of multiplication and division problems that use the words **each** and **per**.	87, 88	
Works problems that describe the division of a quantity into equal-sized parts.	98–100	
Solves word problems that refer to even and odd numbers.	103, 104	
Works word problems that require decimal multiplication.	106, 107	
Works division problems in which the answer refers to non-divisible entities.	115, 116	
Works word problems that require division of a dollar amount.	124	

Inverse Operations

Skills	Taught in these Lessons	Date Lessons Completed
Works 2-step word problems that give the starting number and two operations.	104	
Uses inverse operations to solve pairs of equations and figures out the starting number.	105–108	
Uses inverse operations to solve word problems.	109–111	
Works word problems that generate a series of inverse-operation equations.	112, 114	
Works story problems that involve inverse operations.	124, 125	

Measurement

Skills	Taught in these Lessons	Date Lessons Completed
Completes a series of equivalent fractions, based on equivalent measures.	105, 106	
Works problems that compare different units of measurement.	107–111	

PROBABILITY

Skills	Taught in these Lessons	Date Lessons Completed
Writes fractions that represent the probability of pulling an X from a bag.	112	
Uses information presented as a fraction to generate a set of objects.	113, 114	

Level E Contents

Skills	Taught in these Lessons	Date Lessons Completed
Relates the composition of a set to the number of trials required to give each member one chance of being selected.	114	
Works ratio-table problems that involve probability.	115–119	
Determines which set of objects provides the best chance of drawing a winner.	124	
GEOMETRY **Perimeter and Area**		
Figures out the lengths of sides in quadrilaterals with parallel sides.	56, 57	
Computes perimeters of polygons.	58–61	
Works area-of-rectangle problems shown on the coordinate system using the equation: squares = $x \times y$.	62–65	
Works area and perimeter problems for rectangles shown on the coordinate system.	66, 68	
Works area and perimeter problems for rectangles shown on the coordinate system.	69–72	
Works area-of-triangle problems shown on the coordinate system.	74, 75	
Works area problems for rectangles and triangles that are not shown on the coordinate system.	76, 77	
Works area-of-parallelogram problems shown on the coordinate system.	79, 80	
Works area and perimeter problems for parallelograms shown on the coordinate system.	81, 82	
Works area and perimeter problems for parallelograms that are not shown on the coordinate system.	83, 85	
Works area problems for triangles and parallelograms that are not shown on the coordinate system.	86	

Skills	Taught in these Lessons	Date Lessons Completed
Finds the area of non-right triangles shown on the coordinate system by constructing parallelograms.	96	
Finds the area and perimeter of non-right triangles that are not shown on the coordinate system.	97	
Finds the area and perimeter of parallelograms, rectangles and triangles.	98	
Circles		
Figures out the relationship between the diameter and circumference of a circle.	91	
Uses the equation $\pi \times D = C$ to figure out the circumference of a circle.	92	
Uses the equation $\pi \times D = C$ to figure out the circumference or diameter of a circle.	93–95	
Uses the equation $\pi \times D = C$ to figure out the circumference or radius of a circle.	111, 112	
Uses the equation $\pi \times D = C$ to figure out the circumference, radius, or diameter of a circle.	113	
Uses the equation $A = \pi \times r \times r$ to figure out the area of a circle.	113, 114	
Finds the circumference and the area of circles.	115, 117	
Surface Area		
Computes the surface area of a rectangular prism.	94–96	
Finds the surface area of a rectangular prism from a non-exploded diagram.	97, 98	
Finds the surface area of a pyramid with a rectangular base.	99–101	
Finds the surface area of a pyramid that has a triangular base.	102, 103	

Level E Contents

Skills	Taught in these Lessons	Date Lessons Completed
Volume		
Finds the volume of rectangular prisms.	104, 105	
Finds the volume of a triangular prism.	106, 109	
Finds the volume of rectangular and triangular prisms.	107	
Finds the surface area and volume of a rectangular prism.	108	
Angles and Lines		
Indicates whether pairs of lines are parallel or not parallel.	55	
Answers questions about the number of degrees in angles.	71	
Makes number families to solve angle problems involving an angle that is divided into two smaller angles.	72, 73	
Works problems requiring conversion of a fraction of a circle into degrees.	74, 75	
Uses a fact about a fraction of a circle to make a number family and work problems involving three angles.	77–79	
Makes number families to solve angle problems involving complementary and supplementary angles.	81, 82	
Identifies corresponding angles.	83	
Figures out the degrees in corresponding and supplementary angles.	84–86	
Figures out the degrees in four angles that are formed by two intersecting lines.	88, 89	
Figures out the rule for vertically opposite angles formed by two intersecting lines.	91	
Applies the rule for vertically opposite angles to figure out corresponding sets of angles at parallel lines.	92, 93	
Uses a protractor to measure degrees in an angle.	118	

Skills	Taught in these Lessons	Date Lessons Completed
PROJECTS		
Does the groundwork for building a model of the solar system.	116	
Uses ratio numbers to complete a table about the solar system and makes a scale model.	117	
Completes a circle graph based on a table that shows amounts of time a person spent on various activities.	118	
Constructs a circle graph to show use of time.	119	
Gathers data on favorite colors and complete a table that shows tallies, numbers, and degrees.	119	
Constructs a bar graph and circle graph to display percents for various geometric shapes selected as favorites by 20 different people.	120	
Constructs a bar graph to display the average percents of 10 student surveys conducted in lesson 120.	121	
Compares the ratio of surface area to volume for cubes that are relatively large and small.	122	
Determines the contents of a bag based on experimental data and expected outcomes.	123	
Figures out the threshold of efficiency for a square (the size at which the perimeter and area have the same number of units).	124	
Conducts an experiment and displays the results as a frequency distribution.	125	

For Level E Placement Test, see page 189.

Lesson 52 (Presentation Book)

Materials

- Each student will need a ruler for exercise 3.

Objectives

- **Determine the missing value for orally-presented problems of the form: 7 times some fraction equals 9. What's the fraction?** (Exercise 1)
  Note: For some problems, students answer orally. For others, they write the missing fraction.

- **Complete ratio tables.** (Exercise 2)
  Note: The tables have columns that work like number families, with the total at the bottom of each column. The same "multiplier" is used in each row:

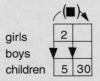

girls	2	
boys		
children	5	30

Students find the missing number in the first column:

girls	2	
boys	▼ 3 ▼	
children	5	30

Then they work a proportion problem that involves a row with two numbers and one of the other rows:

$$\frac{boys}{children} \quad \frac{3}{5}\left(\frac{6}{6}\right) = \frac{18}{30}$$; then figure out the missing number in the last column by adding or subtracting:

girls	2	12
boys	▼ 3 ▼	18
children	5	30

- **Graph points on the coordinate system given their X and Y values.** (Exercise 3)

- Complete division problems in which the whole-number part of the initial answer is either correct or too large. (Exercise 4)

- Use fraction number families to solve word problems that tell about numbers and ask about fractions. (Exercise 5)

EXERCISE 1 MENTAL MULTIPLICATION
Missing Factor

a. You're going to do some mental math.
b. I'll do the first problem: 5 times some fraction equals 3. What's the fraction? 3\5.
c. Your turn: 5 times some fraction equals 4. What's the fraction? (Signal.) *4-fifths.*
- 5 times some fraction equals 9. What's the fraction? (Signal.) *9-fifths.*
- 8 times some fraction equals 9. What's the fraction? (Signal.) *9-eighths.*
(Repeat step c until firm.)

d. Write part O on your paper. Then write A through D. √
- I'll say some more problems. For each problem, you're going to write the missing fraction. Remember, don't write the whole equation, just the missing fraction. Everybody ready?
e. Problem A: 7 times some fraction equals 9. Write the fraction. (Tap your foot 3 times.)
- Problem B: 3 times some fraction equals 4. Write the fraction. (Tap your foot 3 times.)
- Problem C: 8 times some fraction equals 11. Write the fraction. (Tap your foot 3 times.)
- Problem D: 6 times some fraction equals 1. Write the fraction. (Tap your foot 3 times.)

f. Check your work.
- Problem A. What do you multiply 7 by to get 9? (Signal.) *9-sevenths.*
- Problem B. What do you multiply 3 by to get 4? (Signal.) *4-thirds.*
- Problem C. What do you multiply 8 by to get 11? (Signal.) *11-eighths.*
- Problem D. What do you multiply 6 by to get 1? (Signal.) *1-sixth.*

EXERCISE 2 PROPORTIONS
Ratio Tables

a. Open your textbook to lesson 52 and find part 1. √
- (Teacher reference:)

$$\frac{women}{adults} \quad \frac{2}{5} \quad \left(\frac{30}{30}\right) = \frac{\boxed{60}}{150}$$

- I'll read what it says. Follow along: You've worked ratio problems that have two names. Later, you're going to work ratio problems that have three names.
- Look at the table with names for **clean** dogs, **dirty** dogs, and **dogs.**
- You'll use this kind of table to work ratio problems with three names.
- The arrow on top of the table shows that you have to multiply all the numbers in the first column by the same value to get the numbers in the second column.
- The arrows pointing down each column show that the columns work just like number families. The top numbers are small numbers. The number at the bottom of each column is a big number. If you have two numbers in a column, you can figure out the third number.
- Look at the second table. It has numbers.
- How many numbers are shown in the first column? (Signal.) *Two.*
- So you can figure out the missing number in that column. The numbers shown are 3 and 8. A small number is missing.
- What's the missing number? (Signal.) *5.*
- That's the number for **dirty** dogs in the first column.
- Look at the second column.
- Raise your hand when you've figured out the missing number in that column.
- Everybody, what's the missing number in the second column? (Signal.) *32.*
- That's the number for all the **dogs** in the second column.

b. Look at the first table on the next page. It has names for men, women, and adults.
- You can figure out all the missing numbers in that table.
- How many numbers are shown in the first column? (Signal.) *Two.*
- So you can figure out the missing number in that column.
- Everybody, what's the missing number? (Signal.) *3.*
- How many numbers are shown in the second column? (Signal.) *One.*
- So you can't figure out the missing number in that column by adding or subtracting. But you can make a ratio equation.
- You can see the ratio equation showing the number of women to the number of adults.
- The numerators are the values from the women row—2 and box. The denominators are the values from the adults row—5 and 150.
- When you work that ratio problem, you find out that there are 60 women.
- You write that number in the women row of the table. Then you can figure out the missing number for men by subtracting: 150 minus 60.
- The answer is 90. There are 90 men.

Workbook Practice

a. Open your workbook to lesson 52 and find part 1. √
b. Problem A shows a table with the names **boys, girls** and **children.**
- Look at the first column. What's the number for boys? (Signal.) *5.*
- The number for girls is missing. But the number for total children is given. What's the number for children? (Signal.) *8.*
- You can figure out the number of **girls** by subtracting. Write the number for girls in the first column. Raise your hand when you're finished. √
- Everybody, what number did you write? (Signal.) *3.*
c. Now we can make a ratio equation. That equation must have the numbers from the **row** of the table that has two numbers.
- Find the row that has two numbers and look at the name of that row. Everybody, what's the name? (Signal.) *Children.*
- So one of the names in your ratio equation must be children. The other name can be either **boys** or **girls.** We'll figure out the ratio of **girls** to children.

- (Write on the board:)

$$\text{a.} \quad \frac{\text{girls}}{\text{children}} - \left(\quad\right) = \underline{\quad}$$

d. The numbers from the first column of the table go in the first fraction. The number from the second column of the table goes in the last fraction.
- What's the number for girls in the first fraction? (Signal.) *3.*
- What's the number for children in the first fraction? (Signal.) *8.*
- The last fraction has another number for children. What number? (Signal.) *40.*
- (Write to show:)

$$\text{a.} \quad \frac{\text{girls}}{\text{children}} \quad \frac{3}{8} \left(\quad\right) = \frac{\boxed{}}{40}$$

- Here's the ratio equation.
e. Your turn: Next to the table in problem A, write the ratio equation. Figure out the number for girls. Box the answer. Then write that number where it belongs in the second column of the table. Raise your hand when you're finished.
  (Observe students and give feedback.)
- Everybody, what's the number for girls in the second column? (Signal.) *15.*
- Make sure you have 15 for girls in the second column. Now you have two numbers in the second column of your table. So you can figure out the missing number. Subtract and figure out the number of boys. Write it in the table. Raise your hand when you're finished. √
- Everybody, what's the number for boys in the second column? (Signal.) *25.*
- Yes, in the second column, there are 25 boys and 15 girls. So there is a total of 40 children.
f. Table B. Write the missing number in the first column. Raise your hand when you've done that much. √
- Everybody, what's the missing number in the first column? (Signal.) *4.*
- The equation must have the numbers from the **row** of the table that has two numbers. What's the name for that row? (Signal.) *Girls.*
- Write the ratio equation for **boys** to **girls.** Show boys on top. Raise your hand when you have an equation with names, **three** numbers and a box.
  (Observe students and give feedback.)

- (Write on the board:)

$$\text{b.} \quad \frac{\text{boys}}{\text{girls}} \quad \frac{4}{5} \left(\quad\right) = \frac{\boxed{}}{30}$$

- Here's what you should have. Figure out the number for boys. Write it in the table. Then figure out the number of children in the second column. Raise your hand when you've written all the numbers in your table.
  (Observe students and give feedback.)
- Check your work. Everybody, how many boys are there in the second column? (Signal.) *24.*
- How many total children are there in the second column? (Signal.) *54.*
- Yes, there are 24 boys and 30 girls. That's 54 total children. Raise your hand if you got it right.
g. Table C. Write the number for boys in the first column. Raise your hand when you've done that much. √
- Everybody, what's the number for boys in the first column? (Signal.) *2.*
- Yes, 2. What's the name of the **row** that has two numbers? (Signal.) *Girls.*
- Write the equation for the ratio of **girls** to **children.** Show girls on top. Figure out the number of children in the second column. Then figure out the other missing number in the second column. Raise your hand when you've written all the numbers in your table.
  (Observe students and give feedback.)
- (Write on the board:)

$$\text{c.} \quad \frac{\text{girls}}{\text{children}} \quad \frac{3}{5} \left(\frac{9}{9}\right) = \frac{27}{\boxed{45}}$$

- Here's the ratio of girls to children. There are 45 children. You put that number in the table and figured out the number of boys in the second column. Everybody, what number? (Signal.) *18.*
- Yes, there are 27 girls and 18 boys. That's 45 children. Raise your hand if you got everything right.
h. Table D. Write the number for children in the first column. Raise your hand when you've done that much. √
- Everybody, what's the number for children in the first column? (Signal.) *10.*
- Yes, 10. What's the name of the **row** that has two numbers? (Signal.) *Boys.*

- Write the equation for the ratio of **boys** to **girls**. Show boys on top. Figure out the number of girls in the second column. Then figure out the other missing number in the second column. Raise your hand when you've written all the numbers in your table.
  (Observe students and give feedback.)
- (Write on the board:)

d. $\dfrac{\text{boys}}{\text{girls}} \quad \dfrac{3}{7} \left(\dfrac{4}{4} \right) = \dfrac{12}{\boxed{28}}$

- Here's the ratio of boys to girls. There are 28 girls. You put that number in the table and figured out the number of children. Everybody, what number? (Signal.) *40.*
- There are 12 boys and 28 girls. That's 40 children.
i. Raise your hand if you got everything right.

EXERCISE 3 COORDINATE SYSTEM
Graphing Points

a. Find part 2.
   You're going to make points on the coordinate system and write a letter next to each point. Points are little dots. The points you'll make will **always be at the corners of squares on the coordinate system.** The description tells about the X value and the Y value for each point.
b. Point A: X equals 5, Y equals 7. You follow those directions by starting at zero. You go some places along the X axis. How many places? (Signal.) *5.*
- Then you go up some places for Y. How many places? (Signal.) *7.*
- Then you make a dot and write a small capital A above the dot. Do it. Make the point for A. Raise your hand when you're finished.
  (Observe students and give feedback.)
c. Point B. What does X equal? (Signal.) *8.*
- What does Y equal? (Signal.) *10.*
- Go 8 places for X and 10 places for Y. Make the point and write the letter B above that point. Raise your hand when you're finished.
  (Observe students and give feedback.)
d. Point C. What does X equal? (Signal.) *Zero.*
- What does Y equal? (Signal.) *2.*
- Make the point and write the letter C above that point. Raise your hand when you're finished.
  (Observe students and give feedback.)
e. Point D. What does X equal? (Signal.) *3.*
- What does Y equal? (Signal.) *5.*
- Make the point and write the letter D above that point. Raise your hand when you're finished.
  (Observe students and give feedback.)

f. Check your work. Take your ruler and very carefully draw a line through the points you made. Draw the line from one edge of the coordinate system to the other. If you do it the right way, all your points will be on the same line. If your points are not all lined up, you made a mistake. Any point that is off the line is in the wrong place. Check that point and correct it.

EXERCISE 4 LONG DIVISION
Quotient Too Large

a. Find part 3.
   For some of these problems, the whole number part of the answer is too big. For some of these problems, the answer is right. Remember, if the answer to the first problem in the item is right, figure out the remainder. If the answer is too big, work the other problem with an answer that's **1 less.**
b. Your turn: Work the problems in part 3. Raise your hand when you're finished.
   (Observe students and give feedback.)

Key:

a. $24\overline{)175}^{\,8} \quad -192$ $\qquad 24\overline{)175}^{\,7\frac{7}{24}} \quad -168 \atop 7$ $\qquad$ b. $65\overline{)623}^{\,9} \quad -585 \atop 38$ $\qquad 65\overline{)623}^{\,9\frac{38}{65}}$

c. $49\overline{)250}^{\,4} \quad -245 \atop 5$ $\qquad 49\overline{)250}^{\,5\frac{5}{49}}$ $\qquad$ d. $78\overline{)498}^{\,7} \quad -546$ $\qquad 78\overline{)498}^{\,6\frac{30}{78}} \quad -468 \atop 30$

c. Check your work. Find part J on page 168 in your textbook. That shows what you should have for each problem. Check your work over and fix up any mistakes. Raise your hand if you got everything right.

EXERCISE 5 PROBLEM SOLVING
Fraction Number Families

a. Find part 2 in your textbook. √
- These are problems that tell about **numbers** and ask about **fractions.**
b. Problem A. Listen: There were 24 people. 19 of the people were wealthy. The rest were not wealthy. What fraction of the people were wealthy? What fraction of the people were not wealthy?
- Your turn: Make the number family with the names and the three fractions. Box the fractions that answer the questions. Raise your hand when you're finished.
  (Observe students and give feedback.)

- (Write on the board:)

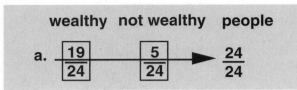

- Here's what you should have. The names are **wealthy, not wealthy** and **people.** The problem gives a number for people. That's 24. So the fraction for the big number is 24/24. That's all the people. What's the fraction for the people who are wealthy? (Signal.) *19-twenty-fourths.*
- What's the fraction for the people who are not wealthy? (Signal.) *5-twenty-fourths.*
- Raise your hand if you got everything right.
- c. Your turn: Work problem B. Raise your hand when you're finished.
  (Observe students and give feedback.)
- (Write on the board:)

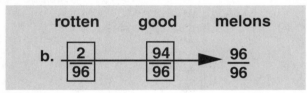

- Here's what you should have. The names are **rotten, good** and **melons.** There are 96 melons. So the fraction that equals 1 is 96/96. What's the fraction for rotten melons? (Signal.) *2-ninety-sixths.*
- What's the fraction for good melons? (Signal.) *94-ninety-sixths.*

- d. Your turn: Work the rest of the problems in part 2. Raise your hand when you're finished.
  (Observe students and give feedback.)
- e. (Write on the board:)

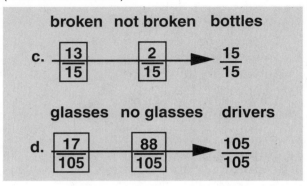

- Check your work. Here's what you should have for problems C and D. Raise your hand if you got everything right.

EXERCISE 6 INDEPENDENT WORK

- a. Do the independent work for lesson 52 of your textbook.
- b. (Assign *Connecting Math Concepts Independent Worksheet* 29 as classwork or homework. Before beginning the next lesson, check the students' independent work.)

Level E, Lesson 52 (Textbook)

This exercise combines what students have learned about number families and ratios/proportions.

Students have learned to solve classification word problems using a number-family strategy.

For example: There are 72 dogs. 48 of the dogs are clean. How many dirty dogs are there?

clean   dirty   dogs
  48   □ ►72

The position of the missing value indicates that students must subtract to find the number of dirty dogs.

Students have also learned to work simple ratio problems that involve two names.

For example: The ratio of women to adults is 2 to 5. If there are 150 adults, how many women are there?

Problems of this type appear in the independent work section of this lesson, textbook **part 4.**

After reading the explanation, students work the ratio-table problems in **part 1** of the workbook (see page 132).

Fraction number families were introduced in lesson 46. For

problem a, students write:

$$\underset{\text{wealthy}}{\boxed{\frac{19}{24}}} \, \underset{\substack{\text{not} \\ \text{wealthy}}}{\boxed{\frac{5}{24}}} \, \xrightarrow{\text{people}} \, \underline{} \; .$$

The problems in **part 2** prepare students for more advanced applications with ratio tables. For example: $\frac{5}{8}$ of the bottles are not broken. 12 bottles are broken. How many bottles are there in all? This type of problem is introduced in lesson 67.

Part 2 **Make a fraction number family for each word problem. Box the answers to the questions the problem asks.**

a. There were 24 people. 19 of the people were wealthy. The rest were not wealthy. What fraction of the people were wealthy? What fraction of the people were not wealthy?

b. At Joe's Market, there are 2 watermelons that are rotten and 94 watermelons that are good. What fraction of the melons are rotten? What fraction of the melons are good?

c. There was a total of 15 bottles. 13 of those bottles were broken. What fraction of the bottles were broken? What fraction of the bottles were not broken?

d. 17 of the drivers wore glasses. 88 drivers did not wear glasses. What fraction of the drivers wore glasses? What fraction of the drivers did not wear glasses?

Independent Work

Parts 3 through 7 are the independent work for lesson 52. These parts review problem types that were practiced in a structured form in earlier lessons.

Part 3 **For each problem, write the whole number as a fraction and work the problem.**

a. $4 - \frac{7}{8} = \blacksquare$ b. $\frac{3}{4} + 8 = \blacksquare$ c. $\frac{3}{4} \times 8 = \blacksquare$

Part 4 **For each item, make a ratio equation and answer the question.**

a. The ratio of posts to beams is 3 to 8. There are 72 beams. How many posts are there?

b. The shadow grows 7 inches every 3 minutes. If the shadow grows 56 inches, how many minutes have passed?

c. A machine uses 6 tons of fuel every 5 days. How many days would it take the machine to use 300 tons of fuel?

Lesson 52   **167**

Part 3 requires students to discriminate between problems in which the whole number must be rewritten with a common denominator (addition/subtraction) and multiplication problems, in which the whole number may be rewritten over 1. The teaching for this discrimination occurred in lessons 32–34.

These problems require students to make a ratio equation. For item c, students write: $\frac{\text{tons}}{\text{days}} \frac{6}{5} (-) = \frac{300}{\square}$. This problem type was introduced in lesson 27, and occurred in nine lessons. It is a component skill for more advanced ratio and proportion problems that involve three names.

The type of multistep problems shown in **part 5** were taught in lessons 39–48. Students use a number-family strategy to work the problems. For item c, students write: They add to find the totals for "in" and "out" values, then work a subtraction problem for the main number family to solve the problem.

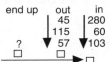

end up	out	in
	45	280
	115	60
?	57	103

Part 5 For each item, make a number family. Answer the question.

a. Mr. Jones had lots of eggs. He delivered 144 eggs to Joe's Market. He delivered 84 eggs to Fran's Market. He delivered 66 eggs to AC Market. Mr. Jones still had 300 eggs. How many eggs did he start out with?

b. A large balloon had 11 pounds of air in it. Then 4 pounds more were pumped into the balloon. Then some air leaked out of the balloon. The balloon ended up with 3 pounds of air in it. How many pounds leaked out?

c. A hat store had 280 hats in stock. On Monday, the store sold 45 hats. The store also received a shipment of 60 hats. On Tuesday, the store sold 115 hats. On Wednesday, the store sold 57 hats. The store also received 103 hats. How many hats did the store have at the end of the day on Wednesday?

Part 6 Copy and work each problem.

a. $6\overline{)1100}$ b. $3\overline{)2103}$ c. $8\overline{)1591}$ d. $5\overline{)703}$

Part 7 Copy and complete each equation. If the fractions are equal, write the simple equation below.

a. $\frac{4}{7}\left(\blacksquare\right) = \frac{40}{63}$ b. $\frac{2}{9}\left(\blacksquare\right) = \frac{420}{1890}$ c. $\frac{1}{15}\left(\blacksquare\right) = \frac{40}{675}$

Students refer to the **part J Answer Key** after they have worked all the problems in the workbook, **part 3** (see page 132).

For the problems in **part 6,** students work a short division strategy that involves "carrying." For example, the work for item c looks like this:

c. $8\overline{)15\,9\,1}$ giving $198\frac{7}{8}$

The carrying strategy was introduced in lesson 22, and work on various problem types continued through lesson 37. **Part 6** presents a full range of problems, including those with a zero in the answer (items b, d) and those where the divisor is larger than the first digit in the dividend (items a, b, c).

The problems in **part 7** require students to discriminate between pairs of fractions that are equivalent and pairs that are not. For equivalent fractions, students write a "simple equation" below. For item b,

students write: $\frac{2}{9}\left(\frac{210}{210}\right) = \frac{420}{1890}$

$\frac{2}{9} = \frac{420}{1890}$ ·

This discrimination was first introduced in lessons 21–23, with simple problems (e.g., $\frac{4}{5} \times - = \frac{12}{15}$). In lessons 43–45, students learned the calculator skills for working problems with larger numbers. The discrimination and calculator skills were combined in lessons 48 and 49.

Level E, Lesson 52 (Workbook)

Students complete **part 1** of the workbook after reading the explanation in **part 1** of the textbook. Problems of this type prepare students for advanced ratio and proportion word problems that involve three names. For example: There were perch and bass in a pond. The ratio of perch to bass is 8 to 5. There is a total of 260 fish in the pond. How many bass are in the pond? How many perch are in the pond?

The coordinate system was introduced in lesson 49. In lessons 49 and 51, students wrote the X and Y values for points shown on a coordinate system. The task in **part 2** occurs in lessons 52 and 53. Starting in lesson 114, students will plot functions on the coordinate system (e.g., y = x + 3).

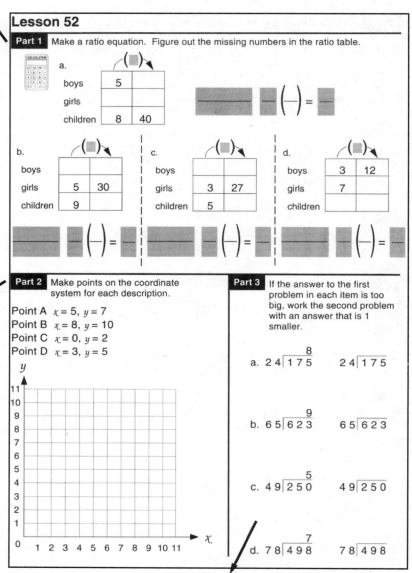

In lessons 46 through 48, students completed 2-digit divisor problems in which the estimated answer was given, and was correct.

The exercise in **part 3** appears for four consecutive lessons. It prepares students for problems in which the estimated answer is too large.

In lessons 58–61, students will work with problems that have estimated answers that are too small.

By lesson 86, students will be estimating answers and working the complete algorithm for a full range of division problems.

Level E

Sample Track: Fraction Number Families

In preparation for work with ratio tables and problems involving proportions, students are introduced to fraction number families. The work begins in Lesson 46. Fraction number families are like whole-number families except that all the values are fractions with the same denominator, and one of the fractions equals one whole.

The word problems introduced in Lesson 47 have the fraction that equals 1 as the big number. All problems involve binary classification. For example:

There are cars on Al's lot. 2/7 of them are dirty. What fraction of the cars are not dirty?

All the cars are represented as one whole: $\frac{7}{7}$. The denominator of the fraction is determined by the other fraction in the problem—$\frac{2}{7}$. The missing fraction is the value that is combined with $\frac{2}{7}$ to give $\frac{7}{7}$.

Beginning with Lesson 74, students work comparison fraction problems. The problem compares some value to 1 or to a letter that is represented by 1.

Example:

M is 7/5 of 1.

M is more than 1. Here's the family:

Dif	One	M
$\frac{2}{5}$	$\frac{5}{5}$	$\frac{7}{5}$

Example:

J is 3/4 of B.

The sentence compares J to B. B is 1. Here's the family:

Dif	J	B
$\frac{1}{4}$	$\frac{3}{4}$	$\frac{4}{4}$

Example:

R is 8/5 of T.

The sentence compares R to T. T is 1. R is more than 1. Here's the family:

Dif	T	R
$\frac{3}{5}$	$\frac{5}{5}$	$\frac{8}{5}$

Here's part of the introduction from Lesson 76:

c. Sample sentence: J is 1/4 of T. That's just like: J is 1/4 of 1. T is 1.

- Listen: J is 1/4 of T. So is J more than T or less than T? (Signal.) *Less than T.*
- So J is a small number. T is the big number. And T is 1.
- (Write on the board:)

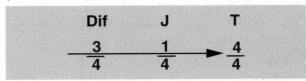

- Here's the number family for: J is 1/4 of T.

d. Problem A: M is 7/3 of B. That's just like: M is 7/3 of 1. B is 1.

- Listen: M is 7/3 of B. Is M more than B or less than B? (Signal.) *More than B.*
- So **M** is the big number. **B** is a small number. And B is 1. Make the number family. Raise your hand when you're finished. √
- (Write on the board:)

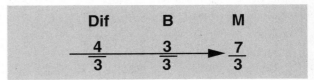

- Here's what you should have. M is 7/3 of B. **M** is the big number. **B** is a small number. It equals 1 whole—3/3. The difference is 4/3. Raise your hand if you got it right.

e. Problem B: R is 5/8 of B. Which letter equals 1? (Signal.) *B.*

- Listen: R is 5/8 of B. Is R more than B or less than B? (Signal.) *Less than B.*
- Make the number family. Raise your hand when you're finished.
  (Observe students and give feedback.)

- (Write on the board:)

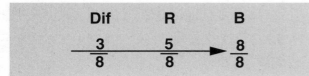

- Here's what you should have. R is 5/8 of B. **R** is a small number. **B** is the big number. B is 1. It's 8/8.
f. Work problem c. Raise your hand when you're finished. (Observe students and give feedback.)
- (Write on the board:)

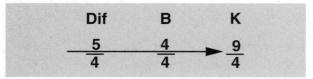

- Here's what you should have. K is 9/4 of B. **K** is more than B. **K** is the big number. **B** is the small number. B is 1. It's 4/4. The difference is 5/4.

In Lesson 78, students make number families from sentences that compare two names. For example:

Donald runs 7/8 as far as Ginger; Fran is 5/4 the height of Ann; Today, we collected 8/5 the amount we collected yesterday.

The procedure is the same as for previous lessons. The name something is compared to is 1. It's the name at the end of the sentence. The other name is either more than 1 or less than 1, depending on the value of the fraction.

Here's part of the introduction from Lesson 78:

c. Sentence A: The train was 3/4 as long as the station.
- Everybody, which name equals 1? (Signal.) *The station.*
- The first thing named is the train. Is it more than the station or less than the station? (Signal.) *Less than the station.*
- Make the number family with three names and three fractions. Raise your hand when you're finished. (Observe students and give feedback.)
- (Write on the board:)

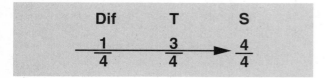

- Here's what you should have. The train is a small number. The station is the big number. It's 4/4. The difference is 1/4.

d. Sentence B: The cost of the book was 5/3 the cost of the radio.
- Everybody, which name equals 1? (Signal.) *The radio.*
- Does the book cost more or less than the radio? (Signal.) *More.*
- Make the number family. Raise your hand when you're finished. (Observe students and give feedback.)
- (Write on the board:)

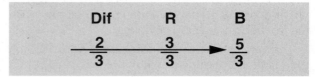

- Check your work. Here's the family you should have. The book is the big number. The radio is a small number. It's 3/3. The difference is 2/3.

With the knowledge of how comparative statements translate into fraction number families, students are prepared to work problems that involve percents.

For example, here's a sentence:

The regular price of shoes is 120% of the sale price.

Here's the family:

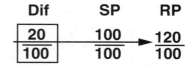

The regular price is more than 1. It's the big number. The sale price is 1. The difference is 20-hundreths or 20 percent.

The work with fraction number families prepares students for later work with complex proportion problems involving fractions, probability, and percents.

Level Bridge

Overview of Level Bridge and Level F

Connecting Math Concepts, Level Bridge is appropriate for students in grades 6 and above, who have not been through the Bridge, and who pass the placement test.

The Bridge is a 70-lesson program designed to prepare students who are new to *Connecting Math Concepts* for Level F (100 lessons).

Connecting Math Concepts, Level Bridge provides students with a thorough understanding of foundational concepts that many sixth graders fail to master, including fractions and mixed numbers, decimals and percents, and operational relationships. Students learn to solve a wide range of word problems, including multi-step problems, ratios and proportions, and problems involving tables and data analysis. Other topics include place value and estimation, area and perimeter, angles and lines, and the coordinate system.

The program may be used as a stand-alone course in preparation for a basic pre-algebra course, or, preferably, in combination with Level F of *Connecting Math Concepts* for a more complete mathematical foundation, including decimal operations, volume, signed numbers, and exponents.

Note: Students who have successfully completed *Connecting Math Concepts,* Level Bridge should not be placed in Level E. They should proceed directly to Level F.

Scope and Sequence for *Connecting Math Concepts, Level Bridge*

The Bridge may be used in preparation for Level F. The Scope and Sequence Chart shows where each track or major topic begins and where it ends.

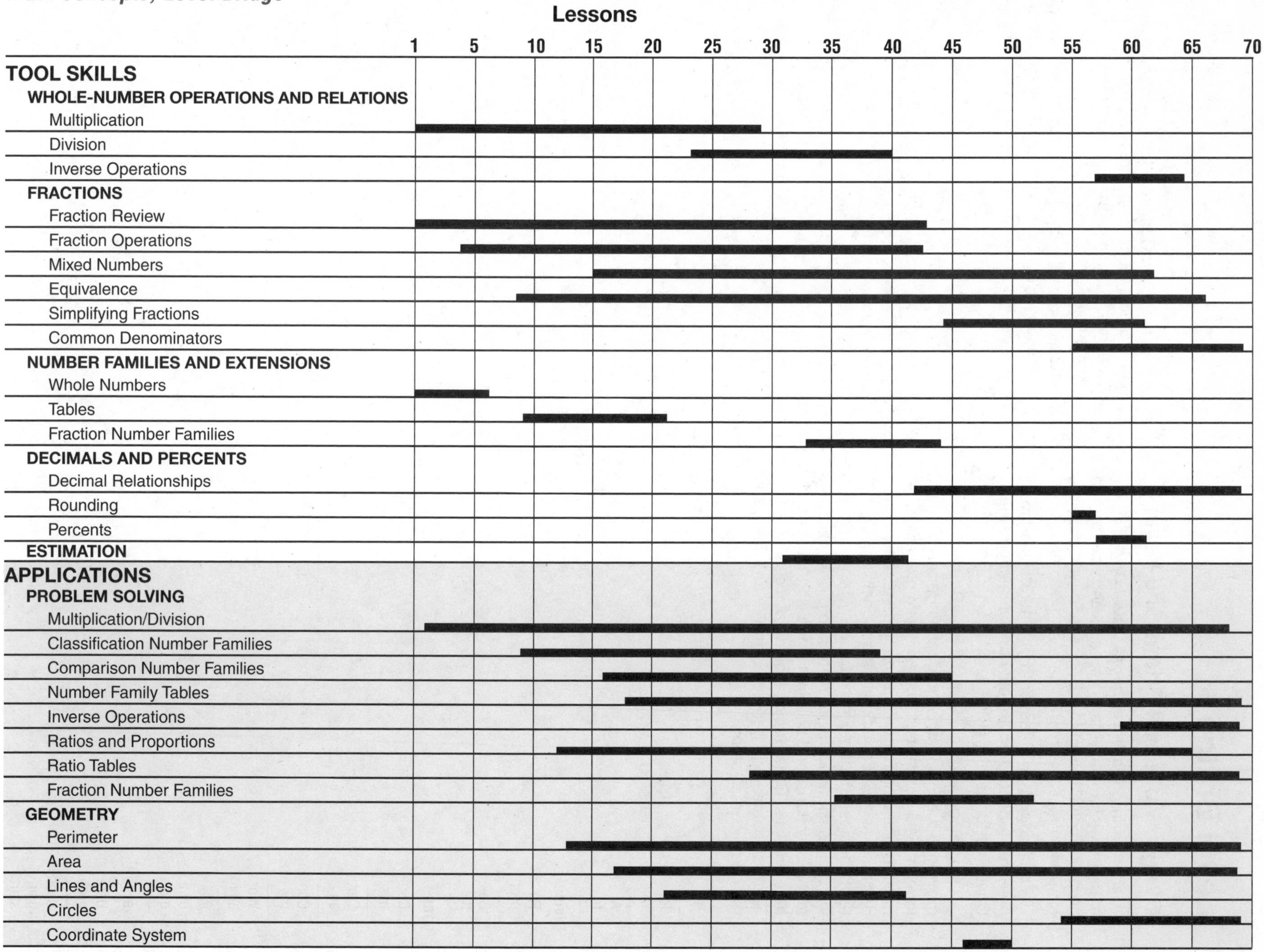

Lessons

(Lesson scale across top: 1, 5, 10, 15, 20, 25, 30, 35, 40, 45, 50, 55, 60, 65, 70)

TOOL SKILLS

WHOLE-NUMBER OPERATIONS AND RELATIONS
- Multiplication
- Division
- Inverse Operations

FRACTIONS
- Fraction Review
- Fraction Operations
- Mixed Numbers
- Equivalence
- Simplifying Fractions
- Common Denominators

NUMBER FAMILIES AND EXTENSIONS
- Whole Numbers
- Tables
- Fraction Number Families

DECIMALS AND PERCENTS
- Decimal Relationships
- Rounding
- Percents

ESTIMATION

APPLICATIONS

PROBLEM SOLVING
- Multiplication/Division
- Classification Number Families
- Comparison Number Families
- Number Family Tables
- Inverse Operations
- Ratios and Proportions
- Ratio Tables
- Fraction Number Families

GEOMETRY
- Perimeter
- Area
- Lines and Angles
- Circles
- Coordinate System

Level Bridge Contents

Skills	Taught in these Lessons	Date Lessons Completed
WHOLE NUMBER OPERATIONS		
Multiplication		
Writes the missing factor in a multiplication fact.	1, 2	
Writes the missing factor or addend in a multiplication or addition fact.	3	
Works a mixed set of multiplication problems, some of which have a missing factor.	4	
Uses division to figure out the missing factor in a multiplication equation.	5	
Completes a table to show a multiplication equation and the corresponding division problem.	6–9	
Rewrites an equation of the form: $15 - 12 = 3$, so that the equation begins with the number that is alone: $3 = 15 - 12$.	12, 13	
Rewrites an equation so it begins with the unknown.	14–17	
Applies a two-operation function to complete a table.	24–29	
Division		
Rewrites the answer to a division problem as a mixed number.	23, 24	
Solves a division problem and writes the answer as a mixed number.	25	
Long Division		
Completes a division problem that has a two-digit divisor.	31, 32	
Completes a division problem with an answer that is not too big.	33, 34	
Completes a division problem that has the correct whole-number answer.	34	
Works a division problem that shows an incorrect whole-number answer.	35, 36	
Works a division problem that divides by a two-digit value and has a one-digit quotient.	37–40	
Inverse Operations		
Uses an inverse operation to undo a problem that has the first value missing.	57–59	
Uses inverse operations to solve a pair of equations and figures out the starting number.	61–64	

Skills	Taught in these Lessons	Date Lessons Completed
FRACTIONS		
Fraction Review		
Classifies a fraction that is more than 1 or less than 1.	1	
Identifies a picture that illustrates a fraction.	1, 2	
Works a problem that adds or subtracts fractions.	1, 2	
Identifies and corrects an incorrect answer to a problem that adds or subtracts fractions.	1, 2	
Classifies a fraction that is more than 1, less than 1, or equal to 1.	2–5	
Identifies and works an addition or subtraction fraction problem that can be worked as it is written.	3, 4	
Completes an equation to show the whole number a fraction equals.	6, 7	
Writes a fraction for a whole number from a description.	11, 12	
Writes a fraction based on a diagram.	42, 43	
Fraction Operations		
Works a problem that requires multiplying fractions.	4, 5	
Works a set of problems involving addition, subtraction, and multiplication of fractions.	6	
Completes an equation to show the whole number a fraction equals.	6, 7	
Figures out the missing factor in a fraction multiplication problem.	6, 7	
Works a set of problems involving addition, subtraction, and multiplication of three fractions.	7	
Uses division or multiplication to figure out the missing fraction in a fraction-multiplication equation.	8	
Obtains a fraction that equals a whole number by substituting fractions in equations of the form: $1 + 1 + 1 = 3$.	8, 9	
Works an addition or subtraction problem that has a whole number and a fraction.	9, 10	

Level Bridge Contents

Skills	Taught in these Lessons	Date Lessons Completed
Writes a division problem as a fraction, and figures out the whole number it equals.	11	
Writes a fraction for a whole number from a description.	11, 12	
Completes a table to show division problems and the corresponding fraction equations.	12	
Completes a table to show a multiplication problem, the corresponding division problem, and the fraction equation.	13	
Treats a fraction as a division problem.	14	
Completes a fraction that equals a whole number.	14, 15	
Solves a set of problems that multiplies more than two values, some of which are fractions.	42, 43	
Writes a fraction based on a diagram.	42, 43	
Mixed Numbers		
Writes an equation that shows an improper fraction and the mixed number it equals.	15, 16	
Writes an equation that shows a mixed number and the fraction it equals.	16–18	
Completes a table to show mixed numbers and the corresponding fractions.	22	
Rewrites a fraction as a mixed number.	26–29	
Rewrites a fraction as a whole number or a mixed number.	27	
Completes a table to show a division problem and a corresponding fraction-to-mixed number equation.	30	
Writes a fraction as a division problem and shows the answer as a whole number or a mixed number.	31, 32	
Rewrites a fraction as a mixed number.	62	
Equivalence		
Determines whether a pair of fractions is equivalent.	8, 9	
Writes a pair of equivalent fractions from pictures.	10, 11	

Skills	Taught in these Lessons	Date Lessons Completed
Completes an equation that shows equivalent fractions by figuring out the fraction that equals 1.	11	
Completes a pair of equivalent fractions.	12–21	
Works a mixed set of equivalent-fraction problems.	13	
Writes a missing middle factor as a fraction.	41–48	
Solves a problem in which the missing middle factor is expressed as a letter.	49–52	
Works a division problem on a calculator and writes the answer as a mixed number.	52, 53	
Writes a complex fraction that equals 1.	53	
Generates a complex fraction that equals a simple fraction equal to 1.	53, 54	
Multiplies a fraction by a complex fraction that equals 1 to generate an equivalent fraction.	55, 56	
Completes a pair of equivalent fractions by generating a complex fraction that equals 1.	57–61	
Writes a statement of equality or inequality for two values.	59, 61	
Works a mixed set of equivalent-fraction problems, some of which require multiplying by a complex fraction equal to 1.	63	
Determines whether a missing factor is more than 1 or less than 1, then figures out the fraction it equals.	65, 66	
Simplifying Fractions		
Writes the prime factors for a number that is not prime.	44–46	
Uses prime factors to simplify a fraction.	47–55	
Simplifies mixed numbers.	60, 61	
Common Denominators		
Adds or subtracts fractions with unlike denominators.	55–59	
Compares two fractions with unlike denominators.	61, 62	
Adds a whole number and fractions with unlike denominators.	65, 66	

Level Bridge Contents

Skills	Taught in these Lessons	Date Lessons Completed
Works a mixed set of problems that involve multiplication, addition, or subtraction of a whole number and fractions.	67, 69	
NUMBER FAMILIES AND EXTENSIONS **Whole Numbers**		
Writes a column problem to find the missing number in a number family.	1–6	
Identifies and corrects an incorrect answer to a number family problem.	1–5	
Identifies number families that are written correctly and figures out the missing number.	4–6	
Makes a number family for a diagram that shows a whole divided into two parts.	5, 6	
Tables		
Computes the missing number in each row of a number-family table.	9	
Computes the missing number in each row or column of a number-family table.	11, 12	
Completes a number-family table by first working rows with two numbers and then columns with two numbers.	13–15	
Completes a number-family table.	17–21	
Fraction Number Families		
Completes a fraction number family that has a big number of 1.	33, 34	
Constructs a fraction number family from a diagram.	38–41	
Completes a fraction number family that does not have a big number equal to 1.	43	
Completes a set of fraction number families, some of which do not have a big number equal to 1.	44	
DECIMALS AND PERCENTS **Reading and Writing**		
Reads and writes decimal values that involve tenths, hundredths, or thousandths.	42–44	
Writes fractions with denominators of 10, 100, or 1000 from decimal numbers.	45–51	
Completes a table to show fractions and equivalent decimal values.	46	

Skills	Taught in these Lessons	Date Lessons Completed
Writes decimal numbers for fractions, some of which are more than 1.	47, 48	
Writes a fraction for a decimal value that is more than 1.	49, 50	
Writes a mixed number from a decimal number.	51	
Rounding		
Rounds a decimal value to the nearest hundredth.	55, 56	
Percents		
Converts decimal values into equivalent percent values and vice versa.	57	
Converts a fraction with a denominator of 100 into the equivalent decimal and percent values.	58	
Completes a table to show fractions, decimals, and corresponding percents.	59, 60	
Writes an equation that shows a fraction, an equivalent fraction with a denominator of 100, and an equivalent percent value.	61	
Conversions		
Writes an equation that shows a fraction, the equivalent decimal number, and the equivalent mixed number.	52, 53	
Completes a table to show fractions, corresponding decimal values, and mixed numbers.	54	
Compares a decimal value and a fraction to determine which is greater.	63–69	
Compares a factor and the product in a multiplication equation.	65, 66	
Determines whether a missing factor in a decimal multiplication problem is more than 1 or less than 1, then figures out the missing value.	67, 68	
ESTIMATION		
Reads a thousands numeral as a hundreds numeral.	31, 32	
Estimates the answer to a problem by rounding values to hundreds.	33–37	
Uses estimation to determine whether a problem has a wrong answer.	35, 36	

Level Bridge Contents

Skills	Taught in these Lessons	Date Lessons Completed
Determines whether a problem has a wrong answer by rounding each value to tens or hundreds.	37	
Rounds two-, three-, or four-digit values according to the first digit of each.	38–41	
PROBLEM SOLVING **Whole Number Operations** **MULTIPLICATION/DIVISION** Works a word problem that requires multiplication or division.	2–5	
Solves a set of multiplication/division word problems by making ratio equations.	66–68	
CLASSIFICATION NUMBER FAMILIES Solves a word problem that describes a whole and the parts.	7, 8	
Makes a number family for a sentence that names binary categories.	9, 10	
Uses a number family to solve an addition or subtraction word problem that involves binary categories.	11, 12	
Makes a number family for a problem that has both a diagram and a comparison statement.	18–22	
Makes number families for a mixed set of problems that involve classification or comparison.	36	
Works a mixed set of word problems that involve classification or comparison.	38, 39	
COMPARISON NUMBER FAMILIES Solves a problem that illustrates two values and the difference between them.	16, 17	
Makes a number family for a comparison sentence.	22	
Uses a number family to solve a comparison word problem.	23–26	
Solves a comparison word problem that asks about the difference.	32	
Solves a set of comparison word problems, some of which ask about the difference.	33	
Makes number families for a mixed set of problems that involve classification or comparison.	36	

Skills	Taught in these Lessons	Date Lessons Completed
Works a mixed set of word problems that involve classification or comparison.	38, 39	
Identifies the larger entity named in sentences of the form: Hilda's weight is 9/8 of Edna's weight.	44, 45	
NUMBER-FAMILY TABLES Answers a set of questions by referring to a number-family table.	17–21	
Completes a number-family table and answers questions by referring to the table.	22, 23	
Uses facts to complete a number-family table and answers questions by referring to the table.	24, 25	
Works a word problem by constructing a number-family table with column and row headings.	26–45	
Uses information shown in a number-family table to work items that compare two quantities.	46–48	
Uses comparison facts to figure out numbers for a number-family table.	51–69	
Inverse Operations Works a two-step word problem that gives the starting number and specifies two operations.	58	
Works a three-step word problem that gives the starting number and specifies three operations.	59	
Works a two-step word problem that asks about the starting number and specifies two operations.	64–66	
Uses inverse operations to solve multistep word problems.	67–69	
Ratios and Proportions Writes names and a fraction for a sentence that gives ratio information.	12, 13	
Refers to a word problem to write a ratio equation.	14, 15	
Writes and solves a ratio equation for a word problem.	16–27	
Identifies whether equations for ratio problems are appropriately written.	18–20	
Works a ratio-equation problem that involves complex fractions.	62–65	

Level Bridge Contents

Skills	Taught in these Lessons	Date Lessons Completed
Ratio Tables		
Completes a ratio table.	28–31	
Completes a ratio table that has headings for the rows.	32–34	
Appropriately places names in a ratio table and completes the table.	35, 36	
Solves a word problem by using a ratio table.	37–39	
Solves a ratio-table problem that involves fractions.	41	
Solves a set of ratio-table problems, some of which involve fractions.	42, 43	
Works a ratio-table problem that has a comparison statement involving fractions.	53–55	
Works a set of ratio-table problems, some of which require a fraction number family that refers to the difference.	56, 57	
Discriminates between problems that require a ratio table and those that require only a ratio equation.	62–64	
Works a ratio-table problem that involves a decimal or a percent value.	68, 69	
Fraction Number Families		
Solves a word problem that involves a whole group by making a fraction number family.	35–37	
Uses a fraction number family to work a problem that tells about numbers and asks about a fraction.	44, 45	
Writes a number family with three names and a fraction for a sentence that compares.	46, 47	
Writes a fraction number family for a sentence that compares two things.	48, 49	
Makes a number family that compares two values shown in a table.	49	
Makes fraction number families from sentences, some of which tell about the difference.	51, 52	

Skills	Taught in these Lessons	Date Lessons Completed
GEOMETRY		
Perimeter		
Computes perimeters of various polygons.	13–15	
Figures out the perimeter of a parallelogram.	22–24	
Area		
Works an area-of-rectangle problem from a diagram.	17, 18	
Computes the area of a parallelogram.	28–30	
Computes the area of a triangle.	33, 34	
Computes the area of a rectangle or a right triangle.	35, 36	
Finds the area of a non-right triangle shown on the coordinate system.	37	
Finds the area of a non-right triangle.	38	
Area and Perimeter		
Computes both the area and the perimeter of a rectangle.	19–26	
Finds the area and perimeter of a parallelogram.	32, 34	
Finds the area and the perimeter of a rectangle, triangle, or a parallelogram.	39, 41	
Given the area of a rectangle and the length for one pair of sides, figures out the length of the other pair of sides.	65, 66	
Works a set of area-of-rectangle problems, some of which ask about the length of a side.	68	
Lines and Angles		
Indicates whether lines are parallel.	21	
Indicates whether non-parallel lines intersect.	22, 23	
Answers questions about angles.	23, 24	
Makes a number family to solve a problem involving an angle that is divided into two smaller angles.	25, 26	
Figures out the degrees in the four angles that are formed by two perpendicular intersecting lines.	27	
Figures out the degrees in corresponding angles formed by a line that intersects parallel lines.	27–29	

Level Bridge Contents

Skills	Taught in these Lessons	Date Lessons Completed
Indicates whether lines are parallel or perpendicular.	28	
Figures out the degrees in the four angles that are formed by two intersecting lines.	31, 32	
Uses the angle symbol ($\angle$) to write an equation that shows the degrees in an angle.	41	
Circles Figures out the relationship between the diameter and circumference of a circle.	54	
Uses the equation $\pi \times d = C$ to calculate the circumference of a circle.	55–57	
Uses the equation $\pi \times d = C$ to figure out the circumference or diameter of a circle.	58–61	

Skills	Taught in these Lessons	Date Lessons Completed
Uses the equation $\pi \times d = C$ to figure out the circumference or radius of a circle.	62, 63	
Uses the equation $\pi \times d = C$ to figure out the circumference, radius, or diameter of a circle.	64	
Area/Perimeter/Circumference Works a mixed set of problems that involve rectangles, triangles, and circles.	69	
Coordinate System Writes the X and Y values for points shown on the coordinate system.	46, 47	
Completes a table to show the X and Y values of points shown on a coordinate system.	48, 49	
Corrects entries in a table to show the X and Y values of points shown on a coordinate system.	50	

For Bridge placement test, see page 196.

Lesson 28 (Presentation Book)

Objectives

- **Indicate whether lines are parallel or perpendicular.** (Exercise 1)

- Work a word problem by constructing a number-family table with column and row headings. (Exercise 2)

- Figure out the degrees in corresponding angles formed by a line that intersects parallel lines. (Exercise 3)

- **Compute the area of a parallelogram.** (Exercise 4)
  Note: Students learn the rule that the height of the figure is shown by a line that is perpendicular to the base.

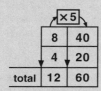

- **Complete a ratio table.** (Exercise 5)
  Note: These tables have columns that work like those in number-family tables. The total is at the bottom of the table. The rows are governed by a multiplication rule, such as times 5. Students multiply the values in the first column by 5 to find the values in the second column.

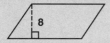

	8	40
	4	20
total	12	60

- Rewrite a fraction as a mixed number. (Exercise 6)

EXERCISE 1 GEOMETRY
Parallel/Perpendicular Lines

a. (Draw on the board:)

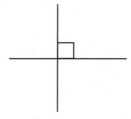

- This angle mark is used for a special angle. How many degrees are in the angle? (Signal.) *90 degrees.*
- And what do we call lines that form a 90-degree angle? (Signal.) *Perpendicular.*
  (Repeat step a until firm.)
b. Open your textbook to lesson 28 and find part 1.
- Some pairs of lines in part 1 are parallel. Some intersect. They are not parallel. Some of the lines that intersect have a square angle marker to indicate that the lines are perpendicular. Remember, perpendicular lines form an angle of 90 degrees.
c. For each item write **parallel, not parallel,** or **intersect** to tell about the lines. Raise your hand when you've done that much.
  (Observe students and give feedback.)

- Tell me what you wrote for each item.
- Item A: What did you write? (Signal.) *Intersect.*
- Item B: What did you write? (Signal.) *Not parallel.*
- Item C: What did you write? (Signal.) *Parallel.*
- Item D: What did you write? (Signal.) *Intersect.*
- Item E: What did you write? (Signal.) *Parallel.*
- Item F: What did you write? (Signal.) *Intersect.*
- Item G: What did you write? (Signal.) *Not parallel.*
d. Circle the letter of each item that shows a pair of perpendicular lines. Remember, those are lines that form a 90-degree angle. Raise your hand when you're finished. √
- You should have circled **A** and **D**. Both those items show lines that are perpendicular.
- Raise your hand if you got everything right.

EXERCISE 2 PROBLEM SOLVING
Number-Family Tables

a. Find part 2.
- You're going to make a table for the problem in part 2.
b. The problem says: In 1980 and 1981, babies were born in Queen's Hospital and Marist Hospital.
- The rest of the problem tells about the numbers and asks the questions. Make the table with the headings. Don't put in any numbers. Raise your hand when you've written the headings.
  (Observe students and give feedback.)

- (Write on the board:)

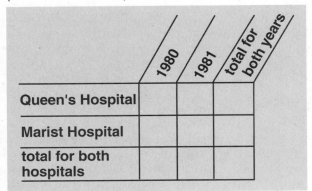

	1980	1981	total for both years
Queen's Hospital			
Marist Hospital			
total for both hospitals			

- Here's what you should have.
c. Put in the four numbers the problem gives. Raise your hand when you've done that much.
  (Observe students and give feedback.)
- (Write to show:)

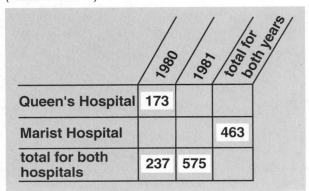

	1980	1981	total for both years
Queen's Hospital	173		
Marist Hospital			463
total for both hospitals	237	575	

- Here's what you should have.
d. Now figure out the missing numbers and write answers to the questions. Raise your hand when you're finished.
  (Observe students and give feedback.)
- (Write to show:)

	1980	1981	total for both years
Queen's Hospital	173	176	349
Marist Hospital	64	399	463
total for both hospitals	237	575	812

e. Check your work.
- Everybody, how many babies were born in Queen's Hospital in 1981? (Signal.) *176.*

- In 1981, were more babies born in Queen's Hospital or Marist Hospital? (Signal.) *Marist Hospital.*
- In which year were fewer babies born in Marist Hospital? (Signal.) *1980.*
- 349 tells about the number of babies born in Queen's Hospital during both years. You should have written **Queen's Hospital** and **both years** or **1980 and 1981.**
- Raise your hand if you got everything right.

EXERCISE 3 GEOMETRY
Corresponding Angles

a. Find part 3.
- Each item has parallel lines and an intersecting line. Remember, corresponding angles formed at parallel lines are equal. Each item gives you information about one of the angles. You'll figure out the corresponding angle that's equal to that angle.
b. Trace figure A. Raise your hand when you're finished. √
- Listen: Angle P is 72 degrees. Write the number of degrees for angle P and for the angle that corresponds to angle P. Raise your hand when you're finished.
  (Observe students and give feedback.)
- (Write on the board:)

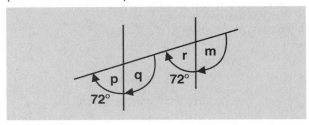

- What's the angle that corresponds to angle P? (Signal.) *Angle R.*
- How many degrees is angle R? (Signal.) *72.*
c. If you know what angle R equals, you can figure out what angle M equals because R and M together make half a circle. Your turn: Figure out angle M. Write the number of degrees. Then write the degrees for the corresponding angle. Raise your hand when you're finished.
  (Observe students and give feedback.)
- (Write to show:)

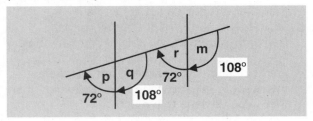

- Check your work. Everybody, how many degrees is angle M? (Signal.) *108.*
- What angle corresponds to M? (Signal.) *Angle Q.*
- How many degrees is angle Q? (Signal.) *108.*
d. Trace figure B. Raise your hand when you're finished.
- Item B gives you information about one of the angles. You'll figure out what the degrees are for all of the marked angles.
- Listen: Angle G is 125 degrees. Figure out all the other marked angles and write the degrees. Raise your hand when you're finished.
(Observe students and give feedback.)
- (Write on the board:)

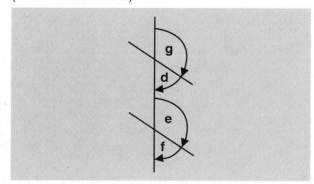

- Check your work. Angle G: Everybody, how many degrees is it? (Signal.) *125.*
- What's the other angle that equals 125 degrees? (Signal.) *Angle E.*
- Yes, angle E corresponds to angle G.
- Angle D: How many degrees does it equal? (Signal.) *55.*
- What other angle equals 55 degrees? (Signal.) *Angle F.*
- (Write to show:)

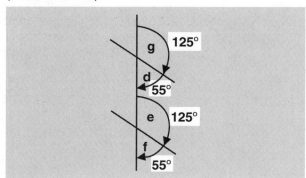

- Here's what you should have.
- Raise your hand if you got everything right.

EXERCISE 4 AREA
Parallelograms

a. Find part 4.
   (Teacher reference:)

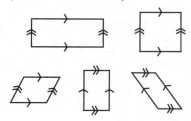

b. I'll read what it says. Follow along: You've worked with figures that have pairs of parallel sides. These figures are called **parallelograms.**
- A **rectangle** is a special kind of parallelogram.
- A **square** is a parallelogram.
- All the figures below the square are also parallelograms.
- You can use the **equation for the area of a rectangle** to find the area of any parallelogram. The area equals the base times the height. But you have to be very careful.
(Teacher reference:)

- For parallelograms that are not rectangles, the **height** of the figure is **not** the length of a side.
- You can see a parallelogram with numbers for two sides. The left side does not show the height. The **height** is a dotted line that is perpendicular to the base of the figure. The height is 8.
- To find the area for the parallelogram, you work the problem 20 times 8. The problem actually tells about a rectangle. You can see the parallelogram with part of it shaded.
- You can make a rectangle that has the same area as the parallelogram. You do that by moving the shaded triangle that is on the left side to the right side.
- You can see a rectangle made from the parts of the parallelogram. Parts haven't been added or taken away, so the parallelogram and the rectangle have the same area.
- Remember, the base times the height gives the area of a parallelogram, but the height may not be the length of a side.
c. Find part 5.
   Find the area of each figure. Remember to show three equations. Raise your hand when you're finished.
   (Observe students and give feedback.)

Level Bridge, Lesson 28 **145**

Key:

a. $A = b \times h$
$A = 16 \times 22$
$A = 352 \; sq \; in$

b. $A = b \times h$
$A = 12 \times 8$
$A = 96 \; sq \; mi$

c. $A = b \times h$
$A = 18 \times 18$
$A = 324 \; sq \; m$

d. $A = b \times h$
$A = 20 \times 14$
$A = 280 \; sq \; ft$

d. Check your work.
- Figure A. What's the base? (Signal.) *16 inches.*
- What's the height? (Signal.) *22 inches.*
- What's the area? (Signal.) *352 square inches.*
- Figure B. What's the base? (Signal.) *12 miles.*
- What's the height? (Signal.) *8 miles.*
- What's the area? (Signal.) *96 square miles.*
- Figure C. What's the base? (Signal.) *18 meters.*
- What's the height? (Signal.) *18 meters.*
- What's the area? (Signal.) *324 square meters.*
- Figure D. What's the base? (Signal.) *20 feet.*
- What's the height? (Signal.) *14 feet.*
- What's the area? (Signal.) *280 square feet.*
- Raise your hand if you got everything right.

EXERCISE 5 RATIOS AND PROPORTIONS
Tables

a. (Write on the board:)

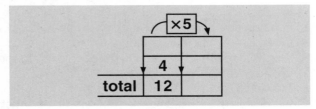

- This is a new kind of table. The total is at the bottom of each column, so if you have two numbers in a column, you can figure out the missing number.
- **You can't add for the rows.** You multiply to go from the first number in the row to the second number in that row. At the top of the table is **times 5.** That means you multiply the first number in each row by 5 to get the other number in the row.
- First work the column. The top number is missing in the first column. Raise your hand when you know the missing number in that column. √
- Everybody, what number? (Signal.) *8.*

b. (Write to show:)

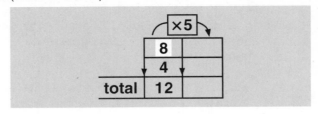

- 8 plus 4 equals 12.
- Now we can multiply to complete each row.
- For the top row, we multiply 8 by 5. What's the answer? (Signal.) *40.*
- For the next row, we multiply 4 by 5. What's the answer? (Signal.) *20.*
- For the bottom row, we multiply 12 by 5. What's the answer? (Signal.) *60.*

c. (Write to show:)

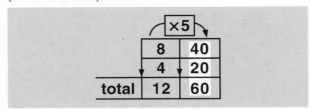

d. Find part 6.
- Copy the table and figure out the missing numbers. Raise your hand when you're finished. (Observe students and give feedback.)

e. (Write on the board:)

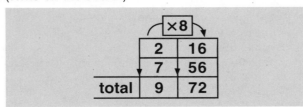

- Here's what you should have. The missing number in the first column is 7. The missing numbers in the last column are 16, 56, 72. 16 plus 56 equals 72.

EXERCISE 6 FRACTIONS
As Mixed Numbers

a. Find part 7.
   You're going to change fractions into mixed
   numbers. To do that, work the division problem
   and write the remainder as a fraction.

b. Fraction A. Read it as a division problem.
   (Signal.) *38 divided by 5.*
- Fraction B. Read it as a division problem.
   (Signal.) *146 divided by 7.*
- Fraction C. Read it as a division problem.
   (Signal.) *27 divided by 2.*
- (Repeat step b until firm.)

c. Your turn: Write the division problem and the
   answer for each fraction in part 7. Remember,
   write the remainder as a fraction. Raise your hand
   when you're finished.
   (Observe students and give feedback.)
   Key:

$$a.\ 5\overline{)38}\ \ {}^{7}\tfrac{3}{5} \qquad b.\ 7\overline{)146}\ \ {}^{20}\tfrac{6}{7}$$

$$c.\ 2\overline{)27}\ \ {}^{13}\tfrac{1}{2} \qquad d.\ 9\overline{)352}\ \ {}^{39}\tfrac{1}{9}$$

d. Check your work.
- Fraction A: 38/5. Say the division problem and the
   whole answer. (Signal.)
   38 divided by 5 equals 7 and 3-fifths.

- So 7 and 3-fifths equals the fraction you started
   with—38/5.
- Fraction B: 146/7. Say the division problem and
   the whole answer. (Signal.)
   146 divided by 7 equals 20 and 6-sevenths.
- So 20 and 6-sevenths equals the fraction you
   started with—146/7.
- Fraction C: 27/2. Say the division problem and the
   whole answer. (Signal.)
   27 divided by 2 equals 13 and 1-half.
- So 13 and 1/2 equals the fraction you started
   with—27/2.
- Fraction D: 352/9. Say the division problem and
   the whole answer. (Signal.)
   352 divided by 9 equals 39 and 1-ninth.
- So 39 and 1/9 equals the fraction you started
   with—352/9.
- Raise your hand if you wrote all the right mixed
   numbers.

EXERCISE 7 INDEPENDENT WORK

- (In addition to independent work in the textbook,
   assign **Connecting Math Concepts,** Level
   Bridge *Independent Worksheet* 8 as classwork or
   homework. Before beginning the next lesson,
   check the students' independent work.)

Bridge, Lesson 28 (Textbook)

The items in **part 1** review the concepts of **parallel** and **intersect,** introduced in lessons 21 and 22. Students also indicate which items show perpendicular lines (a and d). The concept of **perpendicular** was introduced in lesson 27.

The concepts of **parallel** and **intersect** are prerequisites for an understanding of **corresponding angles** (see **part 3**). Similarly, the concept of **perpendicular** is necessary for understanding the height of a parallelogram (see **part 4**).

In earlier lessons (17–19), students were given a completed table and answered questions based on that table. For example, a completed table for **part 2** looks like this:

	1980	1981	total for both years
Queen's Hospital	173	176	349
Marist Hospital	64	399	463
total for both hospitals	237	575	812

In lessons 22–25, students completed a table with missing numbers and answered questions.

In **part 2,** students construct the table themselves.

In later applications, students will work with comparison statements that involve one or more values in the table.

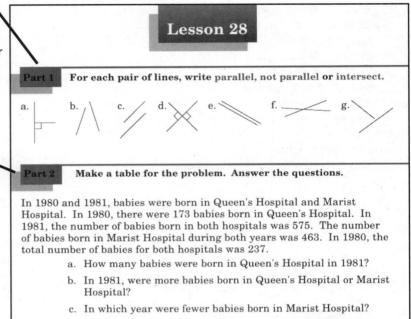

Lesson 28

Part 1 For each pair of lines, write parallel, not parallel or intersect.

a. b. c. d. e. f. g.

Part 2 Make a table for the problem. Answer the questions.

In 1980 and 1981, babies were born in Queen's Hospital and Marist Hospital. In 1980, there were 173 babies born in Queen's Hospital. In 1981, the number of babies born in both hospitals was 575. The number of babies born in Marist Hospital during both years was 463. In 1980, the total number of babies for both hospitals was 237.

   a. How many babies were born in Queen's Hospital in 1981?

   b. In 1981, were more babies born in Queen's Hospital or Marist Hospital?

   c. In which year were fewer babies born in Marist Hospital?

   d. 349 tells about the number of babies born in ▮▮▮▮▮ during ▮▮▮▮▮.

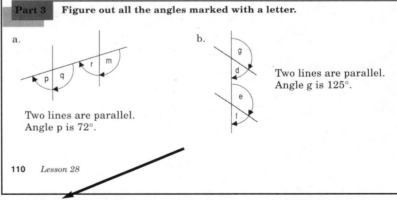

Part 3 Figure out all the angles marked with a letter.

a.

Two lines are parallel. Angle p is 72°.

b.

Two lines are parallel. Angle g is 125°.

110   *Lesson 28*

Corresponding angles were introduced in lesson 27. In lesson 23, students learned that angles forming half a circle total 180°. This fact was applied to angle problems in lessons 25 and 26.

In lessons 31 and 32, students will figure out angles for two intersecting lines and infer the rule for opposite angles (they are equal).

- You've worked with figures that have pairs of parallel sides. These figures are called **parallelograms.**

- A **rectangle** is a special kind of parallelogram.

- A **square** is a parallelogram.

- These figures are also parallelograms.

- You can use **the equation for the area of a rectangle** to find the area of any parallelogram.

Area = base x height

- For parallelograms that are not rectangles, the **height** of the figure is **not** the length of a side.

- The left side does not show the height. The **height** is a dotted line that is perpendicular to the base of the figure.

- To find the area for the parallelogram, you work the problem 20 x 8.

- You can make a rectangle that has the same area as the parallelogram.

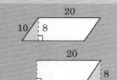

- You do that by moving the shaded triangle that is on the left side to the right side.

- The parallelogram and the rectangle have the same area.

- Remember, the equation for the area of the parallelogram is **Area = base x height,** but the height may not be the length of a side.

Lesson 28   **111**

The concept of perimeter was taught in lessons 13–15. The procedure for finding the area of a rectangle was taught in lessons 17–19.

The explanation in **part 4** demonstrates why the formula used for the area of a rectangle may also be used for any parallelogram.

By the end of the program, students will work mixed sets of problems involving the area and perimeter/circumference of rectangles, triangles, parallelograms and circles.

Following the explanation in **part 4,** students apply the information immediately in **part 5,** using the same formula (A = b × h) for a rectangle (item a) and for other parallelograms (items b-d).

The problem in **part 6** introduces students to the logic of a ratio table.

The position of the missing value in the first column indicates that students must subtract (9 − 2).

In this lesson, students learn that all the values in the first column can be multiplied by a constant value (e.g., 8) to give the values in the second column. This principle will later be applied to complex ratio/proportion problems.

For example: The ratio of green bottles to total bottles is 2 to 9. If there are 56 bottles that are not green, how many are green? How many bottles are there in all?

In lessons 15–17, students wrote equations for fractions and mixed numbers based on a number line. In lessons 16–19 students converted mixed numbers to fractions. The division strategy used in **part 7** for converting fractions to mixed numbers was introduced in lesson 26.

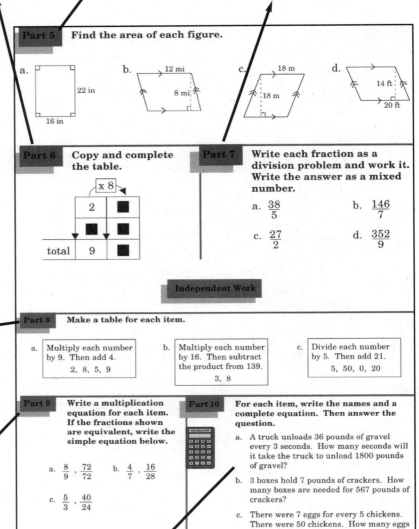

For **part 8** item b, students make this table:

3	91
8	11

Two-step function tables were taught in lessons 24–27.

Part 9 requires students to discriminate pairs of fractions that are equivalent from pairs that are not.

This is what students write for item b:

$$\frac{4}{7}\left(\frac{4}{4}\right) = \frac{16}{28}$$

$$\frac{4}{7} = \frac{16}{28}$$

Equivalent fractions were introduced in esson 8. A variety of equivalent-fraction tasks appeared for five consecutive lessons. A thorough understanding of equivalent fractions is necessary for working basic ratio/proportion problems, as in **part 10.**

Students construct a ratio equation to solve each problem in **part 10.** For item a, students write:

$$\frac{\text{pounds}}{\text{seconds}} \frac{36}{3} \left(\frac{\quad}{\quad}\right) = \frac{1800}{\square}$$

They figure out the missing fraction (50/50) and multiply to solve for the number of seconds. Work with ratio equations began in lesson 12, and appeared in nine lessons prior to lesson 28.

Part 11 reviews addition/subtraction problems that compare. Students use a number-family strategy to solve the problems. For item d, the larger value (the turtle) is the "big number" in the family, and equals the sum of the other two values ("small numbers") in the family. The big number is always at the end of the number-family arrow. Students

write:
dif tree turtle

21 ■ → 134 . The position of the missing value

indicates that students must subtract to find the age of the tree. In lessons 32 and 33, students will also work problems that ask about the difference number. In later lessons, the same logic is applied to advanced ratio/proportion problems that involve comparison statements.

Part 12 reviews the relationship between fractions and whole numbers. This relationship was introduced in lesson 6 and was practiced in lessons 6–18.

Part 12 includes three different problem types (missing numerator, missing whole number, written description). A solid understanding of this relationship is necessary for solving problems involving addition/subtraction/multiplication of a whole number and a fraction, and for simplifying fractional answers to problems.

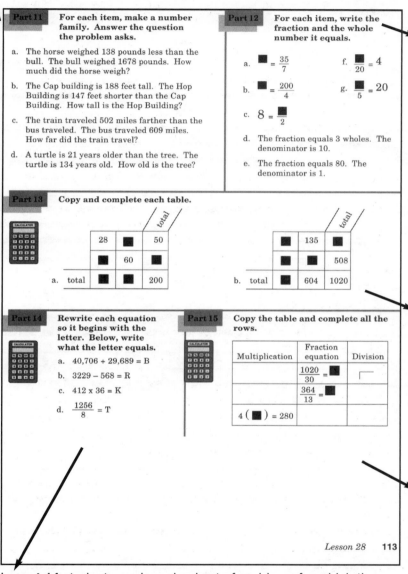

Part 11 For each item, make a number family. Answer the question the problem asks.

a. The horse weighed 138 pounds less than the bull. The bull weighed 1678 pounds. How much did the horse weigh?

b. The Cap building is 188 feet tall. The Hop Building is 147 feet shorter than the Cap Building. How tall is the Hop Building?

c. The train traveled 502 miles farther than the bus traveled. The bus traveled 609 miles. How far did the train travel?

d. A turtle is 21 years older than the tree. The turtle is 134 years old. How old is the tree?

Part 12 For each item, write the fraction and the whole number it equals.

a. $\blacksquare = \frac{35}{7}$ f. $\frac{\blacksquare}{20} = 4$

b. $\blacksquare = \frac{200}{4}$ g. $\frac{\blacksquare}{5} = 20$

c. $8 = \frac{\blacksquare}{2}$

d. The fraction equals 3 wholes. The denominator is 10.

e. The fraction equals 80. The denominator is 1.

Part 13 Copy and complete each table.

a. total

28	■	50
■	60	■
total ■	■	200

b. total

■	135	■
■	■	508
total ■	604	1020

Part 14 Rewrite each equation so it begins with the letter. Below, write what the letter equals.

a. 40,706 + 29,689 = B

b. 3229 − 568 = R

c. 412 x 36 = K

d. $\frac{1256}{8}$ = T

Part 15 Copy the table and complete all the rows.

Multiplication	Fraction equation	Division
	$\frac{1020}{30} = \blacksquare$	
	$\frac{364}{13} = \blacksquare$	
4 (■) = 280		

Lesson 28 113

Part 13 requires students to add or subtract in columns or rows that have two values in order to complete the tables. This component skill enables students to work multistep word problems that can be solved by constructing a table (see **part 2**).

The table in **part 15** requires students to relate multiplication, division and fractions. The relationship between multiplication and division was established in lessons 5–9. Tables of this form first appeared in lesson 13.

In **part 14** students work a mixed set of problems for which they solve for an unknown. In lessons 14 and 15, students worked problems of the form: 501 275 ■. In lessons 16 and 17, the box was replaced with a letter, giving the problem type shown in **part 14.**

The calculator icons indicate that the teacher has the option of permitting students to use calculators for those parts.

Scope and Sequence for

Connecting Math Concepts, Level F

Connecting Math Concepts, Level F prepares students for success in higher math. It is suitable for students who have completed either Level E or the

Lessons

Skill	Lesson Range (bar)
TOOL SKILLS	
WHOLE-NUMBER OPERATIONS	
Division	21–38
Combining Terms & Distributive Property	
NUMBER RELATIONSHIPS	2–38
OPERATIONAL RELATIONSHIPS	
Inverse Operations	2–38
Place Value	2–25
FRACTION OPERATIONS	10–38
Fraction Simplification	10–16
Reciprocals & Fraction Division	
MIXED-NUMBER OPERATIONS	5–38
NUMBER FAMILIES	7–38
DECIMAL OPERATIONS	4–38
COORDINATE SYSTEM	37–38
APPLICATIONS	
PROBLEM SOLVING	
Ratio Equations	14–38
Ratio Tables	6–38
Probability	
Multiplication Problems	24–30
Multi-Step Problems	5–38
Reciprocals	
Mixed-Number Problems	
Time	
Coins and Money Amounts	
Average	
Circle Graphs	
MEASUREMENT	6–38
GEOMETRY	
Area, Perimeter, Circumference, & Diameter	1–38
Volume	
Geometry Facts	
SIGNED NUMBERS	
EXPONENTS	
SIMPLE MACHINES	
PROJECTS	

Bridge. Students learn to solve multi-step problems involving fractions, decimals and percents, tax, and geometry. Other topics include exponents, positive and negative integers, reciprocals, measurement conversion, ratios and proportions, probability, and rate. The Scope and Sequence Chart shows where each track or major topic begins and where it ends.

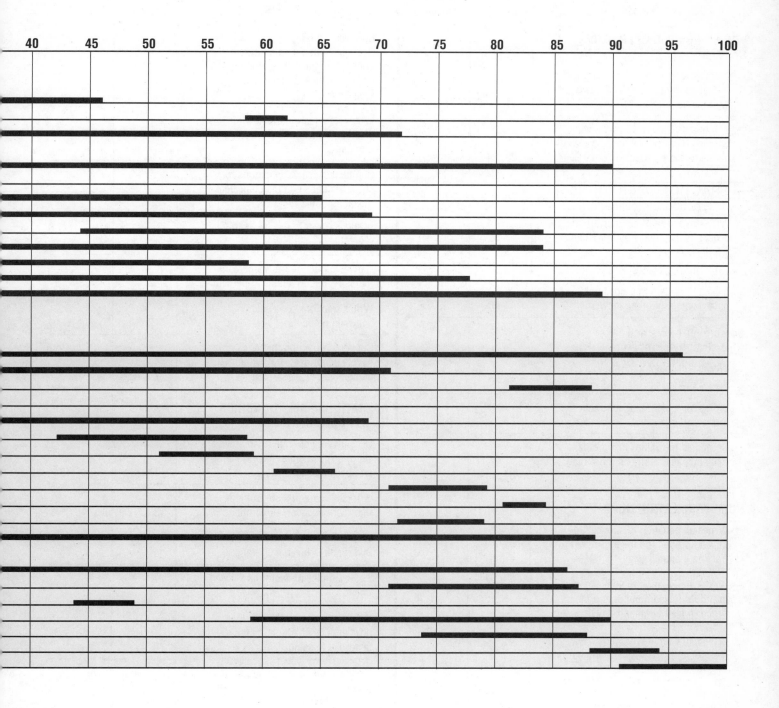

Level F Contents

Skills	Taught in these Lessons	Date Lessons Completed
WHOLE-NUMBER OPERATIONS **Division**		
Works a long division problem that has a two-digit divisor and a two-digit quotient.	21-25	
Works a division problem in which both the dividend and divisor end in one or more zeros.	23, 24	
Uses "shortcuts" to work a mixed set of division problems.	28	
Writes mixed-number answers to problems that divide by 10, 100 or 1,000.	29	
Uses a calculator to work a division problem that does not have a whole-number answer.	44-46	
Combining Terms and Distributive Property		
Works a problem that requires distribution.	58-60	
Works a problem that subtracts more than one value.	59	
Combines the values in a problem that adds and subtracts more than one value.	61, 62	
NUMBER RELATIONSHIPS		
Writes an equation to show a mixed number and the improper fraction it equals.	1-3	
Writes an equation to show an improper mixed number and the proper mixed number it equals.	1-6	
Writes an equation to show a fraction and the decimal value it equals.	1-3	
Completes a table that shows mixed numbers and corresponding decimal values.	3	
Completes a table that shows mixed numbers and corresponding fractions.	4	

Skills	Taught in these Lessons	Date Lessons Completed
Completes a table to show fractions with denominators of 10, 100, 1,000; the corresponding decimal values; and corresponding mixed numbers.	4, 5	
Writes an equation to show the decimal value and the equivalent fraction.	6	
Completes a set of equations to show fractions and the equivalent mixed numbers.	6, 7	
Writes percents for a set of simple fractions.	41-44	
Derives a fraction from a percent that is related to a familiar percent.	42, 43	
Writes fractions for a set of common percents.	42	
Converts a fraction that does not have a denominator of 100 into a percent value.	71, 72	
OPERATIONAL RELATIONSHIPS **Inverse Operations**		
Uses inverse operations to solve a set of problems that have the first number missing.	1, 2	
Works a two-equation problem that requires inverse operations.	3	
Works a three-equation problem that requires inverse operations.	4	
Shows a missing factor as a fraction.	5	
Works a set of multiplication problems in which one of the factors is missing.	6	
Uses inverse operations to solve a problem in which the middle equation has three boxes.	18, 19	
Figures out the missing denominator in an equation that shows a whole number and the equivalent fraction.	45	

Level F Contents

Skills	Taught in these Lessons	Date Lessons Completed
Completes a ratio table with more than three rows.	74, 75	
Works inverse-operation problems to find missing values in a ratio table.	76-80	
Solves an equation that has a single term on the left and the unknown on the right.	89	
Rewrites and solve four-value equations that have the unknown on the right.	89, 90	
Place Value		
Writes an equation to show a decimal value that ends in one or more zeros and the simplified decimal value.	1, 2	
Rounds a decimal value to the nearest hundredth.	24, 25	
FRACTION OPERATIONS		
Constructs a complex fraction that equals 1 to solve an equivalent-fraction problem.	11, 12	
Uses a calculator to work a problem that multiplies a fraction times a whole number.	51	
Uses a calculator to work a problem that multiplies a fraction times a whole number or decimal.	52	
Adds or subtracts fractions with unlike denominators.	61-64	
Works a mixed set of fraction problems with unlike denominators that require multiplication, addition or subtraction.	65	
Fraction Simplification		
Simplifies a fraction in which both the numerator and denominator end in one or more zeros.	16, 17	
Works a multiplication problem that can be simplified by crossing out zeros.	18	

Skills	Taught in these Lessons	Date Lessons Completed
Simplifies fraction-multiplication problems by crossing out fractions that equal 1.	66	
Uses simplification techniques to work problems that multiply fractions.	68, 69	
Reciprocals and Fraction Division		
Expresses the relationship between the fraction for each part and the number of parts in a whole.	44, 45	
Writes a multiplication equation to show the number of equal parts in a whole.	45	
Writes the reciprocal for a fraction or a whole number.	46, 47	
Writes an equation that starts with a given value and multiplies by its reciprocal.	47-49	
Rewrites an equation of the form: $75\% \ (\ ) = \blacksquare = 1.$	51	
Works a two-step word problem that involves reciprocals.	53-55	
Works a mixed set of problems involving the area of a figure divided into equal parts.	56, 57	
Works a division problem as a multiplication problem and vice versa.	81-84	
Rewrites a complex fraction as a division problem; then works a multiplication problem.	84	
MIXED-NUMBER OPERATIONS		
Uses division to figure out the mixed number that equals an improper fraction.	4	
Adds or subtracts mixed numbers.	9, 10	
Works an addition or subtraction problem that involves a whole number and a mixed number.	13	

Level F Contents

Skills	Taught in these Lessons	Date Lessons Completed
Works a renaming problem that involves a whole number and a fraction.	14, 15	
Solves a mixed-number addition problem and expresses the answer as a proper mixed number.	16, 17	
Multiplies mixed numbers.	48, 49	
Adds mixed numbers that have unlike denominators.	67, 68	
Adds or subtracts mixed numbers that have unlike denominators.	69	
Works a mixed-number subtraction problem that requires borrowing.	80, 81	
Works a mixed set of mixed-number problems that require addition or subtraction.	83	
NUMBER FAMILIES		
Makes a complete fraction number family from a single fraction.	7	
Completes a fraction number family that has names.	8, 9	
Writes a fraction number family for a sentence that refers to a decimal or percent value.	11	
Makes a fraction number family for a statement that compares two values.	31	
Makes a complete fraction number family for a statement that compares two values.	32	
Identifies the diagram that shows a specified fractional relationship.	33-49	
Makes percent number families for a set of sentences that compare or classify.	41-59	
Makes fraction number families from sentences, some of which give a percent difference value.	48-51	
Makes a fraction number family that replaces percent values with simple fractions.	48	

Skills	Taught in these Lessons	Date Lessons Completed
Constructs two statements that compare values shown in a number family.	52-58	
DECIMAL OPERATIONS		
Adds or subtracts decimal values.	2-4	
Adds or subtracts a whole number and a decimal value.	5	
Multiplies decimal values.	8-11	
Works a mixed set of problems involving adding, multiplying and subtracting decimal values.	18	
Writes decimal answers to problems that divide by 10, 100 or 1,000.	26, 27	
Works a decimal-multiplication problem as a fraction-multiplication problem.	27-29	
Writes a decimal answer to a division problem.	35, 36	
Shows the answer to a division problem as a mixed number and as a decimal value.	37-41	
Shows a fraction that is less than 1 as a decimal quotient in a division problem.	42, 43	
Divides a decimal value by a whole number.	53, 54	
Converts a fraction that has a decimal in the numerator into a division problem.	55, 56	
Multiplies a decimal value by 10, 100 or 1,000.	61	
Works a decimal-multiplication problem that has a missing factor.	62	
Works a mixed set of decimal-multiplication problems that have a missing factor or a missing product.	63, 64	
Completes equivalent fractions that involve decimals.	65-68	

Level F Contents

Skills	Taught in these Lessons	Date Lessons Completed
Works a division problem based on a fraction that has a decimal denominator.	71-73	
Works a division problem that has a decimal divisor.	74-77	
COORDINATE SYSTEM		
Finds the area of a complex figure shown on the coordinate system.	36-49	
Writes the X and Y value for a point shown on the coordinate system.	87	
Refers to a line on the coordinate system to answer questions.	88, 89	
PROBLEM SOLVING		
Ratio Equations		
Sets up and solves ratio problems that require a ratio equation with equivalent fractions.	2	
Works a ratio and proportion word problem that requires a complex fraction equal to 1.	13, 14	
Finds the lengths of sides for similar triangles.	89	
Completes a ratio equation that uses a colon notation.	96	
Ratio Tables		
Completes a table that has the same multiplier for each row.	7, 8	
Completes a ratio table.	9	
Uses the numerators from a fraction number family as values for the first column of a ratio table.	10	
Makes a fraction number family and a ratio table to solve a word problem.	11	
Makes a fraction number family and a ratio table to work a problem that involves decimals or percents.	12-21	
Completes a ratio table that requires addition or subtraction of a mixed number.	16, 17	

Skills	Taught in these Lessons	Date Lessons Completed
Works a mixed set of problems, some of which require a ratio table.	22-28	
Works a ratio-table problem that gives fractional information to compare two values.	33-35	
Works a ratio-table problem that uses percents to compare values.	36-58	
Works ratio-table percent problems that compare or classify.	43-66	
Works ratio-table problems that compare or classify.	47-59	
Works a ratio-table problem that involves dollar-and-cent amounts.	69, 71	
Probability		
Computes the expected numbers for a probability problem involving a spinner.	81-83	
Matches actual outcomes of a probability experiment with expected outcomes.	83-85	
Expresses probability as a fraction.	86	
Answers a question about probability by referring to a table.	87	
Uses statements about probability to construct a table that shows ratio numbers and expected outcomes.	88	
Multiplication Problems		
Works a multiplication problem that refers to a fraction or percent **of** a value.	21-23	
Works a multiplication word problem that refers to a fraction or percent **of** a value.	24, 25	
Works a multiplication word problem that compares.	26, 27	
Determines whether a word problem can be solved by multiplication.	28-30	
Works a multiplication problem that tells about each like item and the number of items.	31-34	

Level F Contents

Skills	Taught in these Lessons	Date Lessons Completed
Works a mixed set of problems that are solved by fraction multiplication or by a ratio table.	38, 39	
Works a word problem that involves multiplying a decimal by a fraction.	54	
MULTI-STEP PROBLEMS		
Inverse Operations		
Works a word problem that requires inverse operations.	5-12	
Writes an equation with two missing values from a sentence that refers to doubling, tripling or twice.	6	
Solves a two-step word problem by figuring out the missing middle value in the second equation.	9	
Works a mixed set of word problems that require inverse operations.	12-17	
Uses inverse operations to work a word problem that implies a starting value.	12	
Writes an equation with three boxes for a sentence that refers to an operation but does not specify numbers.	18	
Works an inverse-operation problem, part of which refers to an operation without numbers.	21, 22	
Works a mixed set of inverse-operation problems.	23	
Component Calculations		
Works a word problem that involves component problems.	35	
Works a multi-step word problem that involves tax.	36-38	
Works a mixed set of multi-step problems that refer to area, perimeter and tax.	39	
Works a mixed set of multi-step problems that refer to area, circumference, perimeter or tax.	41, 42	

Skills	Taught in these Lessons	Date Lessons Completed
Works a multi-step problem.	43-47	
Finds the area of a figure with a hole.	51, 52	
Finds the area of a figure that has more than one hole.	53, 54	
Works a multi-step problem that involves complex area.	55-59	
Works a multi-step problem involving part of a figure.	58-69	
Reciprocals		
Expresses the relationship between the fraction for each part and the number of parts in a whole.	44, 45	
Works a word problem that involves finding the reciprocal of a common percent value.	52	
Works a two-step word problem that involves reciprocals.	53-55	
Works a mixed set of problems involving the area of a figure divided into equal parts.	56, 57	
Works an area-of-figure problem that asks about one or more than one equal part.	57	
Works a word problem that requires dividing by a fraction.	85, 86	
Mixed-Number Problems		
Works a word problem that requires multiplying by a mixed number.	51, 52	
Works a mixed set of measurement word problems.	57, 58	
Time		
Converts p.m. times to times on a 24-hour clock.	61	
Works an addition or subtraction word problem that involves clock time.	61-63	
Converts times on a 24-hour clock to a.m. and p.m. times.	62, 63	

Level F Contents

Skills	Taught in these Lessons	Date Lessons Completed
Works a word problem that requires converting p.m. time to 24-hour time.	64-66	
Coins and Money Amounts		
Works a multiplication or division problem that involves coins.	73, 74	
Completes a rate-equation coin table.	75-77	
Constructs a coin-table to solve a money problem.	77-79	
Average		
Computes the average for a set of data.	81-84	
Circle Graphs		
Makes a table based on a circle graph.	72-82	
Determines the degrees in a fraction or percent of a circle.	73, 75	
Makes a table that has fractions of a circle in the first column and the corresponding number of degrees in the second.	76, 77	
Works a mixed set of problems that refer to a circle graph.	78, 79	
MEASUREMENT		
Makes fractions that are based on a fact about related units.	7-9	
Writes the unit name for a fraction that shows related units.	11-16	
Rewrites a fraction that refers to related units.	14-16	
Rewrites a mixed number as related units.	17-19	
Given a description of related units, writes a mixed number.	19-21	
Writes a mixed number and unit name for a description of related units.	22, 23	
Completes an equation to show the names for related units.	24-26	

Skills	Taught in these Lessons	Date Lessons Completed
Works a related-unit problem that asks about the smaller unit.	25-27	
Completes an equation to show the names and numbers for related units.	27, 28	
Constructs an equation that shows related units based on a question.	29-32	
Converts a fraction into the equivalent fraction that shows related units.	31-33	
Makes a complete equation for an item that asks about the smaller related unit.	33	
Completes statements of the form: $1\frac{5}{12}$ minutes is ☐ minute and ☐ seconds.	34, 35	
Works a mixed set of related-unit problems.	34-41	
Writes an equation for related units that involves a mixed number.	37-39	
Writes an equation for a sentence that refers to nonconvertible units.	37	
Solves a problem that involves nonconvertible units.	38-44	
Rewrites an incorrect equation that involves nonconvertible related units.	41, 42	
Works a word problem that asks about the rate.	46	
Works a mixed set of nonconvertible-unit problems, some of which ask about the rate.	47	
Rewrites an "improper" expression that refers to related units.	49-78	
Adds related units.	52-54	
Renames values for related units.	54	
Renames and subtracts related units.	55, 56	
Works a mixed set of related-unit problems involving addition or subtraction.	57, 58	

Level F Contents

Name _____

Skills	Taught in these Lessons	Date Lessons Completed
Works a mixed set of measurement word problems.	57, 58	
Works a related-unit word problem that requires addition or subtraction.	59, 60	
Works a problem that multiplies related units.	62, 63	
Works a word problem that requires multiplying related units.	63-79	
Works a mixed set of related-unit word problems that involve multiplication, addition or subtraction.	67	
Works a problem that converts related units into the smaller unit.	68, 69	
Works a mixed set of problems that refer to more than one unit.	87, 88	

GEOMETRY

Area, Perimeter, Circumference and Diameter

Skills	Taught in these Lessons	Date Lessons Completed
Uses the equation $b \times h = A$ to find the area of a rectangle, parallelogram or square.	1, 2	
Finds the perimeter of a triangle or rectangle.	2	
Finds the area and perimeter of a parallelogram or rectangle.	3	
Uses the equation $\frac{b \times h}{2} = A$ to find the area of a triangle.	14	
Finds the area of a parallelogram or triangle.	15	
Uses the equation $\pi \times d = C$ to find the circumference of a circle.	24	
Works a mixed set of problems to find either the circumference or the diameter of circles.	25, 26	
Works a mixed set of problems to find either the circumference or the radius of circles.	27, 28	
Uses the equation $\pi \times r \times r = A$ to calculate the area of a circle.	29-31	

Skills	Taught in these Lessons	Date Lessons Completed
Finds the area and circumference of a circle.	32, 33	
Finds the area of a complex figure shown on the coordinate system.	36-49	
Works a mixed set of multi-step problems that refer to area, perimeter and tax.	39	
Works a mixed set of multi-step problems that refer to area, circumference, perimeter or tax.	41, 42	
Finds the area of a figure with a hole.	51, 52	
Finds the area of a figure that has more than one hole.	53, 54	
Works a multi-step problem that involves complex area.	55-59	
Works a complex-area problem that involves part of a circle.	55	
Works a fraction-of-an-area problem two ways.	56	
Works an area-of-figure problem that asks about one or more than one equal part.	57	
Works a multi-step problem involving part of a figure.	58-69	
Works an area problem that involves mixed numbers.	77-79	
Solves an area problem that involves more than one unit.	86	

Volume

Skills	Taught in these Lessons	Date Lessons Completed
Computes the volume of a rectangular prism.	71, 72	
Computes the volume of a triangular prism.	74	
Works a set of volume problems involving rectangular and triangular prisms.	75, 76	
Uses the equation **Area of $b \times h = V$** to compute the volume of a cylinder.	83	

Level F Contents

Skills	Taught in these Lessons	Date Lessons Completed
Works a mixed set of volume problems, some of which involve a cylinder.	84	
Uses the equation $\dfrac{\text{Area of b x h}}{3} = v$ to compute the volume of figures that come to a point.	85, 86	
Works a mixed set of volume problems including figures that come to a point and figures that have parallel sides.	87	
Geometry Facts		
Writes the number of sides for common polygons.	44-46	
Given a set of common polygons, writes the names.	47	
Answers a question about the degrees in a common angle.	47	
Works a mixed set of items that refer to angles and polygons.	48	
SIGNED NUMBERS		
Combines the values in a problem that adds and subtracts more than one value.	61, 62	
Rewrites and work a problem with signed terms in a different order.	63-65	
Works paired addition and subtraction problems on a number line that has positive and negative values.	64	
Writes an equation for an arrow on a signed number line.	65, 66	
Indicates which of two signed numbers has the greater absolute value.	66, 67	
Completes the number part of the answer for signed-number combination problems.	67-69	
Combines signed numbers.	71-73	
Works a signed-number multiplication problem in which each value has a sign.	78-81	

Skills	Taught in these Lessons	Date Lessons Completed
Works multiplication problems by first combining the signed values on top.	82, 83	
Multiplies by a negative value.	84	
Works a mixed set of problems that multiply by a positive or a negative value.	85, 86	
Works a signed-number multiplication problem of the form: -4×-3.	87, 88	
Works a signed-number problem that has a large operational sign.	88, 89	
Works a problem that divides by a signed value.	89, 90	
Writes a problem that has signed values and a large operational sign.	90	
EXPONENTS		
Writes a base number and exponent for a repeated multiplication problem.	74	
Writes complete equations for a set of exponent problems that show either the multiplication or the exponential notation.	75	
Figures out the value represented by an exponential notation.	76-78	
Shows two groups of repeated multiplication in exponential notation.	83-85	
Rewrites a fraction that shows repeated multiplication as a base and exponent.	86, 87	
Simple Machines		
Works a lever problem.	88-91	
Works a set of problems that involve two types of levers.	90	
Solves a problem that involves a wheel and axle.	92-94	
Solves a problem that asks about the amount of work that is done.	94	

Level F Contents

Level F, Lesson 35 (Presentation Book)

Objectives

- Work a mixed set of related-unit problems. (Exercise 1)

- **Work a word problem that involves component problems.** (Exercise 2)
  Example: A farmer wants to fence a field that is 120 feet by 240 feet. Fencing costs $2.80 per foot. How much is the cost of fencing for the field? Students first find the perimeter of the field, then multiply that distance by the cost of fencing.

- Work a ratio-table problem that gives fractional information to compare two values. (Exercise 3)

- **Write a decimal answer to a division problem.** (Exercise 4)
  Note: Students express the answer with two decimal places:
  $$\begin{array}{r} 10.40 \\ 5\,\overline{)52.00} \end{array}$$

- Complete statements of the form:
  $1\frac{5}{12}$ minutes is ☐ minute and ☐ seconds. (Exercise 5)

EXERCISE 1 MEASUREMENT
Conversion: Equations

a. Open your textbook to lesson 35 and find part 1.
- These are related-unit problems. You'll show the complete equation with names and numbers. Remember, the larger unit goes on the left.
b. Work problem A. Raise your hand when you're finished. (Observe students and give feedback.)
- (Write on the board:)

$$\text{a.}\quad \boxed{\text{8 weeks}} = \frac{56 \text{ days}}{7 \text{ days per week}}$$

- Here's what you should have: 56 days is **8 weeks.** Raise your hand if you got everything right.
c. Work problem B. Raise your hand when you're finished. (Observe students and give feedback.)
- (Write on the board:)

$$\text{b.}\quad \text{28 weeks} = \frac{\boxed{196 \text{ days}}}{7 \text{ days per week}}$$

- Here's what you should have: 28 weeks is **196 days.** Raise your hand if you got everything right.
d. Work problem C. Raise your hand when you're finished. (Observe students and give feedback.)
- (Write on the board:)

$$\text{c.}\quad \boxed{\text{3 years}} = \frac{156 \text{ weeks}}{52 \text{ weeks per year}}$$

- Here's what you should have: 156 weeks is **3 years.** Raise your hand if you got everything right.
e. Work problem D. Raise your hand when you're finished. (Observe students and give feedback.)

- (Write on the board:)

$$\text{d.}\quad \text{12 years} = \frac{\boxed{624 \text{ weeks}}}{52 \text{ weeks per year}}$$

- Here's what you should have: 12 years is **624 weeks.** Raise your hand if you got everything right.

EXERCISE 2 PROBLEM SOLVING
Multi-Step

a. Find part 2.
- (Teacher reference:)

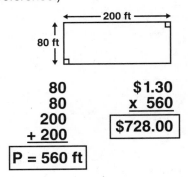

- I'll read what it says. Follow along: Some problems are made up of simpler problems. To work these problems, you solve the simpler problems and then use the answers to work the final problem.
- You can see an example: A rectangular field is 80 feet by 200 feet. A farmer fences the field. The fencing costs $1.30 per foot. How much does the fence cost?

- Before we can figure out the cost of the fence, we have to figure out how much fence to use. So we figure out the perimeter of the field. That's where the fence goes. You can see 80 plus 80 plus 200 plus 200. The perimeter is 560 feet.
- We need fencing for each foot of the perimeter. So we multiply the cost of the fencing by the number of feet. You can see $1.30 multiplied by 560. The answer is $728.
- Remember, work the simpler problems. Then use the answers to work the final problem.

b. Find part 3.

c. Problem A: A farmer plants a field. The field is 240 feet long and 360 feet wide. The farmer plants the field with wheat. The cost of wheat is 3 cents per square foot. How much does it cost to plant the entire field?
- For the first problem, you have to find the number of square feet. Is that the area of the field or the perimeter of the field? (Signal.) *Area.*
- Square feet is the **area.**
- Find the area. Use your calculator. Raise your hand when you've done that much.
  (Observe students and give feedback.)
- (Write on the board:)

> **a.   240 x 360 = | 86,400 sq ft |**

- Here's what you should have. The area is 240 times 360. That's 86,400 square feet.
- The cost of planting each square foot is 3 cents. You want to plant 86,400 square feet, so you multiply. Remember that 3 cents is 3-hundredths.
- Show the problem you'll work and the answer. Raise your hand when you're finished.
  (Observe students and give feedback.)
- (Write to show:)

> **86400 x .03 = | $2,592 |**

- Here's what you should have. The cost is $2,592. Raise your hand if you got it right.

d. Problem B: A farmer wants to fence a square field that is 90 feet on each side. The cost of fencing is $2.58 per foot. What's the cost of fencing for the field?
- The fence goes around the field. So figure out the distance around the field. Raise your hand when you've done that much.
  (Observe students and give feedback.)

- (Write on the board:)

> **b.   90**
> **   90**
> **   90**
> **   + 90**
> **P = | 360 ft |**

- The distance around the field is the perimeter. That's 90 four times. The answer is 360 feet.
- You know the cost of fencing each foot. You need 360 feet of fence.
- Work the problem on your calculator and answer the question. Raise your hand when you're finished. (Observe students and give feedback.)
- (Write to show:)

> **360 x 2.58 = | $928.80 |**

- Here's what you should have. The cost is $928.80.

e. Problem C: A farmer gets 90 cents per gallon of milk and 55 cents for each dozen eggs. In April, the farmer sold 1,235 gallons of milk and 165 dozen eggs. How much money did the farmer receive?
- Work the problem for the milk. Then work the problem for the eggs. Then add the two amounts to find the total. Raise your hand when you're finished.
  (Observe students and give feedback.)
- (Write on the board:)

> ① (milk)   1235 x .90 = | $1,111.50 |
> ② (eggs)   165 x .55 = | $90.75 |
> ③ (total)   1111.50 + 90.75 = | $1,202.25 |

- Here's what you should have. The farmer received $1,111.50 for milk and $90.75 for eggs. You add those two values and get $1,202.25.

f. Work problem D. Raise your hand when you're finished. (Observe students and give feedback.)
- (Write on the board:)

> ① (corn)   1600 x 2.10 = | $3,360 |
> ② (eggs)   284 x .50 = | $142 |
> ③ (total)   3360 + 142 = | $3,502 |

- Check your work. The farmer sold the corn for $3,360. He sold 284 dozen eggs at 50 cents per dozen. That's $142. The total is $3,502.

EXERCISE 3 RATIOS AND PROPORTIONS
Comparison Tables

a. Find part 4.
- These are problems that you can work if you make a fraction number family, then make a ratio table.
b. Problem A: The tank holds 7/5 as much as the barrel. The barrel holds 65 gallons. How much does the tank hold? How much more does the tank hold than the barrel holds?
- The first sentence gives information about a fraction number family. Make the family. Raise your hand when you've done that much.
(Observe students and give feedback.)
- (Write on the board:)

	dif	barrel	tank
a.	$\dfrac{2}{5}$	$\dfrac{5}{5}$	$\dfrac{7}{5}$

- Here's what you should have. Use the ratio numbers and make a table. Figure out the missing numbers. Raise your hand when you've answered the questions for problem A.
(Observe students and give feedback.)
- (Write on the board:)

dif	2	26
b	5	65
t	7	91

- Here's the table you should have. The problem tells you that the barrel holds 65 gallons. So the tank holds 91 gallons. The difference is 26 gallons. That's how much more the tank holds than the barrel.
c. Your turn: Work the rest of the problems in part 4. Raise your hand when you're finished.
(Observe students and give feedback.)
d. (Write on the board:)

	dif	Michael	Walter
b.	$\dfrac{1}{3}$	$\dfrac{2}{3}$	$\dfrac{3}{3}$

dif	1	145
M	2	290
W	3	435

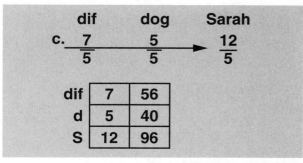

dif	7	56
d	5	40
S	12	96

- Check your work. Here's what you should have for problems B and C.
- Problem B. The ratio numbers are 1, 2 and 3. Walter earned $145 more than Michael. So Walter earned $435 and Michael earned $290.
- Problem C. The ratio numbers are 7, 5 and 12. The problem tells you that Sarah weighs 96 pounds. Her dog weighs 40 pounds. So Sarah weighs 56 pounds more than her dog.

EXERCISE 4 DIVISION
Decimal Answers

a. Find part 5.
- I'll read what it says. Follow along: You've worked division problems that have a mixed number answer.
- You can see 8 divided by 5. The answer's 1 and 3/5.
- You can work those same problems so they have a decimal answer. The decimal answer will show exactly the same value as the mixed number answer.
- Here are the steps for working division problems so the answer shows hundredths: Write a decimal point and two zeros after the decimal point. Then write a decimal point in the answer directly above the other decimal point. Then work the problem.
- You can see the problem worked. The answer is 1 and 60-hundredths. That's the same value as 1 and 3/5.
- Remember the steps: Make a decimal point after the whole number. Make two zeros. Put the decimal point in the answer. Then work the problem.
b. Find part 6.
c. Problem A: 13 divided by 4. Write the problem with the decimal points and two zeros. Raise your hand when you've done that much. √
- (Write on the board:)

$$\text{a. } 4\overline{\smash{)}13.00}$$

- Here it is. Figure out the answer. Raise your hand when you're finished.
(Observe students and give feedback.)

- (Write to show:)

$$\text{a. } 4\overline{)13.00} = \boxed{3.25}$$

- 13 divided by 4 is 3 and 25-hundredths.
d. Your turn: Work problem B so you get hundredths. Raise your hand when you're finished. **(Observe students and give feedback.)**
- (Write on the board:)

$$\text{b. } 2\overline{)7.00} = \boxed{3.50}$$

- Here's what you should have.
e. Work problem C. Raise your hand when you're finished. **(Observe students and give feedback.)**
- (Write on the board:)

$$\text{c. } 8\overline{)12.00} = \boxed{1.50}$$

- Here's what you should have.

EXERCISE 5 MEASUREMENT
Conversion: Mixed Numbers

a. Find part 7.
- These are problems that show mixed numbers and ask about related units.
- Remember, first make an equivalent fraction with the right denominator.
b. Work problem A. Raise your hand when you're finished. **(Observe students and give feedback.)**

- (Write on the board:)

$$\text{a. } \frac{3}{4} \left(\frac{9}{9}\right) = \frac{\boxed{27}}{36}$$

- Here's the equation you worked. 3/4 equals 27/36. So what does 1 and 3/4 yards equal? **(Signal.)** *1 yard and 27 inches.*
c. Work problem B. Raise your hand when you're finished. **(Observe students and give feedback.)**
- (Write on the board:)

$$\text{b. } \frac{2}{3} \left(\frac{4}{4}\right) = \frac{\boxed{8}}{12}$$

- Here's the equation you should have. 2/3 equals 8/12. So what does 6 and 2/3 feet equal? **(Signal.)** *6 feet and 8 inches.*
d. Work problem C. Raise your hand when you're finished. **(Observe students and give feedback.)**
- (Write on the board:)

$$\text{c. } \frac{1}{2} \left(\frac{26}{26}\right) = \frac{\boxed{26}}{52}$$

- Here's the equation you should have for problem C. 1/2 equals 26/52. So what does 3 and 1/2 years equal? **(Signal.)** *3 years and 26 weeks.*

EXERCISE 6 INDEPENDENT WORK
- (Assign *Independent Worksheet* 15 as classwork or homework. Before beginning the next lesson, check the independent work.)

Level F, Lesson 35 (Textbook)

For each item in **part 1,** students construct an equation to show the relationship between units. For example, for item a, students make the basic equation: weeks $= \dfrac{\text{days}}{\text{days per week}}$.

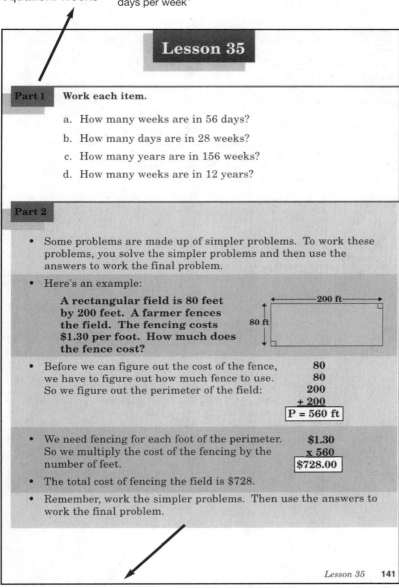

Weeks is the larger unit; days are the parts. The number of days in each week gives the denominator of the fraction—7. Students can also fill in the number given for days and days per week:

$\square$ weeks $= \dfrac{56 \text{ days}}{7 \text{ days per week}}$.

They divide to figure out the number of weeks.

For item b, students have the same basic equation. This time a number is given for weeks:

28 weeks $= \dfrac{\square \text{ days}}{7 \text{ days per week}}$.

Students multiply (7×28) to figure out the number of days.

Prior to lesson 35, students have worked extensively with related units, representing smaller units as fractions of larger units (e.g., 3 days is 3/7 of a week).

Starting in lesson 37, students will work with nonconvertible units (e.g., apples per box or miles per hour). The final application of this analysis enables students to answer questions about the larger unit, the smaller unit, or the rate. An example of the latter type is: A machine produces 126 parts in 6 seconds. How many parts per second does the machine produce? This problem type is introduced in lesson 46.

Part 2 explains a general procedure for working multi-step problems. This procedure will be applied to each item in **part 3.**

Each of the problems in **part 3** requires component calculations. For item a, students first find the area of the field, then calculate the cost of planting. For item c, students find the amount for the milk and the amount for the eggs before finding the total amount.

In lesson 36, multistep problems involving tax are introduced and appear for three consecutive lessons. In lesson 39, students work a mixed set of problems including multistep tax problems and multistep problems similar to those shown in **part 3.** Later, multistep problems involve figures with holes (lessons 51–54) and complex shapes (lessons 55–59).

The calculator icon indicates that the teacher has the option of permitting students to use calculators for this part.

For the items in **part 4,** students represent the comparative statement (e.g., the tank holds 7/5 as much as the barrel) as a fraction number family. The fraction number family for item a is:

$$\begin{array}{ccc} \text{dif} & \text{barrel} & \text{tank} \\ \dfrac{2}{5} & \dfrac{5}{5} & \dfrac{7}{5} \end{array}$$

The object used as the basis for comparison (the barrel) represents one whole. The larger value (the tank) is the "big number" in the family, and equals the sum of the other two values ("small numbers") in the family. The big number is always at the end of the number-family arrow. The difference number is always a small number.

The numerators of the fractions are ratio numbers that can be used in a

ratio table:

dif	2	
barrel	5	65
tank	7	

Each value in the first column is multiplied by a constant (13) to give the corresponding numbers in the second column. The missing top value answers the question: How much more does the tank hold than the barrel holds? The missing bottom value gives the amount for the tank.

Prior to lesson 35, students have worked extensively with ratio tables that classify (see page 132, discussed in the sample lesson from Level E).

Part 3 **Work each item.**

a. A farmer plants a field with wheat. The field is 240 feet long and 360 feet wide. The cost of wheat is $.03 per square foot. How much does it cost to plant the entire field?

b. A farmer wants to fence a square field that is 90 feet on each side. The cost of fencing is $2.58 per foot. What's the cost of fencing for the field?

c. A farmer gets $.90 per gallon of milk and $.55 for each dozen eggs. In April, the farmer sold 1,235 gallons of milk and 165 dozen eggs. How much money did the farmer receive?

d. A farmer receives $2.10 for each bushel of corn and $.50 for each dozen eggs. During one month, the farmer sold 1,600 bushels of corn and 284 dozen eggs. How much did the farmer earn in all?

Part 4 **Make a number family and a ratio table for each problem. Answer the questions.**

a. The tank holds $\frac{7}{5}$ as much as the barrel. The barrel holds 65 gallons. How much does the tank hold? How much more does the tank hold than the barrel holds?

b. Michael earned $\frac{2}{3}$ the amount that Walter earned. Walter earned $145 more than Michael. How much did Walter earn? How much did Michael earn?

c. Sarah's weight is $\frac{12}{5}$ her dog's weight. Sarah weighs 96 pounds. How much does Sarah's dog weigh? How much more does Sarah weigh than her dog weighs?

142   *Lesson 35*

Students first made fraction number families for statements that compare two values in lesson 31.

The type of problems shown in **part 4** were introduced in lesson 33. In lessons 36 and 37, students will apply the same analysis to problems that involve percents.

Part 5 makes the connection between mixed-number answers and decimal answers to division problems. Short division is assumed in Level F and appears in independent exercises from lesson 1. Students were taught to write answers as mixed numbers in both Level E and in the Bridge.

Writing answers as decimals prepares students for conventions of decimal division: adding zeros after the decimal point in the dividend and placing the decimal point in the answer.

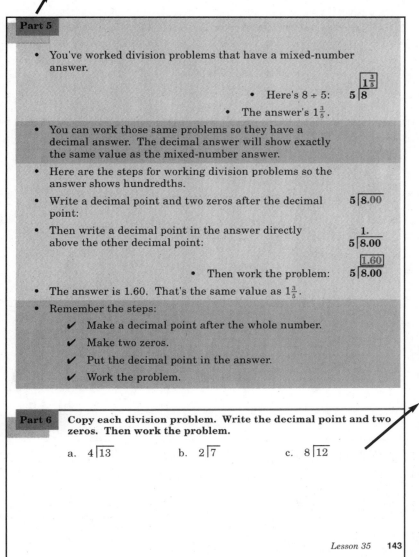

Part 5

- You've worked division problems that have a mixed-number answer.

  - Here's 8 ÷ 5: $5\overline{\smash{)}8}$ $\boxed{1\frac{3}{5}}$
  - The answer's $1\frac{3}{5}$.

- You can work those same problems so they have a decimal answer. The decimal answer will show exactly the same value as the mixed-number answer.

- Here are the steps for working division problems so the answer shows hundredths.

- Write a decimal point and two zeros after the decimal point: $5\overline{\smash{)}8.00}$

- Then write a decimal point in the answer directly above the other decimal point: $5\overline{\smash{)}8.00}$ with $1.$ above

- Then work the problem: $5\overline{\smash{)}8.00}$ with $\boxed{1.60}$ above

- The answer is 1.60. That's the same value as $1\frac{3}{5}$.

- Remember the steps:
  - ✔ Make a decimal point after the whole number.
  - ✔ Make two zeros.
  - ✔ Put the decimal point in the answer.
  - ✔ Work the problem.

Part 6 Copy each division problem. Write the decimal point and two zeros. Then work the problem.

  a. $4\overline{\smash{)}13}$ b. $2\overline{\smash{)}7}$ c. $8\overline{\smash{)}12}$

Lesson 35 **143**

The problem type shown in **part 6** also appears in lesson 36. In lessons 37, 39 and 41, students show answers to division problems as both mixed numbers and decimals.

In lessons 41 and 42, students will apply the same procedure to fractions. For example: 3/4 is written as $4\overline{\smash{)}3.00}$, giving the equivalent decimal value: $4\overline{\smash{)}3.0_20}$ with $\boxed{.75}$ above.

Decimal division will be introduced in lesson 53. Students first learn to divide a decimal value by a whole number. In lessons 71–77, students will learn to work a full range of problems that divide by a decimal value.

For each item in **part 7,** students express the fraction as the number of smaller units. For example: 3/4 of a yard is converted into inches by writing the equivalent fraction with a denominator of 36, i.e., $\frac{3}{4}\left(\frac{9}{9}\right) = \frac{27}{36}$. So 3/4 of a yard is 27 inches. This component task was taught and practiced in lessons 31–33. Complete problems of the form shown in **part 7** were introduced in lesson 34.

The reverse task of writing a mixed number given a description (e.g., given 3 weeks and 5 days, students write 3 5/7 weeks), was taught in lessons 19–23.

Parts 8 through 13 are the independent work for lesson 35. These parts review problem types that were practiced in a structured form in earlier lessons or taught in Level E or the Bridge.

Part 8 is a mixed set of circle problems that review area, circumference, diameter and radius. Circumference and diameter were introduced in lessons 24–26. In lessons 27 and 28, students also found the radius of circles, given the circumference. Area was introduced in lesson 29. Students were required to find both the area and circumference of circles in lessons 32 and 33.

Part 9 reviews various problem types involving fractions or whole numbers and fractions. These problem types were taught in Level E and the Bridge.

Part 10 reviews equivalent fractions, decimals and mixed numbers. These relationships were reviewed in a structured form in lessons 1–6.

To solve each of the problems in **part 11,** students make a fraction number family and a ratio table. (For an explanation of ratio-table word problems, see page 129.) For item a, students construct the number family:

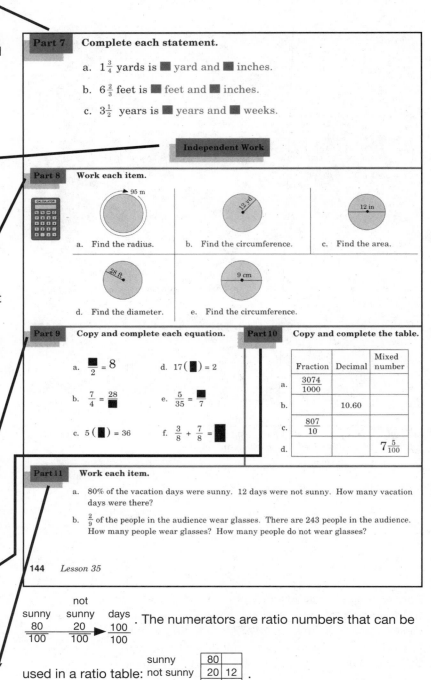

The numerators are ratio numbers that can be used in a ratio table:

sunny	80	
not sunny	20	12
days	100	

The total number of days may now be calculated. Ratio-table problems involving fractions were taught in lessons 10 and 11. Ratio-table problems involving decimals or percents were introduced in lesson 12, and appeared in seven subsequent lessons before lesson 35.

Part 12 requires students to judge which diagram corresponds to a comparative statement. For item a, students determine that they are comparing the height of the elephant to the height of the tree, so the tree represents one whole. Because the elephant is only 3/7 as high as the tree, the tree is the "big number" in the number family:

$$\underset{\text{dif}}{\frac{4}{7}} \quad \underset{\text{elephant}}{\frac{3}{7}} \longrightarrow \underset{\text{tree}}{\frac{7}{7}}$$

. The big number is written at the end of the arrow, and is the sum of the other two fractions.

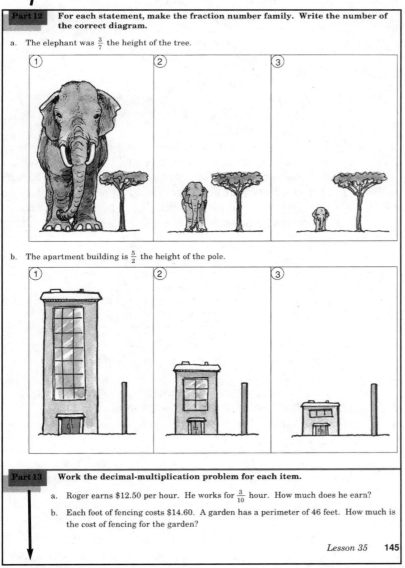

| Part 12 | For each statement, make the fraction number family. Write the number of the correct diagram. |

a. The elephant was $\frac{3}{7}$ the height of the tree.

① ② ③

b. The apartment building is $\frac{5}{2}$ the height of the pole.

① ② ③

| Part 13 | Work the decimal-multiplication problem for each item. |

a. Roger earns $12.50 per hour. He works for $\frac{3}{10}$ hour. How much does he earn?

b. Each foot of fencing costs $14.60. A garden has a perimeter of 46 feet. How much is the cost of fencing for the garden?

Lesson 35 **145**

Having constructed the number family, students select the appropriate diagram—diagram 3 for item a; diagram 1 for item b.

Part 13 reviews decimal multiplication in a word-problem application. For item a, students first convert 3/10 to a decimal value (.3), then multiply. Decimal multiplication was introduced in lesson 8, and reviewed in lessons 10–21. In later lessons (27–29), students represented decimal-multiplication problems as fraction multiplication, and worked each problem both ways.

Multiplication word problems were introduced in lesson 21. A variety of multiplication types were included in lessons 21–34 and discriminated from problems that cannot be solved by multiplication.

Level F

Sample Track: Probability

The work with probability extends the work with ratio tables. Students do not make number families for these applications, and the tables that they construct to show probability have more than three rows. However, the problems are a simple extension of what students learn about ratio tables.

The primary type of probability application students work with in Level F is a spinner on a circle graph. The circle is divided into slices. The probability of the spinner stopping on a particular slice depends on the size of the slice. If the slice is half of the entire circle, the probability is 1/2 or .5.

The work that prepares students for these problems begins in Lesson 72, where students complete ratio tables that have more than three rows and create such tables from information given in a circle graph.

Here's a table that appears in Lesson 72:

%	#
20	■
25	■
40	■
5	4
10	■
total 100	■

The students can't add in the second column. They figure out the missing numbers by first working the problem for the completed row: 5 times some value equals 4. The missing value is 4/5. Therefore, all the numbers in the first column are multiplied by 4/5 to obtain the corresponding numbers in the second column. Here's the completed table:

%	#
20	16
25	20
40	32
5	4
10	8
total 100	80

Problem C in Lesson 72 requires students to construct a ratio table from a circle graph:

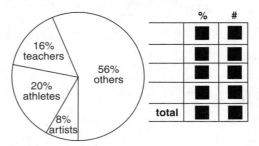

The conventions are:

1. The slices are ordered according to size, with the largest slice first and the smallest slice just above the total.

2. The information shown in the circle graph goes in the first column of the table. This graph gives percents; therefore, the percent numbers (without decimal points or percent signs) go in the first column. The total number of people is 350. That number goes in the second column.

	%	#
others	56	
athletes	20	
teachers	16	
artists	8	
total	100	350

Students complete the table by referring first to the row that has two numbers (100 and 350), figuring out the factor, then using their calculator to work multiplication problems for the rest of the rows.

Here's part of the introduction from Lesson 72:

d. Problem C. The circle graph shows percents for occupations of people at a meeting. The categories are **athletes, teachers, artists,** and **others.** The largest category is **others.**

• Your turn: Make a table. Show percents and the names in order of their size. Show **others** first, then **athletes,** then **teachers,** then **artists,** then **total.** The total is 100 percent because that's the whole circle. Raise your hand when your table has names and percents.

• (Write on the board:)

		%	#
c.	others	56	
	athletes	20	
	teachers	16	
	artists	8	
	total	100	

- Here's what you should have.
- The fact next to the circle graph tells about one of the numbers in the second column: There was a total of 350 people at the meeting.
- Write the number where it belongs and complete the table. Raise your hand when you're finished. (Observe students and give feedback.)
- (Write to show:)

		%	#
c.	others	56	196
	athletes	20	70
	teachers	16	56
	artists	8	28
	total	100	350

- Here's what you should have. You multiplied each row by the fraction 350/100 or the decimal 3 and 5-tenths. You could have simplified that into 35/10. Raise your hand if you got everything right.

For some problems that are presented in later lessons, students will make tables that have percents in the second column, not the first.

Here's an example from Lesson 74.

Make a complete table for the circle graph. Answer each question.

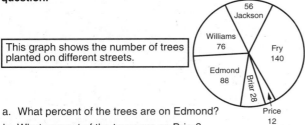

This graph shows the number of trees planted on different streets.

a. What percent of the trees are on Edmond?

b. What percent of the trees are on Briar?

c. What percent of the trees are on Fry?

d. What's the percent for the street that has the largest number of trees?

e. What's the percent for the street that has the fewest number of trees?

Starting in Lesson 79, students work similar problems that do not give a value for every category. Here's a problem from Lesson 79:

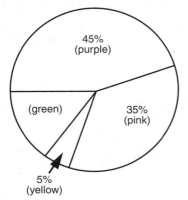

One part (green) is not given. To find it, students add the percents for the other slices and then subtract that total from 100. (In Lessons 76 through 78, students have already practiced the skill of combining values and subtracting.)

Variations of the problem type introduced in Lesson 79 require students to use information about fractions or percents to figure out the degrees for the various slices.

Probability problems are introduced in Lesson 81. The problems are simple extensions of the work with circle graphs. The only difference is the kind of information presented in the two columns of the table. The first column shows percents. The second shows expected numbers based on a total of so many trials. Here's part of the introduction from Lesson 81:

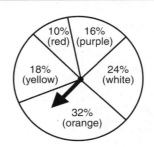

A person spins the arrow 50 times.

b. You're going to work a problem that asks how many times you would expect the spinner to land on different colors.

- You can work probability problems of this type just like other ratio-table problems.
- You'll show the percents in the first column of your table and the second column will show the number of times you would expect the spinner to land on each color. The heading for that column is trials. 1 trial is 1 spin.

c. The circle shows the percents for the parts. The fact above the circle tells the total number of times somebody spins the spinner. That's the total for the second column.

- The most probable color is the color with the largest percent. What color is that? (Signal.) *Orange.*
- List the colors from most probable to least probable. Put percent numbers in the first column and one number in the second column. Raise your hand when you've done that. (Observe students and give feedback.)

- (Write on the board:)

	%	trials
orange	32	
white	24	
yellow	18	
purple	16	
red	10	
total	100	50

- Here's what you should have.
- Make sure your names are in the right order. Then figure out the number of times you would expect the spinner to land on different colors. Remember, you're spinning 50 times. Raise your hand when you've completed the table and answered the questions.
(Observe students and give feedback.)
- (Write to show:)

	%	trials
orange	32	16
white	24	12
yellow	18	9
purple	16	8
red	10	5
total	100	50

- Here's what you should have.
- If you take 50 trials, how many times would you expect the spinner to land on purple? (Signal.) *8.*
- If you take 50 trials, how many times would you expect the spinner to land on yellow? (Signal.) *9.*
- If you take 50 trials, how many times would you expect the spinner to land on orange? (Signal.) *16.*
- If you take 50 trials, how many times would you expect the spinner to land on white? (Signal.) *12.*
- If you take 50 trials, how many times would you expect the spinner to land on red? (Signal.) *5.*
d. Raise your hand if you got everything right.

More difficult probability problems are introduced in Lesson 83. These problems require a table with three columns—one for percents, one for expected numbers, and one for actual numbers. The problems give information about actual numbers, which are not the same as expected numbers. Students first figure out the expected numbers, then place the actual numbers in the table. Students follow the rule of finding the expected number that is close to the actual number and place the actual number in the same row as the corresponding expected number.

Here's the problem from Lesson 83:

Copy and complete the table.

This experiment involves 60 trials.

Facts
1. The spinner landed on this color 14 times.
2. The spinner landed on this color 19 times.
3. The spinner landed on this color 23 times.
4. The spinner land on this color 4 times.

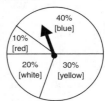

colors	%	expected	actual
	■	■	■
	■	■	■
	■	■	■
	■	■	■
total	■	60	60

Students complete the first two columns. They know that the total number of trials is 60, so they can work the problem: 100 times some value equals 60. Students work the problem on their calculator. The missing value is 6-tenths.

Students multiply the various rows by 6-tenths to complete the first two columns, showing the names for the different colors.

colors	%	expected	actual
blue	40	24	
yellow	30	18	
white	20	12	
red	10	6	
total	100	60	60

Next, students compare the actual values with the expected values and put each actual value next to the value that is closest in size.

In subsequent lessons, students work different variations. For some, not all the percents are given. For some, the information about percents is presented through statements, not by a circle graph.

The final application is a project presented in Lesson 93. Students first figure out the probabilities for different possible outcomes obtained by rolling two dice. Students make a table with the various possibilities in the first column and the expected outcomes for 72 trials in the second column. Finally, students make a circle graph that shows the various possibilities.

Placement Testing

Placement Overview

Levels A through F of *Connecting Math Concepts* are appropriate for regular education students in first through sixth grade. The program is particularly effective with students who are at risk in mathematics. The Bridge program is suitable for older students performing at a fifth- or sixth-grade level.

Each level (except Level F) contains a placement test to determine whether students have the prerequisite skills necessary for success in the program.

Placement in Level F is not determined by a placement test but by successful completion of either Levels E or Bridge.

Note: The placement tests for the various levels of the *Connecting Math Concepts* program provide you with valuable information regarding the performance level of your students. However, for lower-performing students it might be advisable to test on two adjacent levels that you are considering. If a student fails a placement test, you have clear information that the level is too difficult for the student.

In some cases, a student might pass a placement test and still be more appropriately placed in a lower level of the program. This is the case if the lower level covers many objectives that the student has not yet mastered.

If in doubt, place the student in the lower level.

Placement Testing: Level A

Level A is appropriate for any child who meets the placement criteria. A placement test is used to measure the child's ability to:
- count to 10 (part 1).
- count objects (part 2).
- identify numbers that are one more (part 3).
- write numerals from dictation (part 4).

A reproducible copy of the placement test for Level A (taken from the Level A *Teacher's Guide*) follows. *Note:* The test consists of teacher's instructions and the child's sheet.

The test is administered to children individually, not to groups of children.

Administration takes 3–5 minutes per child.

Administering the Placement Test

Arrange to test children in a place that is reasonably quiet. Make sure that each child has a pencil.

The test may be administered by parents or volunteers.

The administrator is to:
- fill out the information at the top of the Teacher's Instructions.
- present parts 1 and 2 as specified.
- circle + or − to indicate pass or fail.

If the child does not pass parts 1 and 2, do not present any more parts of the test. The child should not be placed in Level A.

If the child passes both items 3 and 4, the child should start at Lesson 11 of Level A.

If the child does not pass both parts 3 and 4, the child should start at Lesson 1 of Level A.

Circle the appropriate placement for the child in the placement box at the bottom of the Teacher's Instructions.

Placement Test for *Connecting Math Concepts, Level A*

Teacher's Instructions

Child's Name: _____ Teacher's Name: _____

Date: _____

Note: Test is administered **individually**. Not to groups of children.

1. COUNTING
   "Count to 10." (Cross out missed or omitted numbers. Saying 11 is an error.)

   1 2 3 4 5 6 7 8 9 10 11

   Passing Criteria: No mistakes.

2. OBJECT COUNTING
   a. (Touch stars.) "Count the stars."   (Child counts.) "How many stars?"   +   −
   b. (Touch lines.) "Count these lines." (Child counts.) "How many lines?"   +   −

   Passing Criteria: No mistakes.

   Placement Instructions for parts 1 and 2:
   a. Present parts 3 and 4 to children who passed both parts 1 and 2.
   b. Do not place children who fail either parts 1 or 2 in Level A.
      A possible placement is *DISTAR Arithmetic 1.*

3. ONE MORE
   "My turn: What number comes after 7? 8."
   a. "Your turn: What number comes after 4?"   +   −
   b. "What number comes after 9?"   +   −
   c. "What number comes after 5?"   +   −

   Passing Criteria: No mistakes.

4. NUMERAL DICTATION
   (Point to blanks on child test sheet.)   "You're going to write some numerals."
   a. (Touch the first blank.)   "Write a 7."   +   −
   b. (Touch the next blank.)   "Write a 4."   +   −
   c. (Touch the next blank.)   "Write a 5."   +   −
   d. (Touch the last blank.)   "Write an 8."   +   −

   Passing Criteria: No mistakes. (Count correct numbers written backwards as correct.)

   Placement Instructions for parts 3 and 4:
   a. Children who do **not** pass both parts 3 and 4 begin *Connecting Math Concepts, Level A* on **Lesson 1**.
   b. Children who pass both parts 3 and 4 begin **Lesson 11**.

   Note: Children who pass both parts 3 and 4 and who know answers to simple addition problems such as **5 + 1** and **6 + 2** could be given the placement test for *Connecting Math Concepts Level B.*

PLACEMENT:

DISTAR 1	*CONNECTING MATH CONCEPTS, LEVEL A*	
Lesson 1	Lesson 1	Lesson 11

Name: _____

Placement Test for _Connecting Math Concepts, Level A:_ Child Test Sheet

☆ ☆ ☆ ☆ ☆ ☆

| | | | | | | | | |

———————————————————————————

—— —— —— ——

———————————————————————————

Placement Testing: Level B

Level B is appropriate for any child who successfully completes Level A and for any child who has the skills assumed by Level B. The test measures the child's ability to:
- write the counting numbers through 10 (part 1).
- count objects and write the appropriate numeral (part 2).
- write answers to addition-subtraction facts (part 3).
- write 2-digit numerals (part 4).
- write counting numbers for 2-digit sequences (part 5).

A reproducible copy of the placement test for Level B (taken from the Level B *Teacher's Guide*) follows. The test is group administered and requires about 10 minutes for children to complete. The script for presenting the test appears below.

Administering the Placement Test

Try to test children on the first day of instruction.

Pass out a test form to each child. Present the wording in the test administration script.

Note: What you say is shown in **blue** type.

Circulate among the children as you present the items.

When observing the children, you should make sure that they are working on the correct part or correct item of the test. Do not prompt them in a way that would let them know the answer to the item.

TEST ADMINISTRATION SCRIPT

Make sure each child has a copy of the placement test.

Direct children to write their name on the top line.

PART 1. Everybody, touch part 1. √ (Check children's responses.)
There are **X**s below each box. You're going to count the **X**s and write the correct numeral in the box.
Touch box A. √
Count the **X**s under box A and write the numeral. Raise your hand when you're finished.
(Observe children. Make sure they understand what they are supposed to do. Do not help them in writing the appropriate numeral.)

Touch box B. √
Count the **X**s under box B and write the numeral. Raise your hand when you're finished.

PART 2. Everybody, touch part 2. √
That's a number line, but a lot of the numbers are missing. Here's what the numbers should say: Zero, 1, 2, 3, 4, 5, 6, 7, 8, 9, 10.
The first number shown is zero. Touch zero. √
The next number is 1. Touch 1. √
The next number is 2. Touch 2. √
The next number is missing. What should that number be?
Write 3 where it belongs. Then write the rest of the numbers through 10. Raise your hand when you're finished. (After no more than 1 minute, present Part 3.)

PART 3. Everybody, touch part 3. √
The top problem is completed. You're going to complete the bottom problem. The top problem in A is 6 plus 1 equals 7. Your turn: Complete that problem. Write the answer in the box. Raise your hand when you're finished.
(Observe children. Make sure they are working the appropriate problem. Do not tell them the answer.)

PART 4. Everybody, touch part 4. √
You're going to write a 2-digit numeral on each line.
Touch line A. √
Write the numeral 18. 18. Raise your hand when you're finished.
Touch line C. √
Write the numeral 46. 46. Raise your hand when you're finished.

PART 5. Everybody, find part 5. √
These are number lines for large numbers. The numerals are supposed to show what you'd say when you count. But some numbers are missing on each number line. You'll write the missing numbers.
Touch row A. √
The numbers shown are 42, 43, and 44. Write the numbers that come next when you count. Raise your hand when you're finished.
(Observe children.)
Touch row B. √
The numbers are 67, 68, and 69. Write the numbers that come next when you count. Raise your hand when you're finished.

Connecting Math Concepts, Level B

Placement Test

Name _____ Score _____

Part 1

a.
[ ]

x x x
x x x
x x

b.
[ ]

x x x x x
x x x x x
x x

Part 2

Write the numbers on the number line.

0   1   2   __ __ __ __ __ __ __ __ __ __

Part 3

a. 6 + 1 =   7

6 + 2 =   [ ]

b. 5 − 1 =   4

5 − 2 =   [ ]

Part 4

a. _____

b. _____

c. _____

Part 5

a.   42   43   44   __   __

b.   67   68   69   __   __

Scoring the Test

- To score the test, mark each error, count the total errors and write the number at the top of the sheet.

- Reversals of digits are not to be treated as errors:

  Ɛ for 3, 2I for 12.

- Transposition of digits in 2-digit numerals **is** a mistake:

  81 for 18 is an error.

Answer Key

Connecting Math Concepts, Level B

Placement Test

Name _____ Score _____

Part 1

a.

8

x x x
x x x
x x

b.

12

x x x x x
x x x x x
x x

Part 2

Write the numbers on the number line.

0   1 3 4 5 6 7 8 9 10

Part 3

a. 6 + 1 =

6 + 2 = 8

b. 5 − 1 =

5 − 2 = 3

Part 4

7 a. 18

b. 81

c. 46

4

Part 5

a.   42   43   44   45   46

b.   67   68   69   70   71

Placement Criteria

Children pass the test if they make no more than 4 errors.

Children fail the test if they make 5 or more errors.

If 80% of the children pass the test, present these lessons: Transition Lesson A, Transition Lesson B, then Lessons 16, 17, 18, and so on through Lesson 120.

If fewer than 80% of the children pass the test, present these lessons: 1, 2, 3, 4, 5, and so on through Lesson 120.

Children who make 9 or more errors on the test may not have the skills required for Level B and would be more appropriately placed in Level A or in a program that teaches basic counting and writing skills.

> **Note:** This placement procedure assumes that all children in the class will work on the same lessons. If the class is divided into small groups for math instruction, children can be grouped according to their placement-test performance (with some groups starting on Transition A and, others starting on Lesson 1).
>
> Note also that the Transition lessons A and B review skills that are taught in Level A. These transition lessons permit children who have not gone through Level A to transition to the conventions in Level B.

If children who have completed *A* are very solid on the placement test, most of them making no mistakes, you may begin on Lesson 16, rather than on Transition Lesson A. See page 4 for options with first graders. Here's a summary of the placement criteria for second graders:

PLACEMENT CRITERIA FOR SECOND GRADERS

80% or more pass	Transition Lessons A, B, then 16–120
Less than 80% pass	Lessons 1–120
Children making 9 or more errors	Place in a first level program

Placement Testing: Level C

Level C is appropriate for any student who meets the placement criteria. A placement test is used to measure the student's ability to:
- Write numerals from dictation.
- Write answers to addition and subtraction facts.

A reproducible copy of the placement test (taken from the Level C *Teacher's Guide*) follows. Administration takes 3–5 minutes.

Administering the Placement Test

Try to test students on the first day of instruction.

Pass out a test form to each student. Present the wording in the test administration script.

Note: What you say is shown in **blue** type.

Circulate among the students as you present the items.

When observing the students, you should make sure that they are working on the correct part or correct item of the test. Do not prompt them in a way that would let them know the answer to the item.

TEST ADMINISTRATION SCRIPT

- (Direct students to fill out their names on the top of the test form.)
- Everybody, find part 1. I'm going to dictate 2-digit numbers. You'll write them on the appropriate lines, starting with line A.
- Touch line A.
  Write 70 on line A. 70. (Pause 3 seconds.)
- Line B. Write 17 on line B. 17. (Pause 3 seconds.)
  (Repeat for remaining numerals: 51, 42, 96, 15, 20, 71.)
- Pencils down.
- Everybody, find part 2.
  For part 2, you'll write answers to the addition problems and subtraction problems. I will time you. You will have two minutes to write all the answers.
- Be careful. Pencils ready . . . Go.
  (Time students. At the end of two minutes, say:)
- Everybody stop and put your pencils down.
  (Collect test forms.)

Placement Criteria

The criteria for passing the test are:

	Pass	Fail
Part 1	0 or 1 error	2 or more errors
Part 2	0–3 errors	4 or more errors
Total Test	0–4 errors	5 or more errors

Students who fail a particular part should receive remedial work on the skill tested by the part (writing numerals, addition facts, subtraction facts). Students who make a total of five or more errors should not be placed in Level C. They should either be placed in Level B or in a program that addresses basic fact and number relationships.

If more than 40% of the students fail the test, Level C is inappropriate for the class. Students should either work on Level B or should receive a great deal of practice on basic fact and number relationships before entering Level C.

Connecting Math Concepts, Level C

Placement Test

Name _____ Score _____

Part 1

a. _____   b. _____   c. _____   d. _____

e. _____   f. _____   g. _____   h. _____

Part 2

| a. $\begin{array}{r}6\\+3\\\hline\end{array}$ | b. $\begin{array}{r}4\\+2\\\hline\end{array}$ | c. $\begin{array}{r}2\\+9\\\hline\end{array}$ | d. $\begin{array}{r}1\\+6\\\hline\end{array}$ | e. $\begin{array}{r}2\\+3\\\hline\end{array}$ | f. $\begin{array}{r}3\\+8\\\hline\end{array}$ | g. $\begin{array}{r}3\\+5\\\hline\end{array}$ |

| h. $\begin{array}{r}1\\+1\\\hline\end{array}$ | i. $\begin{array}{r}5\\+2\\\hline\end{array}$ | j. $\begin{array}{r}6\\+1\\\hline\end{array}$ | k. $\begin{array}{r}8\\+2\\\hline\end{array}$ | l. $\begin{array}{r}5\\+0\\\hline\end{array}$ | m. $\begin{array}{r}3\\+3\\\hline\end{array}$ | n. $\begin{array}{r}7\\+3\\\hline\end{array}$ |

| o. $\begin{array}{r}9\\-2\\\hline\end{array}$ | p. $\begin{array}{r}4\\-0\\\hline\end{array}$ | q. $\begin{array}{r}5\\-1\\\hline\end{array}$ | r. $\begin{array}{r}7\\-7\\\hline\end{array}$ | s. $\begin{array}{r}7\\-2\\\hline\end{array}$ | t. $\begin{array}{r}8\\-1\\\hline\end{array}$ | u. $\begin{array}{r}10\\-1\\\hline\end{array}$ |

| v. $\begin{array}{r}2\\-0\\\hline\end{array}$ | w. $\begin{array}{r}2\\-1\\\hline\end{array}$ | x. $\begin{array}{r}2\\-2\\\hline\end{array}$ |

Connecting Math Concepts, Level C

Placement Test Answer Key

Part 1

a. 70   b. 17   c. 51   d. 42

e. 96   f. 15   g. 20   h. 71

Part 2

a.
$$6 + 3 = 9$$
b.
$$4 + 2 = 6$$
c.
$$2 + 9 = 11$$
d.
$$1 + 6 = 7$$
e.
$$2 + 3 = 5$$
f.
$$3 + 8 = 11$$
g.
$$3 + 5 = 8$$

h.
$$1 + 1 = 2$$
i.
$$5 + 2 = 7$$
j.
$$6 + 1 = 7$$
k.
$$8 + 2 = 10$$
l.
$$5 + 0 = 5$$
m.
$$3 + 3 = 6$$
n.
$$7 + 3 = 10$$

o.
$$9 - 2 = 7$$
p.
$$4 - 0 = 4$$
q.
$$5 - 1 = 4$$
r.
$$7 - 7 = 0$$
s.
$$7 - 2 = 5$$
t.
$$8 - 1 = 7$$
u.
$$10 - 1 = 9$$

v.
$$2 - 0 = 2$$
w.
$$2 - 1 = 1$$
x.
$$2 - 2 = 0$$

Placement Testing: Level D

Level D of *Connecting Math Concepts* is appropriate for any student who completes Level C or who passes the placement test. A reproducible copy of the placement test (taken from the Level D Teacher's Guide) follows.

Administering the Placement Test

Try to test students on the first day of instruction.

Pass out a test form to each student. Present the wording in the test administration script.
Note: What you say is shown in **blue** type.

When observing the students, you should make sure that they are working on the correct part or correct item of the test. Do not prompt them in a way that would let them know the answer to the item.

If the class is particularly weak on parts of the placement test, work on these skills before starting with Level D. Present items similar to those of the test.

TEST ADMINISTRATION SCRIPT

- Find part 1.
  These are multiplication facts. You have one minute to finish these problems. Read them carefully. Get ready. Go.
- (At the end of one minute, say:) Stop writing. Pencils down.
- Find part 2.
  You're going to write numerals that I dictate. You can see three hundred twenty-four is already written. That shows where you'd begin a hundred numeral.

Numeral A. Seven hundred forty-eight. Write it.
Numeral B. Six hundred two. Write it.
Numeral C. 17. Write it.
Numeral D. 300. Write it.
- You'll work the rest of the parts on your own. For part 3, read each problem. Write the number problem and the answer.
- For the rest of the parts, just write the answer to each problem. Raise your hand when you're finished.
- (Collect test forms.)

Placement Criteria

The criteria for passing the test are:

	Pass	Fail
Part 1	0–2 errors	3 or more errors
Part 2	0 errors	1 or more errors
Part 3	0 errors	1 or more errors
Part 4	0–1 errors	2 or more errors
Part 5	0–1 errors	2 or more errors
Part 6	0 errors	1 or more errors
Part 7	0–1 errors	2 or more errors
OVERALL	Students pass 5–7 parts.	Students pass 4 or fewer parts.

Is Level D appropriate for your classroom? A rule of thumb is that three-fourths or more of the students in the class should pass the placement test. If more than one quarter of the students fail the placement test, it may be difficult to present Level D to the entire class. A recommendation is to place the lower performers in Level C.

Placement Test

Name _____ Score _____

Part 1

a. $5 \times 4 =$ ___ e. $4 \times 0 =$ ___ i. $8 \times 5 =$ ___

b. $2 \times 6 =$ ___ f. $9 \times 1 =$ ___ j. $1 \times 2 =$ ___

c. $7 \times 2 =$ ___ g. $4 \times 4 =$ ___ k. $3 \times 2 =$ ___

d. $8 \times 10 =$ ___ h. $3 \times 5 =$ ___ l. $0 \times 10 =$ ___

Part 2

```
3 2 4
```
a.

b.

c.

d.

Part 3

a. Hiro Moto had 47 nuts. Somebody ate 30 of his nuts. How many did he end up with?

b. A man had 23. Then he got 16 more. How many did he end up with?

Part 4

a. $\begin{array}{r} 14 \\ + 79 \\ \hline \end{array}$ b. $\begin{array}{r} 370 \\ + 98 \\ \hline \end{array}$

c. $\begin{array}{r} 39 \\ + 95 \\ \hline \end{array}$ d. $\begin{array}{r} 12 \\ 46 \\ + 599 \\ \hline \end{array}$

Part 5

a. $2\,\overline{)14}$ b. $5\,\overline{)30}$ c. $9\,\overline{)27}$

d. $8\,\overline{)8}$ e. $1\,\overline{)8}$

Part 6

a. $\begin{array}{r} 54 \\ \times 2 \\ \hline \end{array}$ b. $\begin{array}{r} 43 \\ \times 5 \\ \hline \end{array}$

Part 7

a. $\begin{array}{r} 360 \\ - 218 \\ \hline \end{array}$ b. $\begin{array}{r} 37 \\ - 18 \\ \hline \end{array}$ c. $\begin{array}{r} 647 \\ - 134 \\ \hline \end{array}$ d. $\begin{array}{r} 409 \\ - 136 \\ \hline \end{array}$

Placement Test Answer Key

Part 1

a. $5 \times 4 =$ _20_   e. $4 \times 0 =$ _0_   i. $8 \times 5 =$ _40_

b. $2 \times 6 =$ _12_   f. $9 \times 1 =$ _9_   j. $1 \times 2 =$ _2_

c. $7 \times 2 =$ _14_   g. $4 \times 4 =$ _16_   k. $3 \times 2 =$ _6_

d. $8 \times 10 =$ _80_   h. $3 \times 5 =$ _15_   l. $0 \times 10 =$ _0_

Part 2

	3	2	4
a.	7	4	8
b.	6	0	2
c.		1	7
d.	3	0	0

Part 3

a. Hiro Moto had 47 nuts. Somebody ate 30 of his nuts. How many did he end up with?

$$\boxed{}\, 30 \longrightarrow 47 \begin{array}{r} 47 \\ -\,30 \\ \hline 17 \text{ nuts} \end{array}$$

b. A man had 23. Then he got 16 more. How many did he end up with?

$$23\ \ 16 \longrightarrow \boxed{} \begin{array}{r} 23 \\ +\,16 \\ \hline 39 \end{array}$$

Part 4

a. $\begin{array}{r} {}^{1}14 \\ +\,79 \\ \hline 93 \end{array}$ b. $\begin{array}{r} {}^{1}370 \\ +\,98 \\ \hline 468 \end{array}$

c. $\begin{array}{r} 39 \\ +\,95 \\ \hline 134 \end{array}$ d. $\begin{array}{r} {}^{1}12 \\ 46 \\ +\,599 \\ \hline 657 \end{array}$

Part 5

a. $2\overline{)14}$ → 7   b. $5\overline{)30}$ → 6   c. $9\overline{)27}$ → 3

d. $8\overline{)8}$ → 1   e. $1\overline{)8}$ → 8

Part 6

a. $\begin{array}{r} 54 \\ \times\,2 \\ \hline 108 \end{array}$ b. $\begin{array}{r} {}^{1}43 \\ \times\,5 \\ \hline 215 \end{array}$

Part 7

a. $\begin{array}{r} {}^{5}3\!\!\!/60 \\ -\,218 \\ \hline 142 \end{array}$ b. $\begin{array}{r} {}^{2}3\!\!\!/7 \\ -\,18 \\ \hline 19 \end{array}$ c. $\begin{array}{r} 647 \\ -\,134 \\ \hline 513 \end{array}$ d. $\begin{array}{r} {}^{3}4\!\!\!/09 \\ -\,136 \\ \hline 273 \end{array}$

Placement Testing: Level E

There are two placement tests. Placement Test A is for any student who has not gone through Level D of *Connecting Math Concepts*. Placement Test B is for any student who has completed Level D. Reproducible copies (taken from the Level E *Teacher's Guide*) follows.

Administering the Placement Test

Administer the placement test that is appropriate for the class. If none of the students went through Level D, administer Placement Test A. If some of the students went through Level D, administer Placement Test A. If all or nearly all of the students when through Level D, administer Placement Test B. If possible, complete the testing on the first day of instruction.

Pass out a test form to each student. Present the wording in the test administration script.

Note: What you say is shown in blue type.

When observing the students, make sure that they are working on the correct part or correct item of the test. Do not prompt them in a way that would let them know the answer to the item.

TEST A ADMINISTRATION SCRIPT:
FOR NEW STUDENTS ONLY

- Find part 1.
  You're going to write numerals that I dictate. You're going to line them up the same way you would if you were adding them. You can see 7 thousand, 3 hundred 24 is already written. That shows where you'd begin a thousands numeral.
  Numeral A. 2 thousand, 6 hundred 50. Write it.
  Numeral B. 11 thousand, 9 hundred 3. Write it.
  Numeral C. 7 hundred 9. Write it.
  Numeral D. 20 thousand, 45. Write it.
- You'll work the rest of the parts on your own. For part 3, read each problem. Write the number problem and the answer.
- For the rest of the parts, just follow the directions for working each item. Raise your hand when you're finished.
- (Collect test forms.)

TEST B ADMINISTRATION SCRIPT:
FOR CONTINUING STUDENTS ONLY

- This is a test. Follow the directions for working each part. Raise your hand when you're finished.
- (Collect test forms.)

Placement Criteria

The criteria for passing Test A are:

	Pass	Fail
Part 1	0–1 errors	2 or more errors
Part 2	0–1 errors	2 or more errors
Part 3	0–1 errors	2 or more errors
Part 4	0 errors	1 or more errors
Part 5	0–2 errors	3 or more errors
OVERALL	8 or fewer errors	9 or more errors
PLACEMENT	CMC Level E Lesson 1	CMC Level D Administer placement test

Is Level E appropriate for your classroom? A rule of thumb is that three-fourths or more of the students in the class should pass the placement test. If more than one-fourth of the students fail the placement test, it may be difficult to present Level E to the entire class. A recommendation is to place the lower performers in Level D.

The criteria for passing Test B are:

	Pass	Fail
Part 1	0 errors	1 or more errors
Part 2	0–1 errors	2 or more errors
Part 3	0 errors	1 or more errors
Part 4	0–1 errors	2 or more errors
Part 5	0 errors	1 or more errors
Part 6	0–2 errors	3 or more errors
Part 7	0 errors	1 or more errors
OVERALL	5 or fewer errors	6 or more errors
PLACEMENT	CMC Level E Lesson 16	CMC Level E Lesson 1

If more than one quarter of the students fail test B, begin instruction at Lesson 1 of Level E.

If three-fourths or more of the students pass the placement test, begin instruction at Lesson 16 of Level E.

Note: Students who failed the test need additional teaching and practice if they are to keep pace with classmates who start at Lesson 16. Try to provide that additional work, or place these students in a group that is working on material that is appropriate for these students (possibly at Lesson 1 of Level E).

Connecting Math Concepts, Level E

Placement Test A (for new students)

Name _____ Score _____

Part 1 Write the numbers your teacher says.

	7,	3	2	4
a.				
b.				
c.				
d.				

Part 2 Work each item.

a.
$$411 - 306$$

b.
$$1075 \times 6$$

c.
$$417 + 94 + 159$$

d.
$$380 \times 9$$

Part 3 Figure out the answer to each question. Show your work.

a. There are 37 students on the playground. 16 of the students are boys. How many girls are on the playground?

b. Phyllis had 48 dogs. She bought another 103 dogs. How many dogs does Phyllis have now?

c. A man had 59 stamps in his collection. He traded some stamps for coins. Now he has 45 stamps. How many stamps did he trade?

d. A truck started out with 2190 pounds of gravel. It delivered 2000 pounds of gravel. How many pounds of gravel were still on the truck?

Part 4 Work each item.

a. $\dfrac{10}{3} - \dfrac{8}{3} =$

b. $\dfrac{2}{12} + \dfrac{9}{12} =$

c. $\dfrac{9}{10} - \dfrac{7}{10} =$

Part 5 Work each item.

a. $8 \times 7 =$

b. $9\overline{)68}$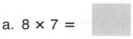

c. $4\overline{)0}$

d. $0 \times 56 =$

e. $7 \times 6 =$

f. $7\overline{)42}$

g. $9 \times 8 =$

h. $1\overline{)9}$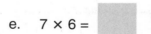

i. $14 \times 1 =$

j. $7\overline{)45}$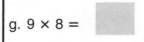

Placement Test B (for students continuing from Level D)   Name _____ Score _____

| **Part 1** | Work each item |

a.   8 8
   × 4 7

b.   1 5 6
   × 4 2

| **Part 2** | Complete the table. |

Multiplication	Division
a. 4 × ▨ = 12	▨
b. 9 × ▨ = 54	▨

| **Part 3** | Answer each question. |

This table shows the number of deer and squirrels that live in Hill Park and River Park.

a. How many deer live in River Park? _____

b. What's the total number of squirrels for both parks? _____

c. In which park do fewer squirrels live? _____

d. What is the total number for both animals in both parks? _____

	Deer	Squirrels	Total for both animals
Hill Park	23	19	42
River Park	40	86	126
Total for both parks	63	105	168

| **Part 4** | Write the fraction for each lettered arrow. |

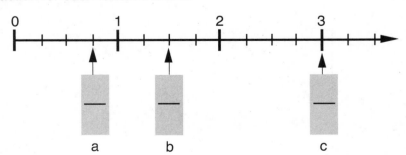

Part 5 Complete the table.

Fraction Equation	Division
a. $\dfrac{24}{3}$ = ▨	▨ $3\overline{)2\ 4}$
b. $\dfrac{28}{7}$ = ▨	▨

Part 6 Complete the table.

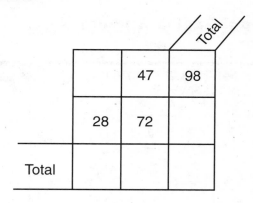

		Total
	47	98
28	72	
Total		

Part 7 Figure out the answer to each question. Show your work.

a. Robert is 25 pounds heavier than Adam. Robert weighs 96 pounds. How many pounds does Adam weigh?

b. The chess club has 31 fewer members than the band. There are 68 people in the chess club. How many people are in the band?

Connecting Math Concepts, Level E

Placement Test A Answer Key

Part 1 Write the numbers your teacher says.

	7,	3	2	4
a.	2,	6	5	0
b.	1 1,	9	0	3
c.		7	0	9
d.	2 0,	0	4	5

Part 2 Work each item.

a.
$$\begin{array}{r} 411 \\ -306 \\ \hline 105 \end{array}$$

b.
$$\begin{array}{r} 1075 \\ \times\ \ \ 6 \\ \hline 6450 \end{array}$$

c.
$$\begin{array}{r} 417 \\ 94 \\ +159 \\ \hline 670 \end{array}$$

d.
$$\begin{array}{r} 380 \\ \times\ \ \ 9 \\ \hline 3420 \end{array}$$

Part 3 Figure out the answer to each question. Show your work.

a. There are 37 students on the playground. 16 of the students are boys. How many girls are on the playground?

21 girls

b. Phyllis had 48 dogs. She bought another 103 dogs. How many dogs does Phyllis have now?

151 dogs

c. A man had 59 stamps in his collection. He traded some stamps for coins. Now he has 45 stamps. How many stamps did he trade?

14 stamps

d. A truck started out with 2190 pounds of gravel. It delivered 2000 pounds of gravel. How many pounds of gravel were still on the truck?

190 pounds

Part 4 Work each item.

a. $\dfrac{10}{3} - \dfrac{8}{3} = \dfrac{2}{3}$

b. $\dfrac{2}{12} + \dfrac{9}{12} = \dfrac{11}{12}$

c. $\dfrac{9}{10} - \dfrac{7}{10} = \dfrac{2}{10}$

Part 5 Work each item.

a. $8 \times 7 =$ 56

b. $9\overline{)68}$ $\quad 7\frac{5}{9}$

c. $4\overline{)0}$ $\quad 0$

d. $0 \times 56 =$ 0

e. $7 \times 6 =$ 42

f. $7\overline{)42}$ $\quad 6$

g. $9 \times 8 =$ 72

h. $1\overline{)9}$ $\quad 9$

i. $14 \times 1 =$ 14

j. $7\overline{)45}$ $\quad 6\frac{3}{7}$

Placement Test B Answer Key

Part 1	Work each item

a.
```
    8 8
  × 4 7
   6 1 6
+ 3 5 2 0
  4 1 3 6
```

b.
```
    1 5 6
  ×  4 2
    3 1 2
+ 6 2 4 0
  6 5 5 2
```

Part 2	Complete the table.

	Multiplication	Division
a.	4 × **3** = 12	**3** / 4⟌12
b.	9 × **6** = 54	**6** / 9⟌54

Part 3	Answer each question.

This table shows the number of deer and squirrels that live in Hill Park and River Park.

a. How many deer live in River Park? **40 deer**

b. What's the total number of squirrels for both parks? **105 squirrels**

c. In which park do fewer squirrels live? **Hill Park**

d. What is the total number for both animals in both parks? **168**

	Deer	Squirrels	Total for both animals
Hill Park	23	19	42
River Park	40	86	126
Total for both parks	63	105	168

Part 4	Write the fraction for each lettered arrow.

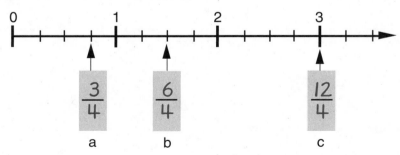

a. $\dfrac{3}{4}$ b. $\dfrac{6}{4}$ c. $\dfrac{12}{4}$

Part 5   Complete the table.

	Fraction Equation	Division
a.	$\frac{24}{3}$ = **8**	$\begin{array}{r} 8 \\ 3\overline{)24} \end{array}$
b.	$\frac{28}{7}$ = **4**	$\begin{array}{r} 4 \\ 7\overline{)28} \end{array}$

Part 6   Complete the table.

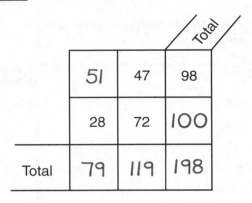

			Total
	51	47	98
	28	72	100
Total	79	119	198

Part 7   Figure out the answer to each question. Show your work.

a. Robert is 25 pounds heavier than Adam. Robert weighs 96 pounds. How many pounds does Adam weigh?

b. The chess club has 31 fewer members than the band. There are 68 people in the chess club. How many people are in the band?

Dif A R

25 → 96

$\begin{array}{r} 96 \\ -25 \\ \hline 71 \text{ pounds} \end{array}$

Dif C B

31 68 →

$\begin{array}{r} 31 \\ +68 \\ \hline 99 \text{ people} \end{array}$

Placement Testing: Level Bridge

Connecting Math Concepts, Level Bridge is appropriate for any student in grades 6 or above who has not been through Level E of *Connecting Math Concepts* and who passes the placement test.

A reproducible copy of the placement test (taken from the Level Bridge *Teacher's Guide*) follows.

Administering the Placement Test

Try to test students on the first day of instruction. Allow 20 minutes.

Pass out a test form to each student. Give the following directions:

- You'll do the test on your own. Read each problem. Show the work for each problem and the answer. Raise your hand when you're finished.
- (Collect test forms.)

Placement Criteria

The criteria for passing the test are:

	Pass	**Fail**
Part 1	0–1 errors	2 or more errors
Part 2	0–1 errors	2 or more errors
Part 3	0–1 errors	2 or more errors
Part 4	0–1 errors	2 or more errors
Part 5	0–1 errors	2 or more errors
Part 6	0–1 errors	2 or more errors
OVERALL	Students pass 4–6 parts and make no more than 7 errors.	Students pass 3 or fewer parts.

Is the Bridge appropriate for your classroom? A rule of thumb is that three-fourths or more of the students in the class should pass the placement test. If the class is particularly weak on parts of the placement test, work on these skills before starting with the Bridge. Present items similar to those on the test.

Placement Test Summary

Name	Mark parts passed (0 or 1 error per part)						Pass 4-6 parts passed and fewer than 8 errors	Fail 0-3 parts passed and/or more than 7 errors
	1	2	3	4	5	6		
1.								
2.								
3.								
4.								
5.								
6.								
7.								
8.								
9.								
10.								
11.								
12.								
13.								
14.								
15.								
16.								
17.								
18.								
19.								
20.								
21.								
22.								
23.								
24.								
25.								
26.								
27.								
28.								
29.								
30.								
Number of students Passed = P								
Total number of students = T								
Present the program if P/T = 75% or more								

Placement Test (Pre-Program)

Name _____ Score _____

Part 1 Answer each question.

| 408 | 4008 | 4807 | 480 | 3964 | 478 |

a. Which number is largest? _____

b. Which number is smallest? _____

c. Which number has the smallest hundreds digit? _____

d. How many digits are in 3964? _____

e. What is the hundreds digit in 3964? _____

Part 2 Figure out the answer to each question.

a. Phyllis had 48 dogs. She bought another 36 dogs. How many dogs does Phyllis have now? _____

b. A man had 74 stamps in his collection. He traded some stamps for coins. Now he has 46 stamps. How many stamps did he trade? _____

c. A truck started out with 2085 pounds of gravel. It delivered 1290 pounds of gravel. How many pounds of gravel were still on the truck? _____

Part 3 Work each item.

a. $14 + \boxed{} = 14$

b. $\boxed{} - 9 = 0$

c. $3 \times 6 = \boxed{}$

d. $1 \times \boxed{} = 37$

e. $26 \times \boxed{} = 0$

f. $58 - \boxed{} = 53$

g. $\boxed{} + 1 = 74$

Part 4 Write the fraction for each diagram.

a. 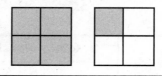 _____

c.  _____

b. 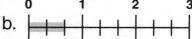 _____

d.  _____

Part 5 Work each item.

a.
```
  3 4
×   9
```

b.
```
  6 3
× 1 3
```

c.
```
6 0 0 5
− 9 0 4
```

d.
```
  4 1 7
    9 4
+ 1 5 9
```

e.
```
  4 0 6
− 3 1 8
```

f.
```
  5 8 4
×   7 5
```

Part 6 Work each item.

a. 9⟌9 3 6

b. 4⟌2 8 8

c. 9⟌8 9

d. 3⟌7 6 5

Placement Test (Pre-Program)

Answer Key

Part 1	Answer each question.		

Part total	Passing
5	0–1 errors

408	4008	4807	480	3964	478

a. Which number is largest? __4807__

b. Which number is smallest? __408__

c. Which number has the smallest hundreds digit? __4008__

d. How many digits are in 3964? __4__

e. What is the hundreds digit in 3964? __9__

Part 2	Figure out the answer to each question.

Part total	Passing
3	0–1 errors

a. Phyllis had 48 dogs. She bought another 36 dogs. How many dogs does Phyllis have now? __84 (dogs)__

b. A man had 74 stamps in his collection. He traded some stamps for coins. Now he has 46 stamps. How many stamps did he trade? __28 (stamps)__

c. A truck started out with 2085 pounds of gravel. It delivered 1290 pounds of gravel. How many pounds of gravel were still on the truck? __795 (pounds)__

Part 3	Work each item.

Part total	Passing
7	0–1 errors

a. $14 + \boxed{0} = 14$

b. $\boxed{9} - 9 = 0$

c. $3 \times 6 = \boxed{18}$

d. $1 \times \boxed{37} = 37$

e. $26 \times \boxed{0} = 0$

f. $58 - \boxed{5} = 53$

g. $\boxed{73} + 1 = 74$

Part 4 Write the fraction for each diagram.

Part total	Passing
4	0–1 errors

a.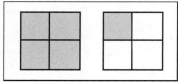
$$\frac{5}{4}$$

c.
$$\frac{6}{6}$$

b.
```
0   1   2   3
├┼┼┼┼┼┼┼┼┤
```
$$\frac{2}{3}$$

d.
```
0   1   2   3
├┼┼┼┼┼┤
```
$$\frac{3}{2}$$

Part 5 Work each item.

Part total	Passing
6	0–1 errors

a.
```
   3 4
 ×   9
 3 0 6
```

b.
```
    6 3
  × 1 3
  1 8 6
+ 6 2 0
  8 0 6
```

c.
```
  6 0 0 5
 −  9 0 4
  5 1 0 1
```

d.
```
    4 1 7
      9 4
  + 1 5 9
    6 7 0
```

e.
```
   4 0 6
 − 3 1 8
     8 8
```

f.
```
      5 8 4
    ×   7 5
    2 9 2 0
 + 4 0 8 8 0
  4 3,8 0 0
```

Part 6 Work each item.

Part total	Passing
4	0–1 errors

a.
```
    1 0 4
9 ⟌ 9 3 6
```

b.
```
    7 2
4 ⟌ 2 8 8
```

c.
```
     9 8/9
9 ⟌ 8 9
```
(or 9 r8)

d.
```
     2 5 5
3 ⟌ 7 6 5
```

Placement Testing: Level F

There is no placement test for Level F. Any student who has completed either Level E or Level Bridge and has passed the respective end-of-program test is eligible for Level F.

Placement Procedures

School-Wide Implementations Connecting Math Concepts, Levels D, E, Bridge, and F

The following placement procedures are for schools in which students can be placed in *Connecting Math Concepts* (CMC) groups that are homogeneous and may comprise students from different grade levels. These placement procedures include new criteria for current placement tests and new fact tests. The Level D fact test is used for placing students only in Level D. The Level E fact test is used for placing students in Levels E and Bridge.

Placing Students in CMC D in a School-Wide Implementation:

1. Administer the existing Level D placement test.
2. After students have completed the placement test for CMC Level D, administer the fact test for CMC Level D.

INSTRUCTIONS:

(Pass out fact test sheets face down.)
- Write your name on the back of your sheet. √
- When I tell you to start, you will turn the sheet over and you will have two minutes to complete it. When you are finished, or after I tell you that time is up, promptly turn your sheet over.
- Get ready. Begin.
  (After two minutes:)
- Stop and turn your papers face down.
  (Collect the papers and grade them)
3. Grade the placement test and the fact test. Use the answer keys to determine the items students missed.

PLACEMENT TEST CRITERION

Students fail the Level D placement test if they make 3 or more errors.

FACT TEST CRITERION

Students fail the fact test if they make 3 or more errors. Items that were not completed should be considered errors.

For Grades 1 through 5, students who fail either test should not be placed in CMC Level D. Place them in a group at a lower level.

For Grades 6 through 12, if students fail the placement test and/or the fact test, you may remediate the facts and/or specific skills in the part(s) students failed, then place them in the CMC program at Level D.

Note: It may be necessary to provide supplemental fact instruction throughout the year.

Placing Students in CMC E or Bridge in a School-Wide Implementation:

The procedure and criteria for placing students in CMC Level E or in CMC Level Bridge are the same as those for CMC Level D. Teachers should give each student the placement test from the respective program level and the Level E fact test.

CRITERIA

Criteria are the same as those for Level D. Students who make 3 or more errors on either test fail the test.

For grades 6 through 12, if students fail the placement test and/or the fact test, you may remediate the facts and/or specific skills in the part(s) students failed, then place them in the CMC program at that level.

Note: It may be necessary to provide supplemental fact instruction throughout the year.

Fact Test for *Connecting Math Concepts,* Level D

$$\begin{array}{r} 2 \\ \times\,7 \\ \hline \end{array}$$

$$\begin{array}{r} 14 \\ -\,6 \\ \hline \end{array}$$

$$\begin{array}{r} 7 \\ +\,9 \\ \hline \end{array}$$

$5\overline{)35}$

$8 + 6 =$

$16 - 8 =$

$4 \times 5 =$

$2\overline{)18}$

$7 \times 1 =$

$$\begin{array}{r} 57 \\ +\,0 \\ \hline \end{array}$$

$$\begin{array}{r} 17 \\ -\,8 \\ \hline \end{array}$$

$$\begin{array}{r} 6 \\ +\,7 \\ \hline \end{array}$$

$10\overline{)80}$

$9 \times 2 =$

$7 + 4 =$

$1 \times 7 =$

$12 - 5 =$

$5 \times 6 =$

$3\overline{)15}$

$$\begin{array}{r} 8 \\ +\,5 \\ \hline \end{array}$$

$$\begin{array}{r} 10 \\ \times\,6 \\ \hline \end{array}$$

$$\begin{array}{r} 7 \\ +\,8 \\ \hline \end{array}$$

$$\begin{array}{r} 6 \\ \times\,2 \\ \hline \end{array}$$

$$\begin{array}{r} 14 \\ -\,8 \\ \hline \end{array}$$

$$\begin{array}{r} 8 \\ \times\,0 \\ \hline \end{array}$$

$$\begin{array}{r} 11 \\ -\,6 \\ \hline \end{array}$$

$3\overline{)30}$

$6 + 7 =$

$17 - 0 =$

$2\overline{)16}$

$$\begin{array}{r} 2 \\ \times\ 7 \\ \hline 14 \end{array} \qquad\qquad \begin{array}{r} 14 \\ -\ 6 \\ \hline 8 \end{array} \qquad\qquad \begin{array}{r} 7 \\ +\ 9 \\ \hline 16 \end{array}$$

$5\overline{)35}$ → 7 $\qquad\qquad$ $8 + 6 = 14$ $\qquad\qquad$ $16 - 8 = 8$

$4 \times 5 = 20$ $\qquad\qquad$ $2\overline{)18}$ → 9 $\qquad\qquad$ $7 \times 1 = 7$

$$\begin{array}{r} 57 \\ +\ 0 \\ \hline 57 \end{array} \qquad\qquad \begin{array}{r} 17 \\ -\ 8 \\ \hline 9 \end{array} \qquad\qquad \begin{array}{r} 6 \\ +\ 7 \\ \hline 13 \end{array}$$

$10\overline{)80}$ → 8 $\qquad\qquad$ $9 \times 2 = 18$ $\qquad\qquad$ $7 + 4 = 11$

$1 \times 7 = 7$ $\qquad\qquad$ $12 - 5 = 7$ $\qquad\qquad$ $5 \times 6 = 30$

$3\overline{)15}$ → 5 $\qquad\qquad$ $\begin{array}{r} 8 \\ +\ 5 \\ \hline 13 \end{array}$ $\qquad\qquad$ $\begin{array}{r} 10 \\ \times\ 6 \\ \hline 60 \end{array}$

$$\begin{array}{r} 7 \\ +\ 8 \\ \hline 15 \end{array} \quad \begin{array}{r} 6 \\ \times\ 2 \\ \hline 12 \end{array} \quad \begin{array}{r} 14 \\ -\ 8 \\ \hline 6 \end{array} \quad \begin{array}{r} 8 \\ \times\ 0 \\ \hline 0 \end{array} \quad \begin{array}{r} 11 \\ -\ 6 \\ \hline 5 \end{array}$$

$3\overline{)30}$ → 10 $\qquad$ $6 + 7 = 13$ $\qquad$ $17 - 0 = 17$ $\qquad$ $2\overline{)16}$ → 8

Fact Test for *Connecting Math Concepts*, Levels E, Bridge, and F

$$\begin{array}{r} 8 \\ \times\, 7 \\ \hline \end{array} \qquad \begin{array}{r} 14 \\ -\, 6 \\ \hline \end{array} \qquad \begin{array}{r} 7 \\ +\, 9 \\ \hline \end{array}$$

$7\overline{)42}$ $\qquad\qquad$ $9 + 6 =$ $\qquad\qquad$ $16 - 8 =$

$6 \times 7 =$ $\qquad\qquad$ $6\overline{)54}$ $\qquad\qquad$ $28 \times 1 =$

$$\begin{array}{r} 57 \\ +\, 0 \\ \hline \end{array} \qquad \begin{array}{r} 17 \\ -\, 8 \\ \hline \end{array} \qquad \begin{array}{r} 6 \\ +\, 7 \\ \hline \end{array}$$

$8\overline{)48}$ $\qquad\qquad$ $9 \times 3 =$ $\qquad\qquad$ $7 + 4 =$

$4 \times 7 =$ $\qquad\qquad$ $12 - 5 =$ $\qquad\qquad$ $7 \times 9 =$

$3\overline{)21}$ $\qquad\qquad$ $\begin{array}{r} 8 \\ +\, 5 \\ \hline \end{array}$ $\qquad\qquad$ $\begin{array}{r} 6 \\ \times\, 4 \\ \hline \end{array}$

$$\begin{array}{r} 7 \\ +\, 8 \\ \hline \end{array} \quad \begin{array}{r} 6 \\ \times\, 6 \\ \hline \end{array} \quad \begin{array}{r} 14 \\ -\, 8 \\ \hline \end{array} \quad \begin{array}{r} 10 \\ \times\, 0 \\ \hline \end{array} \quad \begin{array}{r} 11 \\ -\, 6 \\ \hline \end{array}$$

$3\overline{)18}$ $\qquad$ $6 + 7 =$ $\qquad$ $17 - 0 =$ $\qquad$ $8\overline{)32}$

$$\begin{array}{r} 8 \\ \times\ 7 \\ \hline 56 \end{array} \qquad \begin{array}{r} 14 \\ -\ 6 \\ \hline 8 \end{array} \qquad \begin{array}{r} 7 \\ +\ 9 \\ \hline 16 \end{array}$$

$7\overline{)42}$ quotient 6 $\qquad$ $9 + 6 = 15$ $\qquad$ $16 - 8 = 8$

$6 \times 7 = 42$ $\qquad$ $6\overline{)54}$ quotient 9 $\qquad$ $28 \times 1 = 28$

$$\begin{array}{r} 57 \\ +\ 0 \\ \hline 57 \end{array} \qquad \begin{array}{r} 17 \\ -\ 8 \\ \hline 9 \end{array} \qquad \begin{array}{r} 6 \\ +\ 7 \\ \hline 13 \end{array}$$

$8\overline{)48}$ quotient 6 $\qquad$ $9 \times 3 = 27$ $\qquad$ $7 + 4 = 11$

$4 \times 7 = 28$ $\qquad$ $12 - 5 = 7$ $\qquad$ $7 \times 9 = 63$

$3\overline{)21}$ quotient 7

$$\begin{array}{r} 8 \\ +\ 5 \\ \hline 13 \end{array} \qquad \begin{array}{r} 6 \\ \times\ 4 \\ \hline 24 \end{array}$$

$$\begin{array}{r} 7 \\ +\ 8 \\ \hline 15 \end{array} \quad \begin{array}{r} 6 \\ \times\ 6 \\ \hline 36 \end{array} \quad \begin{array}{r} 14 \\ -\ 8 \\ \hline 6 \end{array} \quad \begin{array}{r} 10 \\ \times\ 0 \\ \hline 0 \end{array} \quad \begin{array}{r} 11 \\ -\ 6 \\ \hline 5 \end{array}$$

$3\overline{)18}$ quotient 6 $\qquad$ $6 + 7 = 13$ $\qquad$ $17 - 0 = 17$ $\qquad$ $8\overline{)32}$ quotient 4